UNFUC KWITH ABLE

HALEY BOWLER - COOKE

UNFUCKWITHABLE is a work of divinity
For individual empowerment and collective ascension
It's time to free yourself of your limitations

Copyright @ 2023 by Haley Bowler-Cooke

Written by Haley Bowler-Cooke

Interior and Cover Design by Haley Bowler-Cooke & Jenna Rose

2023 First Edition @ Haley Bowler-Cooke

Bowler-Cooke, Haley, Author, Thought Leader
UNFUCKWITHABLE – Haley Bowler-Cooke

For information about events, client work, bulk purchases, interviews etc. please contact author directly

UNFUCKWITHABLE
Issued in Print and Electronic formats

ISBN: 978-1-7390206-0-6 (Hardcover)
ISBN: 979-8-399018-6-0-7 (Paperback)
ISBN: 978-1-7390206-1-3 (Ebook)

UNFUC KWITH ABLE

HALEY BOWLER-COOKE

Published 2023 Toronto

This book is for…

The soul, who knows they're having a human experience

The one who is ready to live a life by their own design

With plenty of room for divine intervention of course…

Welcome to the realm of infinite possibility

Life by design is absolutely the path less traveled

…But it is 100% the most beautiful path.

Being Unfuckwithable is a coming home to all that you are.

*Unapologetic, Gushing in Love, Innately Brilliant, **You.***

Welcome to a New Paradigm of Holistic Success

LOVE - WELL BEING - WEALTH - PURPOSE - IMPACT - JOY

A love note, for the reader.

If you are reading this…

I know a little bit about You…
You are FAR from average.

You are a high level being, and you are
here to live an extraordinary life.

A life by design. One that is dripping in pleasure,
gushing in love, and overflowing in abundance.

It's time to elevate and it's time to expand.

You have been building momentum all along…
I promise You, it's all adding up.

Now, it's time to: unlock, heal, release, upgrade and ascend.

It is time to BE Unfuckwithable, and reap all the rewards.

The divine timing is now...To claim it…To actually LIVE it.

I see You, and I am so proud of You.

Let's dive in.

CONTENTS

You know that song that's like…
"Mount Everest ain't got shit on me…
Cuz I'm on top of the world…
I'm on TOP of the world…"

It's like that. That's the vibe.

You are here because you ARE Unfuckwithable,
and it is your time to be fully embodied in that power.

Before we begin, before it all changes for you…

Take a moment with me here.

Close your eyes, place your hand over your heart…

And take a few deep breaths.

You are here.
You have arrived.
There is nowhere else you need to be.
So land here.

I'm proud of You.
I'm so excited for You.

Thank YOU for being here.

Now let's dive in.

CHAPTER 1

REMEMBERING WHO THE FUCK YOU ARE

I have spent a lifetime living with unshakeable embodied confidence, a lifetime of BEING Unfuckwithable. A lifetime of accessing new levels of my innate personal power, refining it, elevating it, and deeper awakening to the truth of my infinite potential. This is the *Dimension of Openness*…A dimension where there is no separation, a dimension where we exist in circular flow with life. A dimension where it is always adding up, we are ALIVE in our *life by design,* and it is all happening FOR us. **We are in a realm of infinites, and it is ALL possible for you.** If you know in your heart that you are here for MORE, then that *more* is MEANT for you. The work and integrations within these pages will facilitate you in actualizing that *more*…Actually HAVING what you desire, and having what LIFE desires *for* you.

I couldn't be better positioned to be writing this book for you.
I SEE, FEEL and EMBODY my power effortlessly…
And I SEE and FEEL your power, too.

Evolution, ascension, manifestation…It's a BIG fucking deal. It's an act of devotion to decide that you want more, that you are worthy of more, and that you are ready and committed to *more.* So with that all being said. One thing I need to make clear straight off the hop my love, is that–*I will be holding you to your highest standard.* On the journey of reading this book, implementing the work and long after you've passed this book on to every single person you know…I will be HOLDING you to this standard–the highest standard of living. I will be HOLDING you to your desires.

Holding you to your HIGHEST timeline. I won't tip toe around the facts, I won't allow you to stay in your woundology, and I will never stop REMINDING you *who the fuck you are*. This is the realm of infinite possibility, limitless potential and a lived reality beyond your wildest dreams. You will not play small. You will not shrink your magic and you will not dim your light.

Whoever you are, wherever you are, and no matter what your story has been up until now…You have something so powerful to move with–DECISION. Making the decision that the time is *now*. The decision that it's ALL adding up. The decision that you are loved, supported, and that something mystical beyond comprehension is unfolding FOR you, now. Deciding that the time is now for a MASSIVE upgrade in your energetic and physical reality. A decision that the divine timing to RISE is–now. Your life can change in the most abundant, love filled and expansive way possible, in *one single moment*. The work however, is TRUSTING yourself to move with it. Whether the season you are in right now feels like flow, ease and abundance…Or struggle, lack and uncertainty, I promise you, it's not happening *to* you…It's happening *for* you. Make the decision now. The decision that you are worthy and committed to the life of your dreams. The decision that you *get* to live a life that you are obsessed with. The decision that it is YOUR time, and that you are ready now. *Make the decision now, that your entire life gets to upgrade.*

Remember Love…You are a divine God/Goddess from the stars. You're a high level being, and life CHOSE you. You're the Main Character…It's time to act like it. As we rise up into our alignment and higher self consciousness, we are called to deeper levels of awareness. We are asked to enhance our observation of self, and observation of the life surrounding, and within us. Sometimes this invitation is propelled by resistance. This resistance may be experienced by challenging thoughts and/or situations. Sometimes this invitation is propelled by desire. A desire to live differently, to have more, and to live in your truest alignment. *Nonetheless, it is all part of the great unfolding that is happening FOR you.* When you can deepen your sense of trust, and begin to embody the *knowing* that it is all happening for you...The resistance transmutes into magic and possibility. *Uncertainty transmutes into curiosity, and the unknown transmutes into the sexiest most exciting foreplay you've ever been a part of.* You feel a new sense of inner peace. You know that no matter what is occurring in the physical/material dimension, or in your mind and in your energy...You know it's happening for you...You have certainty. You know it's all adding up, and you know you are supported. You know that you are always taken care of, and that everything you desire is *here now–or close, and on its way.*

All your manifestations are on their way...Nothing is good, nothing is bad, it all just is. Life is a circular flow of wanting and having, and giving and receiving. Life is circular–always fluid, always moving. Remembering that you are a co creator, and an active participant in this life allows you to yield more results, and experience so much more fulfillment out of the ever changing seasons. You are powerful. You have the capability within your energetics, thoughts, beliefs and in your action–to determine the life of your dreams, and to then actually *live it.* One of my favorite quotes by me goes like this *"Your standards determine how the world responds to you."* I often say...It's not about boundaries at this level of alchemy...It's about standards. When we are operating at such high levels of self awareness, love and acceptance our reality becomes shaped by our standards–what we *are and are not* available for. You really are getting what you're available for–period. A moment of presence here, take a moment to acknowledge yourself. Deep breath in as you honor your perfect body, your essence, and the expression of ALL that you are.

Life chose You.
The Universe chose You.
The Creator chose You.
Now it's time for YOU, to choose You.

You are a rare human being to be reading this book, picking up a book titled "Unfuckwithable" *–is a power move in itself.* A move of an open, enlightened and badass individual. *I see you Boo.* Now it's time for YOU to see you. We are operating from this point forward from a KNOWING space…**A wisdom FAR beyond logic.** A space of certainty in our desires, in our vision, and in our dreams—both big and small. We are operating from a space of devotion. We're building momentum, moment to moment in alignment with our truth. We are cashing in that momentum, and actually HAVING our desires. As we operate from KNOWING we hold a unique and undeniable amount of power. At this level, we are operating from an INsourced certainty—*rather than from needy attachment to external validation.* **We are operating from personal power, a foundation of wholeness and fullness.** An unconditional space of creation and receptivity. No limits, no conditions…But rather infinite realities, and infinite results.

As I will mention many times in this book, I am holding you to the highest standard of your highest self. Standards are energetic, they are felt. ***The world responds to YOUR standards.*** When it's time to clean up and refine your life—raise the standard. When things are going beautifully, and you decide you're ready for *more*—raise the standard. Hold yourself (first and foremost), your circle, your colleagues, your clients, your friends, partner(s), family, experiences, products and visions to a HIGHER standard. **You are the leader of your life, the main character—the leading energy.** Everything is always responding to YOU. This level of responsibility means that your energetic and physical intentions and actions create your lived reality. **The world responds to your standards babe—so set them high.** Consciously do your part, and devote yourself to them. Hold yourself to the integrity of healthy assessment and realignment. Cultivate the strength to hold them HIGH—*and hold yourself to the expansive evolution of all that comes with that.*

On our journey together you will also become familiar with the phrase ***"Life By Design."*** It is my favorite way to live, and an absolute standard when BEING Unfuckwithable…Living a life by your own design means:

YOU, are the designer.
Not your parents.
Not your teachers.
Not what everyone in your friend group/community is doing, and certainly not the ideologies of the conditioned and suppressed societal standards.

Life by design is a life designed by YOU. *Living a life by your own design is absolutely the path less traveled…But it is 100% the most beautiful path.* Life by design is NOT the life, lifestyle or experience that the greater conditioned society has celebrated or naturalized… **Life by design is an act of rebellion.** As my poetic sister puts it *"Your life drenched in love is the greatest act of rebellion"* - Jenna Rose. Life by design doesn't happen by accident, it's not something that is normalized or nurtured in society–it is something you co create. A life by design is a reclamation of your aliveness, your desires and your ultimate fulfillment. It's not the norm, it is RARE.

Thank God you're not here to fit in. You are here to stand out, to build your empire, to leave your legacy and to amplify your impact of love, consciousness, creation and empowerment to the collective. You are here to have everything you want–and more. Here to be expanded and surprised with the abundance of the Universe. You are here to heal, alchemize, to rise and to become the aligned creator that you innately already are. You are here to *embody AND observe* your stunning life. You are walking this life as an embodied being, with infinite intelligence, and the highest forms of soul consciousness. You are here for a STUNNING life. You are willing to lean into the uncomfortableness to create what it is your soul truly desires. You are ready for it to be aligned, ease and joy filled in every way. You are here for a LOT of expected success, and *many more* unexpected miracles. I see you, you are a high level being, and you have decided that the time is *now* to accelerate and actualize things.

We're here because we are rare, ambitious and we are not settling for less. I've personally spent my entire life desiring high-level success and aligning myself with it. Success in my work, path, purpose, businesses, finances, relationships, health, wellness and freedom. *I always knew that it was within my power to decide how life would go for me.* I decided early on in my journey that I would not deprive myself of my desires. It was either–*yes I'm having this now, creating or receiving this NOW, or I am working toward it.* I wanted it all… and I still do. The difference between then and now is that now I KNOW that my success, desires and dreams are indeed inevitable (and yours are too). I live a life of *"Thank You, More Please"* (more on this later). A life where I am BUILDING momentum while simultaneously cashing in on all the previous momentum built. **My success is certain, and more of that success is always available.** No question, my desires were divinely placed into my consciousness, my desires are MEANT for me and they can't miss me. The same is true for you, if you choose it. You may have heard healers, speakers and spiritual teachers say things like this, and it likely resonated with your soul. Your logical mind and your conditioning however likely questioned the "How" or the legitimacy of it all. I know this feeling, because I was there too. I felt the resonance but never FULLY believed or understood it as completely true.

What you WANT must be in congruence with who you ARE

Our journey together, chapter by chapter will integrate the **codes of understanding** (the exact formula) and the **proper embodiment** (ways of living) to therefore vibrate at the level of certainty required for actualized manifestation. The level of power and knowing to actualize and materialize your desires while simultaneously living a lifestyle of ease and purpose. **Through the work, the wisdom and the practices in this book, we are encoding the most potent KNOWING of your power and your innate Unfuckwithableness as the creator and receiver of your most stunning life.** It's all adding up, it's happening for you now–and the journey is as delicious as the destination when you walk with certainty. It's time to create *more* in alignment, while already *overflowing* in the most abundant fulfilling life. You are ALIVE in this, you are tapped in and ALWAYS co-creating babe, you can't turn it off...But you CAN optimize it.

So...Let's talk about manifesting high level success–*I'm talking rich and famous vibes, empire vibes, healing and awakening the world vibes, leaving a fucking mark on every single person you meet vibes.* A little on my journey–I have always wanted to make a difference and I am dead serious about doing so. As I'm sure you are too–you are exceptional–you chose to embark on this journey through my book and in that I SEE YOU. Thanks to the various systems of oppression, hegemonic structures, capitalism and the patriarchal old paradigm (which is rooted in scarcity and delusion by the way). For a while there my success journey looked like: misaligned hustle and trying WAY too hard. I was burning out, exhausted, over-working and looped up in the illusion of scarcity without even knowing it– all in the name of so-called "freedom". How backwards! Luckily there is a better way, a way in which I **have mastered**, continue to evolve and share with the world. Now I get it, now I understand, I've integrated and I EMBODY the truth. The truth is–**your success is inevitable** (in every area of your life) when you do it your way, a way led by your highests elf and a way led by love. When you are DEEPLY supported, when you are regulated and when you believe wholeheartedly that there is no other option.

After realizing that hustling my way to success was so out of alignment, and frankly-killing me slowly. My deep innate personal power came through. The part of me that KNOWS myself, who I am and how I want to live. This part of me KNOWS that there is a much more pleasurable, ease filled and aligned way to have and hold it all. Creating the impact I desire, the life I KNOW is meant and natural for me. Honoring my soul path here on Earth, and doing so in a way that prioritizes my human waves, my energy and my physical body. Truly LIVING, expanding into infinite possibilities (and actually living them), deeply aligned success that nourishes me, my family, my clients AND the collective. It ultimately all comes down to my BEING, my alignment and my flow. It is completely about *who I BE* not *what I DO*. My openness to what's MEANT for me, what has been written in the stars and designed for me. It came down to surrendering to my absolute destiny while also honoring my conscious desires. My purest frequency… my truth. This state is the state where I flourish, where I am led and where I can create the most stunning impact from. This state of soul beingness, pure knowingness–this is the embodied state I am leading you into as we continue this journey together.

So my love, this is the time to decide, to declare, to OWN all that you are. It's always a decision, and the decision is the catalyst to the next opening, the next opportunity, and the next reward. Each decision and aligned way of BEING builds the aligned momentum and catapults you into your next reward, and OH BABY are we here for the rewards. I often say "divine timing is when we decide it's divine timing". Let's layer onto that. Once you decide…The universe will *get* you ready. Are you willing to fully claim it? Claim the desire? Claim the knowing? Within that decision, you are declaring that you are worthy and READY for more. There's something BEGGING to be expressed from deep within you, now is the time to unleash it all. I am not the exception, the people you have pedestalled, and the "Greats" you look up to, are not exceptions. This level of freedom is available to you. Your desires are not separate from you–there is no separation. It all becomes natural for you when you remember *who the fuck you are.* Our higher self KNOWS when enough is enough. The point when what IS just doesn't fucking cut it anymore. There comes a point on everyone's journey where what IS no longer aligns with what's MEANT for you. It's time to expand. You want MORE, you want different, you want a gushing *in-love FUCK YES life.*

You are ready to be swept up into this work, and so fucking grounded in what that looks like in the day to day. This book is your facilitator, and you owe it to yourself to dive all the way in. Hand your gorgeous self over to this work and bask in the upgrades. You are done seeking permission and you're done repeating the same patterns over and over again. You're done wondering if it's enough, if you're enough and you are absolutely done falling just short of what's ACTUALLY meant for you. It's TIME my angel, to revel in the overflow that is so authentic to you...so NATURAL for you. *It's time to live a life by your own design.* A life that is self led with pure devotion and surrender to the divine path.

So... this power that you have...*This POWER that you ARE.* It cannot be turned off, you are always co creating. Your life gets bigger, more aligned, way sexier, way wealthier and WAY more impactful when you UNDERSTAND and learn to harness this power—to FOCUS this power. When you are INTENTIONAL about what you consume, what you think, what you believe, what you do and what you don't do. When you are conscious about connecting to your SOUL, to your truth and to what feels like a true YES in your body (no matter how unconventional or wild it may seem). That's when Life gets YUMMY. It gets abundant and joyful as fuck when you follow your innate brilliance, versus following a borrowed identity or belief system. You are constantly creating—it doesn't turn off. Moment to moment you are perceiving a reality and generating the next image. You ARE the creator AND the receiver of this stunning life. Now what does this mean? Well first off... Energy rules the world, energy runs your physical, emotional, spiritual and mental body. Energy runs finances, energy runs communities, energy runs all connections and energy is a FELT phenomenon. When you understand your power as the co-creator, your power as an INNATELY INHERENTLY powerful being, and you walk the walk accordingly. Your energy is felt in a higher frequency and therefore you receive in relation to that higher coherence. If you fail to understand the laws of energy...*You will live a life of illusion.*

I have mastered energetics. I was born this way and managed to decondition any false programming that attempted to dim my radiance. The most common thing I hear is "I LOVE YOUR ENERGY!" My energy is my currency and this is my magnetism. My energy is FELT far and wide and it is NOT conditional to any time or space reality... it is FELT infinitely within the *Dimension of*

Openness. I have incredible energy, I experience an incredible reality AND it's no coincidence. It is an intentional practice day in, day out. The practice becomes a lifestyle and you never have to think about– it is simply your BEING. Your energetic currency will naturally upgrade as you deepen in your intention through our journey here together. So get ready for that magnetism to be FELT.

Let's take a quick pause…

Close your eyes, reflect on this question…Breathe this in…

How is YOUR energy felt?
How do you think others feel when they think of You?
What "vibe" are you vibrating on?
Take some time here, no rushing ahead. The work is meant to be integrated. When you can become aware of how you are FELT you can begin to understand how the universe (and those who inhabit it) is/are responding to YOU.

Being **Unfuckwithable** is all about personal power, and it is all about energetics and embodiment. Within the coming chapter you will be asked to sit with yourself, allow the stillness within you to speak and to really get real with who you are and how you're living. Like I said, this is a path less traveled. **Doing these levels of introspection and showing up, powerfully in alignment, in the outer world is not for the faint of heart…*But I believe in you babe.***

So, let's talk about embodiment. As we calibrate to higher levels of consciousness, frequency and therefore LIVED realities, we must become the masters of embodiment. **In order to embody a life, lifestyle and reality that is TRUE and aligned for us we must first become aware of our current ways of being.** Becoming mindful of our thoughts, beliefs, patterns, lifestyle, energetic and physiological embodiment. These are often cycles we repeat unknowingly, and until we bring conscious awareness to them they will continue to run the show, hindering our evolution, success and overall well being. **We repeat the cycles not**

because they were serving us…But because they're familiar, and the brain loves familiarity. The ego is here to survive, not thrive and the brain is a slave to the ego. So the old outdated programs, patterns and cycles that have been playing out in your life have kept you alive. You survived despite the pain, trauma, cyclical toxicity, limiting beliefs etc. etc. you survived. Therefore, your ego associates these old patterns with safety and will continue to run these programs subconsciously to keep you there. Safe, yes, but stuck in robotic misaligned repetition until we bring our consciousness to it. The unknown of what I call *"Thrival"* (aka living your best fucking life, turning heads and smiling your face off) is scary to the ego, and requires conscious moment to moment calibration. Stepping into your full power is unfamiliar, and that is what I am here to teach and lead you into so it becomes the SAFE and regulated norm for ALL parts of you.

Okay love, as this chapter comes to an end…I am bringing you some homework, some devotional work that requires your self leadership. At the end of each chapter you will be met with an invitation to dive deeper into the components of each chapter to ensure proper integration of the teachings. **In order to get out of old programs and remember who the fuck we are…our intention, action and alignment IS required.**

No matter who you are, where you come from, what your story is (was) you must BE the *Main Character.* You've outgrown your limitations, you wouldn't be reading this if you weren't ready for massive evolution. The old programs and paradigms no longer serve you (read it again). It's no longer yours to uphold, let it go and let's step into true alignment. The conditioning up until this point has attempted to keep you small…But it's time. It's TIME to BE the *Main Character.* Whoever you are, wherever you are…always remember that you have something SO powerful to move with…DECISION.

Making the decision that the time is now, the decision that it's all adding up, the decision that you are loved, supported and that something mystical beyond comprehension is unfolding

FOR you. Deciding that the time is now for a MASSIVE upgrade in all areas of your energetic and physical reality. A decision that the divine timing to RISE is NOW, trust yourself and MOVE with it. You are the MAIN character my love, now ACT like it.

Homework / Daily Devotionals …

Feel into, BREATHE into, and journal on the following–we are bringing it ALL into our awareness, we are becoming EMPOWERED by our lives, what has been our reality up until this point and what IS our truth.

Before each numbered reflection, take a few deep breaths, close your eyes and drop into your body.

- Where are You NOW? What is going well? What could use an upgrade? What could be better/more delicious/more expansive in your life? Where are you playing small? Where do you desire to go BIGGER?
- Who are you BEING in your moment to moment and day to day current reality? What role are you playing in your "Thrival" OR in your suffering? What old programs are running? What old cycles and patterns are playing out? Now, from that high level awareness and honest observation of SELF… jump to question 3.
- What beliefs/patterns/programs need to be REcoded, REwired and RE-programmed? (in order to properly align with your soul's desires, your innate knowing and your highest self timeline) From this awareness, your job is noticing, observing and witnessing yourself. Notice each time you run an old program, nothing needs to change… just witness it. From this observation day in day out you will start to see how these old programs no longer serve you, and from that awareness you can simply begin to upgrade or transmute the thought, belief and pattern into something of higher service to self. **One of my radical beliefs is that** *"once you are aware of something, you can consider it healed."* **So let go of the** *fixing,* **and just start noticing.**

Your life can change in the most abundant, love filled and expansive ways possible and it can change in **one single moment.** The work is TRUSTING yourself to MOVE with it. Remember, when you serve SELF from the highest love consciousness…You serve LIFE, and all forms of life benefit.

Like all alchemy, ascension and self improvement, your self leadership is required. You will be led, you will be supported, you are a CO-creator and it is absolutely *not* all in your hands. However, you have the personal power to make the moves, shift, choose again, choose differently, perceive differently, and live more fully each and every day. The work is required, and I invite you to fully devote to these prompts above. Fully embody them, move with them, and fully surrender to that work. Once you feel you have devoted fully to the work of chapter one, move forward and layer in the codes within chapter two.

CHAPTER 2

LIFE BY DESIGN

The Highest Timeline Path is absolutely the path less traveled…
But it is 100% the most beautiful path

Living a life by your own design means one thing…*You are the designer.* We have collectively entered a new world, a new Earth, a new paradigm—one of limitless possibilities. **You however have to choose to live in this way.** There's living by default, then there's living by *design*. Wanting what you want then *having* what you want. Deciding to empower yourself in the TRUTH that you are the designer of your life…(and if you're anything like me, you're also leaving lots of room for magical and divine intervention). **This empowerment work, highest self actualization and existing within the infinite reality of the *Dimension of Openness* means that you are not only going to be supported in manifesting everything YOUR heart desires…you will also manifest everything that LIFE desires for you.** *You are a powerful CO creator—and this lifetime gets to absolutely blow you away.* Like we covered in chapter one, no matter who you are and what your story is/was/has been, you have something SO powerful to move with…your DECISION. Deciding to live *a life by design* is literally step number one. *Devoting and aligning to that decision day to day…moment to moment—now that is the work.* As always…the Universe wants you to have everything you desire AND it wants you to be the most whole and complete version of yourself on that journey. **There's no seeking or chasing in this reality—there is simply naturalizing what is meant for you.**

Let's take a check in together…Breathe in, breathe out.

What are you healing?
What are you rising into?
What are you creating?
Who are you BEING as you build your legacy?

Now actually take a minute here, breathe and drop into those prompts–take your time.

Life by design isn't a destination–it's a journey. This work of co-creation and cultivating a *life by design* WILL undoubtedly get you mind blowing results in the material world…AND the work is about so much more than that. The work is about INsourced and INborn identity, beingness and embodiment. Regardless of what appears in the material world–you are powerful…*AND you get to have everything you have ever fuckign wanted.* This is a physical world, we desire physical things and we GET to have them. Taking it deeper however, this work is for the **high level being who KNOWS these physical manifestations are inevitable.** You are whole and complete regardless of what is being validated in their external reality. *Life by design* is about the journey of becoming, undoing, healing, awakening, emotional intelligence, self awareness, observation and embodiment to LIVE within each moment with intention. **Fulfillment is the focus–abundance naturally follows.** The focus is to BUILD aligned momentum in the direction of your desires from a place of wholeness. You move in the aligned direction with full honoring of your TRUTH, while also *inevitably and absolutely* cashing in your desires and all the rewards along the way. **Again–there is no destination…it is all happening NOW, and you are ALIVE in this life by design.** This is the path your highest self walks, in devotion, alignment and in surrender. It is the path of ease, (yet by no means is easy to do). **There is focus, devotion and deep surrender required.** The *Highest Timeline Path* is absolutely the path less traveled… *AND it is 100% the most beautiful path.*

So my love…The results are a no brainer. You want xyz…you CAN and you WILL have it. YOU will co create it, receive it, manifest it, generate it and cultivate it when you integrate this work. *However, I encourage you to focus more on the internal and inborn shifts and manifestations that will occur for you on this journey–as that is where the true power lies.* You will learn to create, receive and attract from a place of personal power and TRUE Unfuckwithableness. **Anything outside of you is simply a guarantee, to be expected and a lovingly anticipated cherry on top.** The work is truly about unconditionally LOVING who you are on this journey–through ALL the seasons. Setting true heartfelt intentions, taking the aligned action and expanding into new paradigms. Focussed intention on the path, all the while feeling into ease and surrender in ways like never before. This flow with life, where you are an active co creator AND open to all the magic that is unfolding before you, effortlessly and in pure divine timing. You are on your soul path, it's all divine, in perfect order, it's all inevitable. *What's meant for you…it's adding up… it's done…absolutely guaranteed.* You get to have it all, you WILL have it all…AND…This work goes even deeper. Your power does not come from validation in your external world, your power does not come from all the things you manifest. You ARE the power and naturally you create, attract and magnetize all that you desire as you walk this powerful walk. We're in the realm of… of course you can BE, DO and HAVE all that you desire… AND I invite you deeper.

Who do you want to BE on the journey?
How do you want to be felt by those in your realm, remembered, known?
How do YOU want to feel?

Your desires, goals and dreams are a guarantee with this work, *but the true fulfillment comes from the intentional honoring of the path.* This co-creation of a *life by design* is your EMPIRE, and your legacy *will* live on. Abundance in every way, ease, pleasure and wealth simply GETS to be the bi-product of you LIVING in your alignment–living from a place of undeniable personal power. *Life by design* simply GETS to be a path, a journey with various seasons AND continuous stacked and cashed momentum. You must release the illusion of "when I get there" or "once this happens." Those are distortions that exist within a dimension of separation. The work of this book however, is foundational within what I like to call *"The Dimension of Openness"*. **Within the dimension of openness there is no separation.** *The Dimension of Openness* is a circular, naturalized, and fluid existence where everything is co-existing in union and flow. ***The Dimension of Openness* is responsive to your coherence, and a higher coherence is always available.** *A life by design* is a moment-to-moment choosing of love, openness and feeling good. *The inevitable outcome of that is naturally: more love, more money, more impact, more joy and more aligned purpose.* **Are you willing to do the work?** Truly, are you HERE for it? If the answer is **YES!!** –give yourself the gift of a deep breath, a massive smile, a big hug and ***lets fucking GO.*** As you already know, living a *life by your own design* is 100% the path less traveled. *Life by design* does not conform to the norms of society or the illusions of separation. ***Life by design* takes bravery, courage and devotion**. If you have made it this far, and you are serious about being ALIVE in your dream, then I absolutely believe in you, **I SEE YOU** and it is my greatest honor to continue to lead you on this journey of self actualization and LIFE by design.

Let's talk about SELF BELIEF, gorgeous. I can tell almost immediately when someone in my world (friends, family, clients etc.) is/are going to manifest/actualize and receive what they desire by this one trait. I can tell immediately if they will be successful (and not the boring limited conventional success you hear about) but the gushing in love, mind blowing results and out of this world JOY on their journey of the manifestation by this one trait...SELF BELIEF. Life is CHOOSING you all day long. SOURCE is choosing you all day long. GOD is choosing you all day long. The UNIVERSE is choosing you all day long. But YOU have to CHOOSE you. I'm willing to go deep with the ones who choose themselves, and I truly hope that THIS is the catalyst that prompts you to CHOOSE you, if you haven't already. *Decide now that you are committed, worthy and READY for this beautiful life to unfold.*

Are you ready? I lead the ones who have that deep knowing within, the self belief that they are chosen and they are ready for more. Those who hold this level of self belief and those who are DEVOTED to their alignment. **THEIR success is GUARANTEED.** I can immediately tell no matter how much doubt, fear or uncertainty they may be experiencing temporarily. No matter how many blocks, no matter how much rewiring and reprogramming is needed. Self-belief is a potent essence that I can FEEL, and no matter what, no matter who you are, and no matter what your past experiences have been up until now…LIFE CHOSE YOU and YOU get to choose you. No matter how much confidence, competence and clarity someone may hold…*or lack thereof.* I can SEE and FEEL their level of PERSONAL POWER and SELF BELIEF *–and I KNOW in that moment that their success is GUARANTEED.* BEING **Unfuckwithable** is the innate knowing and aligned embodiment that YOU are here to live an extraordinary life, and you are WILLING to do and BE what it takes to allow that to unfold.

My guess is…If you're the type of person reading this book you want a life where the JOURNEY is as delicious as the destination. A life of **THANK YOU**, **MORE PLEASE**, the kind of life that's oozing in gratitude while you walk forward with desire and a hunger for more. THIS is *life by design.* You picked this book up because you on some level have a deep curiosity in something more, you may have the knowing already, or maybe just a flicker of aliveness that is pulling you from the mundane into the pulse of this new paradigm of life. You're rare babe, I already feel that in you, you wouldn't be reading this if you weren't. *The truth is, we were all born with the pull to experience life here on Earth, we were pulled from the cosmic bliss to the density of Earth because deep within us, in our soul consciousness we KNEW we could be ALIVE in our dreams.* To live a soul fulfilling life while honoring the physical desires, manifestation and actualization within the material world. The soul came here pure, curious and open to receive. Each of us have our own unique amounts of programming, some positive and aligned with our desires, and some not. The undoing, unbecoming and unraveling is where we can unleash the truth. We ALL have this level of certainty in our dreams, we all have soul desire…some of us just have more de/reconditioning to do than others. As you deepen into the integration of this work, even simply the proximity to the energetics and language within the coming chapters, you will begin to unravel and *come home* to your truest, purest self. I'm excited for you babe, stay in this work.

Life CHOSE you, now you have to CHOOSE you. This work is for the ones who know they want more. More for this life, for this world, for the Earth, for the collective, for their own universe and the universe at large. You have a desire(s) and you have the knowing(s). *You have the codes. The work is an unwinding process to uncover your innate brilliance, and help you discover your soul essence and highest self consciousness already within you.* A remembering, with some high level facilitation and some new, rather radical ways of thinking and living. Your pinky toe has more wisdom than any book ever written (even this one). Your cells hold the knowings, and your body keeps the score. My channel, this work, these devotions… are simply here to validate and clarify the TRUTH of you, your truth, your purpose and the invisible string that continues to pull you forward. *This work is a gift… but you are the present.* **In order for you to THRIVE in this life by design, we must get your self belief on POINT.** Your ability to create, achieve, receive and manifest comes from you KNOWING your power, your TRUTH and your unfuckwithableness. This book is pure wisdom with so many codes, this book is BRILLIANT and is channeled from infinite intelligence…AND…You…Yes–YOU Babe, *ARE* infinite intelligence.

In order for you to elevate in the ways in which you desire, you MUST know your innate personal power and walk the walk with that next level self belief. You must know that

NOTHING outside of you can fuel you the way your own soul can, and that YOU are the source–*all day long*. One of my potent quotes by me goes like this "Your self belief determines the actualization of your desires, and your alignment determines how *fast*." Meaning… BELIEF is required and that belief makes it all inevitable for you…AND the alignment in your action, energetics and embodiment determine the speed in which it all manifests. I hold you now to the highest standard of self belief, and I promise you that this book will get you aligned.

Now, let's talk about being ALIVE in your dream. The moments each day where you feel that sense of bliss, you feel the knowing, the appreciation, you feel that pure success and satisfaction in all that you are, where you're at, what you've accomplished and what you've received from your pure beingness. The vibe of ***"I've arrived, I'm here…Alive in my dream."*** The feeling of fulfillment, purpose, serenity and certainty as you powerfully move through each day knowing that it's all adding up, and it's all happening now". Let's create more of this–let's expand and amplify it. *Thank You, More Please is the focus.* A focus on feeling so good in each moment that the next feel good moment naturally aligns. Living a life of intentionality, mindfulness and FULLNESS naturalizes for you–*a compounding effect of pleasure. A life that is "pleasure led" allows you to feel that unfolding and unraveling into the aliveness of life and the wholeness of all that is.* The more you bring magic, intention and miracle energetics to the mundane, the more joy you will feel. That joy overtime stacks into internal and embodied happiness in which you leave that legacy for future generations to build on–*you are literally changing the world.* The compounding effect of a life lived with intention, is a life where you are stacking and cashing momentum of aligned energy, aligned experiences and therefore desired results. A life of *"the better it gets, the better it gets"* –THIS is life by design–THIS is being ALIVE in the dream.

Before you even get to the homework/devotional portion of this chapter… can you take a moment now. Put this book down BREATHE and ask yourself are you BEING alive in this life? Alive in your connection to *all that is?*

Alive in the present moment?

Alive in the pleasure and joy that is presently available to you NOW?

If the answer is yes–amplify it, if the answer is not yet–check yourself, shift it and align.

Breathe slowly, land in the body…

You are WORTHY and DESERVING of a life you can't stop smiling about.

Close your eyes and smile now. It is ALL adding up, it's happening FOR you, it's here–it's now.

Let's talk about being ALL IN on yourself. Let's dive into the POWER of that *"all in"* energy. You didn't arrive here to be half of what you came here to be. You didn't come to scratch the surface of your potential…again, LIFE chose YOU now it's time for YOU to choose you. This frequency that you begin to vibrate on when you DECIDE that life is fucking precious and you are ready and devoted to going all in on what's aligned and meant for you. This is the frequency that magnetizes and actualizes desires. This is allure, this is UNFUCKWITHABLENESS…a MAGNETISM that is unmatched. What if you decided to go all in? What if you actually decided to fulfill your FULL potential? What if you KNEW and LIVED in such a way that MONEY, LOVE, IMPACT and PURPOSE were natural bi-products of you choosing YOU all day long? All of these supportive energies are working for you–your most devotional support systems. All here to guide, hold and amplify YOU in living your life by design. The practices within this book are about encoding these truths into every cell in your body. *You should be really proud of yourself for doing this work, it's all adding up babe–get excited.* I want to see you ALIVE in your dream. You are here for it all, to stand out, to build your empire, to leave your legacy and to amplify your impact of love, consciousness, creation and empowerment to the collective. You are here to have everything you want and more. Here to be expanded and surprised with the abundance of the Universe. You are here to alchemize, to rise, to master self, your emotions and your ways of being. You are here to embody and observe your stunning life. Walking as soul consciousness and experiencing all the pleasure, joy and wealth along the way. A higher coherence is always available, and a life by design is a beautiful choice. *What will you choose?*

Part of owning that "all in" energy and being a STAND for the life of your dreams, is the practice of continuously noticing what is no longer aligned. The high level individual, the UNFUCKWITHABLE human has a pure frequency and is NOT energetically available for anything less. This pure frequency is a life of alignment. Anything that is not of that alignment essentially is no longer a part of your life. I always say to my clients– "it either upgrades to your new level OR it's not coming with you". If there is a desire for "more" in alignment, you must create spaciousness for it. *You must be open and receptive, with a clean and clear energetic bandwidth, and aligned capacity to receive.* I am notorious for saying *"it's not about boundaries… It's about standards."* As you RISE, your standards for what comes with you also elevates. A constant refining process is required as we live a life by design. You are constantly getting what you are available for. *When you go all in on you–you must make the decision that you are no longer available for _____ and ONLY available for _____ if not that, something better.*

This clean clear communication with the Universe, creates a clean clear landing strip of ALIGNED receptivity. Communicating often with words, actions, journaling, beliefs and conscious thoughts will amplify this clarity between you and your co creator. With every up-level, there must be a healthy assessment energy of "what do I want?" and "what is no longer aligned?" *What are you still available for that no longer serves your next level?* Get real with yourself, if you truly desire the shift(s). Embodying this energy of refined clarity and being Unfuckwithable is an INSIDE job, there are high levels of awareness and action (energetically and physically) required. You move–the universe responds. You put out the signal–the universe aligns. What needs cleaned up, rearranged, healed or released in your life? Every time you deeper align to your truth–you are refining. *Things stay, things elevate, and things go.* Take a deep breath, create safety in your inner being and trust that it is safe for you to evolve beyond what no longer aligns.

High level individuals move quickly, intentionally and strategically. We move with LOVE as our discernment, and we intentionally refine through healthy assessment energy. Releasing what is no longer aligned, upgrading what can be upgraded and stepping bravely into our TRUTH. This is a behind the scenes moment to moment intentional devotion. *You are here for a stunning life...right?* With that, you must be willing to lean into the uncomfortableness to create what it is your soul truly desires. *You must be willing to want what you want, more than fear what you fear.* Willing to get uncomfortable, lean into an edge and expand into unchartered territory and unknown paradigms. The ease, joy and alignment with each up-level requires naturalization. Conscious naturalization of the next level–means calibrating to a higher coherence and creating safety in that new paradigm. The new level just feels normal, natural and safe for your system. *The naturalization process allows you to continue to grow and evolve– the ceiling becomes the floor and you get SO MUCH MORE out of this life.*

"Every act of creation begins with an act of destruction"
-Pablo Picasso

As we evolve, rise in our alignment and standards, and determine what is no longer the vibe–we must leave behind the outdated versions of ourselves and ways of relating. This refinement process can inevitably include a grieving process...*Again, not everything will rise with you, as you rise.* **Trust what is meant to fall away.** With the higher standards of fulfillment and success...your courage and willingness to go *all in* on yourself becomes critical. Part of living a life by design and BEING **Unfuckwithable** is getting comfortable with change. Being willing to shatter the old, before stepping into the new. Being bold enough to destruct what no longer aligns, before creating what is meant for you. *"Every act of creation begins with an act of destruction,"* Pablo Picasso. Your next evolution, your new paradigm, your new reality WILL involve the shattering and/or the upgrading of the old. **Trust that process, and lean all the way in babe.**

Doing the same thing gets you the SAME results... Energetically and physically. If you want to feel different or experience a different reality in small or massive ways, I can promise you that doing the same thing will NOT yield a new experience, feeling or result. **Life by design–means knowing when to make the move, when to make a shift and when to choose differently.** If you want something you've never had, if you want to do something you've never done and BE someone you've never been...I am 100% sure that there is something that needs to shift. Be it a thought pattern, belief, action, energy or embodiment... something must shift to catalyze the actualization of what's next. Either things needs to elevate or you simply need to lean the fuck back. I hope it's clear by now–but you are NOT in this alone. You are a CO creator and sometimes the answer is taking a step back, and letting the divine do its thing.

Sometimes doing it differently is simply being present with yourself, and your progress. Sometimes it is as simple as acknowledging all the things you've done both physically and energetically that support your manifestation. **Self acknowledgment is sometimes the missing ingredient that emulsifies our desires into manifest.** Maybe your new and next move is simply honoring how far you've come, all that you've done and simply deciding that it is all adding up. Or maybe your shift is completely restructuring your physical and energetic reality to create space for what is truly meant for you. **Regardless...If you desire newness, you must embody newness.** Mix it up Queen/King, start saying YES to the flow of what IS and begin experiencing what fluidity looks and feels like in your stunning life. *Move with desire and intuition, change up your routine, get out of your comfort zone and step into something new.* This is what having your finger on the pulse of life looks like. **This open aliveness is what adds up to a life lived by design.**

Everyone can imagine what their dream life would look like, but not everyone is willing to actually LIVE it.

This work of actualization (actually materializing your desires) is high level–it's not for everyone. Yet it's so natural, once it's integrated. A profound remembering once embodied, and the pinnacle of truth once experienced. The concepts of a life by design are simple "live presently, moment to moment and lead with your highest self leadership". So simple, yet so nuanced. The real work here is overcoming the old and outdated programming and conditioning that stands in the way of what is natural and TRUE for You.

Living a life by design requires ongoing self inquiry:

"What would my highest self like to do?"
"How would I like to feel?"
"What would I like to experience?"
"What is my truth?"

Then go do that…BE that…Live that.

There's autopilot living, where old programs and patterns run your show. Then there's actually being ALIVE and ATTUNED to the pulse of life. There's stagnancy (yawnnn) and then there's healthy assessment energy– observation, elevation and up-leveled embodiment. There's saying YES to pleasure, opportunity and abundance like never before. This YES to life, this YES to your pleasure body, this YES to your highest self requires elite levels of focus and intention. Energetic and physical upgrades encode when you devote yourself to this work. It's the ON GOING devotion to this life–*this life is one of miracles.* Again, *"The Highest Timeline Path is absolutely the path less traveled… but it is 100% the most beautiful path"*

The highest timeline path is one of readiness and commitment, success and failure, pain and pleasure. It doesn't have to be perfect, but try hard as hell to make it intentional. Remember, if it were easy…everyone would be doing it. Everyone would be unconditionally loving, conscious impactful benevolent billionaires with mind blowing, soul fulfilling relationships. This work is WORK, and my GOD is it ever rewarding. This is evolution over a lifetime. *It's fucking exciting, it's a big fucking deal to live a life with such intention and boundless desire.* Passion! Is a fucking gift. Walking the walk, doing the work, CHOOSING the highest path over and over and over again, moment to moment. This is something I too work at every single day. BECAUSE I am committed to evolution...I am constantly getting uncomfortable. Ease, joy, bliss, abundance, purposeful living requires high standards of DEVOTIONAL living and an ongoing assessment of what is no longer aligned. This devotion isn't always pleasure filled, indulgent and luxurious. I can promise you that...But what I CAN promise you, is that walking this walk is the best fucking deision you could ever make for yourself, your life, your legacy. This walk of observation (soul) and embodiment (human), is the walk of a soul having a human experience, and living a life by design—and this life is PRICELESS!

Okay Love, as this chapter comes to an end... I am bringing you some homework, some devotional work that requires your self leadership. The work within these upcoming devotionals will single handedly transform your life, we're starting off strong with a bang. So don't rush through it. In order to live a life by design you must DESIGN your dream life (while of course leaving room for the magic of what LIFE desires FOR you). *It's time to release the old programs, and rewrite your story.* This work WILL meet you where you're at, so as you devote yourself to this work—I want you to be true to your present vision, present truths, present healing and present desires as possible. *Come back to this work as your desires evolve and shift throughout this precious unrepeatable life—again—the work meets you where you're at.* This doesn't have to be executed perfectly, this doesn't have to encapsulate every desire that exists within your being, you simply are PRACTICING the development of self awareness, honoring your desires and witnessing what needs to be elevated and upgraded along the way. I have to be completely honest with you…I am far from "perfect" with my alignment AND I deeply believe that that's why I evolve so fast, my success exists (and is ever evolving and growing) because I value EXCELLENCE over perfection and PROGRESS over perfection. I move, I start, I build, I upgrade, I tear it all down and I rebuild. *It is the meeting yourself where you're at, and deepening into the work that is PRESENTLY true for you that catalyzes evolution, progress and materializes your results.* So, in this journaling practice simply honor what is TRUE for you, today.

Homework / Daily Devotionals …

Feel into, BREATHE into and journal on the following…We are bringing ALL of it into our awareness. We are becoming EMPOWERED by our lives, what has been our reality, and what is *actually* our truth. Not only are there journal prompts, reflection and meditation prompts within this homework section–there are also mini trainings and teachings on some high level concepts to empower your understanding of co-creation.

Before each numbered reflection…

Take a few deep breaths, close your eyes and drop into your body.

1. **If this moment was a completely fresh start, new slate, new beginning (because it is) what would you DECIDE?** What would you CHOOSE your life to look, feel and BE like? This is a paradigm that is available to you now… One where you receive everything you want… for your highest good and the highest good of all, *but* you have to design it that way, and you have to choose it. So, in your journal, on your mood board, in your own precious mind–design it.
   *Pro Tip –get super detailed, feel the feelings of this design, see yourself living this design so much to the point that it begins to feel NATURAL.

2. **What would stand between you living this life by design? What fears or illusions are in the way?** Fear deeply served our ancestors...now however... All it does is keep your lived reality boring, average and limited. Fear is part of the human experience, fear is inevitable. Especially if you walk your highest timeline and CHOOSE moment to moment to live life by your own stunning design (which DUH that's why you're reading this). When you walk the path less traveled, you will have to stand up and walk with more and more fear than the average person who is choosing a safer, more conditional lifestyle. Fear is an emotion that penetrates the nervous system and it is an emotion that is and has been felt by every single person you look up to. Fear is to be expected. It DEEPLY served our ancestors as humans and kept us alive, for that I am thankful for my fear every single day. However, thanks to evolution...Fear no longer serves the purposes it used to. Contextually speaking, the fear response no longer saves our lives in the day to day. Instead, it is actually just something we get to observe and move with. If we allow it to take over, if we allow our hindbrain to run the show we stay incredibly average, unhappy, we squash our dreams and we intensely limit ourselves. The UNFUCKWITHABLE being absolutely feels fear, they just don't let it fuck with them, they don't let it inhibit their movement or get in their way. They see it, hold it and walk with it. They make the moves, anyway. So the work is—getting real and raw with yourself in your journal, out loud or in your head... **What IS your deepest fear?** How is that fear blocking you now? Can you become acquainted with this fear in such a way that you will walk forward with it?

3. **"You get what you expect"** My love, a life by design is nuanced and high level because you are building expectations from a place of soul knowing and excitement *before* you have the evidence that it *is* to be expected. **Our brain creates pathways of expectation, we visualize things, experience things and the brain naturalizes**

that, learns to expect it and therefore co creates it through that anticipation and expectation energy–powerful eh!? This is an INCREDIBLE feature of being human AND it can be your worst nightmare (if you are unaware of the power of it, and not in the driver's seat of these anticipations and expectations). The first half of this 3rd piece of homework is being real with yourself, honest with where you're at, and starting to see what programs of expectation are running. **What do you expect of your financial life, your love life, your work life, your impact, your outcomes, your behaviors and your mood? What do you expect you will earn and generate this month in your finance? What do you expect you will experience this month in your intimate relationships? What do you expect in any area of your life?** Be REAL and TRUE to what actually comes up. Once you really see the truth of what you have been expecting, what you have been AVAILABLE for, and therefore co creating…You get to decide if it stays or elevates. Is this going to cut it? Is this enough? Is this true for me? Is this aligned? You decide. This healthy assessment energy is so necessary in building and creating a life by design. If what you are expecting is not up to the standard of your life by design and your dreams…It's time to start expecting MORE.

4. **How do I naturalize more? How do I GENUINELY start expecting more? How do I start creating that more?** Well my love, you should by now be pretty clear on what it is you want–if you're not, take your time getting clear on what you truly desire (not the life you think you should want…the life you ACTUALLY want). Now in order to expect it to exist for you (and therefore naturalize it), there is a period of time where we practice aligning to that, being the energetic match for that, vibrating at the same coherence as that, and begin to see and feel it as true for us. This is a practice, again healthily assess…*Does the version of me who has xyz act in this way, think in this way, live in this way, believe in this way?* If it's a no…Clean it up

and shift it. Healthily assess—Are there even pathways for what you desire to reach you? Are you physically, energetically and emotionally available for this next level? Are you truly open to this new reality? Are you in coherence with this LIFE by design? If the pathways are not yet in place—set them up. YOU are a CO creator, and you must do your part. Once you have ensured that the portals and pathways are open, your energy and physical reality is clear and ready to receive it, and it FEELS natural for you...From this foundation, you can easily get into the energetics of excitement and therefore expectation about what you desire as on its way, as a standard for you, and to be EXPECTED for you!

Wowza! That was a lot, this homework is no joke.

This devotion to self is intense at times and really requires work. So I hope you took your time, I hope you didn't rush through this work and I deeply encourage you to continue to come back to this work (especially as your desires shift and evolve throughout the seasons of your life). Continue to hold the duality of what is aligned, and what needs to shift. Continue to deepen the relationship with your beautiful self, life and legacy. Choose your highest timeline—moment to moment. Walk with fear, don't let it slow or stop you. Be insanely grateful and present—while also staying focussed and committed to creating what's next. Stay in your own lane AND uplift those around you. DEVOTION to this life is just that...It's devotional living.

Staying in your lane isn't a concept to know...It's a lifestyle to EMBODY. Doing "the work" is not for the faint of heart. Living life by your own design is not the norm, not widely accepted or understood by the average person. It's a decision. **A moment to moment decision.** To make a new choice, consciously CHOOSING differently and elevating your standards. Different thoughts, beliefs, patterns, behaviors, actions, embodiments, energetics...You get the point. *Choose different, choose again and make not having habits your habit.* You are here for massive things. It's GO time. Move toward your desires in alignment with their frequency. The frequency of your highest self. Call them in. Claim them. Then actually BE in the moment. Enjoy the journey.

The journey is you, living your life. *So truly LIVE it.*

CHAPTER 3

HIGH LEVEL ENERGETICS

You can listen to a million self development podcasts,
*but until you start actually **living** in that way...Nothing changes.*

The age of knowing has shifted to the age of integration. This is a new-higher paradigm, a higher collective coherence. This means that simply knowing what's good for you and being informed–is not enough to create change. Information is important-but it's not enough. You must actually live it. Integrate the knowings and live in alignment with those knowings. Learn it, integrate it, and then actually **live** it. *Life by design,* this high level experience of life on Earth, and it comes down to your intention AND your action. **You can read a million self help books but until you align your mindset, energetics and actions you will continue to get the same results.** Your devotion to the path means you are aligning, re-aligning, calibrating and re-calibrating on a moment to moment basis–actually doing the work. *The external validation and the rewards of this work take time– because this level of alignment takes time.* This work is not for someone who wants instant gratification from an external validating marker. This work is for the person who wants instantaneous elevation, ascension, and raised internal frequency. You will feel incredible immediately in this work, but it may take time before your external world shows up for you the way your heart desires. *One of my favorite quotes by me is this: "This life is artistry-it is the behind the scenes that determines the audience- the audience may never show- but do it for you, anyway."* This life... *life by design,* one of such intentional service and such aligned receptivity, new paradigm leadership... a life of **devotion**. Led by faith in the knowing, it is (for the most part) **ART**

with no audience. It is the devotion behind the scenes of self actualization–the audience will come later if you want it. Devotional living is obedience to the path (while maintaining the most tender care for the desires of your body on the journey). It is striving, while also anchoring in moments of acceptance. **It is being with what is, while actively creating... more.** *Life by design* is discovery and presence. Being a high level individual means you are actively elevating and upgrading your life through conscious observation and aligned action-moment to moment.

Quick moment of awareness:
Have you truly been living intentionally?
Have you truly been taking aligned action?
Have you truly been living in alignment with the **life you desire**?
Do you consider yourself a high level individual?
How can you elevate that as **TRUTH**?

The high level individual living a *life by design* is inevitably leaving their legacy. **Legacies are BUILT behind the scenes.** My personal legacy is: unapologetic self love, boundless love for all that is, devotion to my work, devotion to my loves, holistic success all around, truly being and feeling ALIVE! My legacy is boundless desire and infinite abundance in ALL areas of my life. My legacy is a profound relationship with energy and all that exists within the *dimension of openness*. My legacy is confidence so powerful it heals timelines of souls who ever forgot their power. My legacy is dripping pleasure that reclaims timelines and generations of shame. My legacy is taking elite care of self and elite care of those who come into my realm. My legacy is SEEING people only as their highest most divine selves, as God created them. My legacy is **"Thank You, More Please"**. Basking in all that's *good* and amplifying it. My legacy is reclamation, empowerment, energetic and material wealth. My legacy is rewriting, recoding and rewiring any thoughts, beliefs or patterns that aren't my ultimate truth. **My legacy is being built moment to moment-behind the scenes, and yours is too.** Within this chapter we are building foundations, lifestyle, strategies, energetics and embodiment practices of the high level being. **Creating a life to be witnessed and**

remembered. In life, love, purpose, creation, spirit, wealth, and of course illogical success in every way. Throughout this chapter, as I share high level energetics that I embody and lead my clients into embodying, **I want you to begin to observe yourself and see where you can attune to higher frequencies of existing.** This meaning, higher standards for yourself, how you show up, and what/who you interact with.

Take a few moments here…
Breathe in… breathe out.
What is Your Legacy?
How are you choosing to live?
How do you want to be remembered?

Embodying and observing your beautiful life…

I always say…"The high level individual both embodies and observes their beautiful life." Essentially, **you are both the observer and the experiencer of life.** You must be deeply present with life, embodied in life and living *within* the experience to get the most out of it. In order to refine, upgrade, and improve your life, you must be observing it as well. Fully embody pain as it arises and fully embody the pleasure. The high level being does not shy away from the realness and rawness of what *is*. **They feel it all, to have it all**—plain and simple. With every edge, there is evolution. There's no shying away from the shadows, no suppressing, no leaving behind. **It's about falling in love with all of you**- when you do that, you are truly *Unfuckwithable.* That's the Embodiment, THAT is the work. The observation however, is knowing and *living* in such a way that your **awareness of self guides your life.** Your awareness that there is something bigger, your awareness that there is always another choice, a better way, a higher love…Something divine is leading you. **Your awareness of self is your edge,** it is your brilliance and it is the key to all your success. Your ability to observe your *human* self in its fullness—in every detail of their precious self. The seeking, the presence, the highs, the lows, the desire, the patience, the magic… all of it.

When you can fully *see* yourself and hold yourself up– miracles happen.

Embodiment moves mountains. When your embodiment is experienced and fully expressed in a safe, open, and intentional space-you become ***Unfuckwithable.*** This embodiment is a deep honoring of your spirit, your *femininity* and your creatrix energy. This safe held space however is created through the observer, your inner *masculine*, your higher self, the part of you that creates spaciousness to fully embody what *is* in a regenerative- high level way. **Observation and embodiment is the *way* of the high level being-always flowing and always intentional.** It's nuanced, it's complex (until Integrated within this work), then, it becomes automatic, effortless, natural, it's *just the way you live*. The high level being gets it, and the high level being lives it. It takes practice being the one embodying and observing their beautiful life. Fully immersed-yet highly aware of your actions, intentions, and patterns. Being in the driver's seat and the passenger seat simultaneously. **Life in the fast lane, yet witnessed in ultra slow motion.** This deep honoring of your innate feminine and your innate masculine. **The divinity within embodied polarity and attuned harmonization creates a deeply fulfilling life.**

You are more divine than you know–act accordingly.

A little about being a high level individual, from my personal experience/perspective...

A fully expressed unapologetically beautiful, powerful, and abundant woman WILL trigger the shit out of You... shining light on the aspects of yourself that deserve a whole lotta love. We've all been there-the one being triggered, and the one triggering. There is medicine on "either side". So don't shy away, lean into the edges...always. **If you're not in full celebration of this type of woman then be gentle with yourself, get curious, and get healing.** The sequence of events for me tends to look like this (not always, but often). My confidence and certainty triggers another innately brilliant, bad ass, powerful, and wildly capable woman. Make the brave decision to lean into it with curiosity, and dive deep into my world, into my work, my offers, and naturally rise to new heights in confidence, personal power, success, and enlightenment. *Many* of the women who I get to witness rise in massive ways often say to me, "You used to trigger me so much." As a High Level Woman, I hold this sacred space for you. **I hold the duality of being an expander for women while also triggering them.** I don't love that I trigger good people, and it's not a comfortable experience. However, for the amount of people I expand, heal, activate, inspire, and motivate- it's 100% worth it! In turn, naturally, I also trigger a tonne of people and they may choose to hate on my very unapologetic existence, and that's okay too.

Part of living life in the fast lane, and operating in HIGH level energetics means that you aren't really relatable to the masses, your drive, your genius, your alignment and your devotion is not relatable–and absolutely not repeatable. I am deeply grateful for the women who came before me–those women who both expanded *and* triggered me. I am SO grateful to have been shown a better and free-er way. Any trigger, or uncomfortable expansion was always an invitation to better understand myself, my power, my vulnerability AND my personal alignment. It was always an opportunity to heal, hold the edges of myself, and fully accept where I was at each moment. With love, understanding, and a tonne of grace of course. **Part of being a high level being who chooses to live a life by your own design- is that you will not be understood or celebrated by all.** It is triggering to the masses to see someone walk with high self love and pure expression. **It is a great act of rebellion to love your life and show that to the world.** It is a great act of rebellion to unapologetically live your *High Level Life,* and own your success, brilliance and own the *speed* in which you evolve. The high level being however, is brave enough to do this.

Our highest timeline requires our fullest expression. **Your fullest expression is your most innate attraction point.** It also happens to be a way of being that most people are uncomfortable witnessing. We've had lifetimes of conditioning as women to be threatened by another woman's beauty, power, magnetism, and success. This being said, be super gentle with yourself if you feel triggered, or even just uncomfortable when you see a fully expressed genuinely happy, brilliant, abundant, gorgeous woman living her best life freely. Be with it, embody it, observe it and return to the truth that is, "When she thrives, I thrive, we ALL thrive." **You are the main character of your life, so act like it–be a rebel, and do YOU.** Old paradigms are fading and new paradigms are rising. High level energetics are foundational in these new paradigms. Energetics of individuals owning and expressing their individuality with high levels of kindness, integrity, and consciousness. **So stop tip-toeing around what you want, who you are, and what your truth is- and claim it.** We're meant to live free, joyful, abundant lives. Step into it now, make one move today that feels like a FUCK YES in your body–and continue to build off that.

You are the main character Babe-act like it.

High Level Beings don't get stuck in lack, doubt, fear or waiting. Do they feel the feels? –Yes, absolutely. Do those feelings take over their life? No, absolutely not. It's time to really start to program the high level embodiment and observation of honoring what comes up, being with the uncomfortableness, honoring the duality, moving into a better feeling, and choosing to do it again. **It's easy to get stuck in lack-based frequencies when you don't take the time and space to pull yourself up and out of it.** When you don't live in observation you lose out on the higher perspective of it all. Society, MSM, and the general mass hypnosis perpetuates lack and misalignment (more on this in upcoming chapters). Misalignment through hustle culture, not-enoughness and perpetual fear mongering. The old outdated paradigms perpetuate woundology, stangnancy and fear. **You must be really intentional, conscious and devoted to break**

free of that old programming. It takes intention and devotion to be the high level person who constantly pulls themself up and out, and chooses again. This choosing again, this moving into a higher frequency… this is the observation self, this is your Highest Self or your soul perspective of your life. This is something I have mastered, and continue to enhance. This is something I support my clients in experiencing and something you will experience as you devote yourself to this work within this chapter. **Being in observer mode of your life, while still embodying all of it… now that's a vibe.** This is high level living. It's a multidimensional way of being of various realms playing together, intertwining, and collapsing into one. This is what I call, *"The Dimension of Openness"* where *all-that-is,* exists simultaneously. It's life changing and REALLY really fun to learn, integrate, and to eventually experience this synergy and union as natural… as "life itself."

It's time to normalize the "both-and". You can be completely in your power, feel successful, and radiant while also feeling sad about the version of you who no longer exists. The grief reaction when you come up against the edges and the paradigms that no longer align. Each day, and each week I, personally, feel all of it. Emotions *higher than high* and emotions *lower than low,* I allow myself to feel it all. I have a neutral baseline of peace, satisfaction, wellbeing, and holistic success, and I constantly CHOOSE to return to my baseline as a standard of living. A high level way of being, high vibrational, open and holistically successful–as non negotiable. *I am constantly embodying and processing emotions as they show up to ensure that I have an open and clear system.* An open and clear system is a magnetic and receptive system. **An unobstructed system IS a receptive system.** If you want to receive more (love, money, impact, success etc.), then You want to practice immediately embodying and processing when things come up… more on this in later chapters. *This emotional processing allows my baseline to be abundant, clear, blissful, successful, and satisfied.* This allows my nervous system to be extremely regulated as I continue to rise into more while holding more on this natural ascension path. I celebrate often. I also grieve. I cry, I laugh, sing, dance, and I collapse into the fetal position when I just need to be held. I hold myself in a child's pose asking for guidance. I stand powerfully in a mountain pose declaring my power– my truth. **I embody all of it.** I feel anger and rage fully. I feel pleasure and joy in ways like never before. You get to feel it all while you have it all. **As a matter of fact there is no way to have it all without feeling it all.**

The High level being moves quickly, strategically and intentionally. *High Level Individuals do not hesitate, they do not waiver and they are FAR from indecisive.* They move. They trust themselves, they have the belief system that it is always happening for them, there is no failure, only growth, only learning and they make bold moves that catalyze their next level powerfully and often. **They know that everything's adding up for them–so that's just how they live.** There is no room for questioning, doubting, or living in stagnancy. They trust themselves. Their life just keeps getting better. They make bold moves in alignment with their next level. Bold moves made in alignment with their highest self. **They choose better feeling thoughts, they choose joy over and over again.** They trust their desires. They lead themselves and they allow themselves to be led. High Level Individuals do the inner work to heal, awaken, and thrive. A constant recalibration process to their truth, to their knowing, to their soul, spirit, and highest level identity. Recalibrating future anxieties or from the past to the now– their path and their purpose. This is a dialed, focused, and deeply devotional path. Having the courage to live *life by your own design* in a time where living freely, happily, and on your own terms is not the norm. **Amidst the chaos, amidst the fear…Can you choose to be wildly, freely and openly, You?** Can you choose to believe that there's a better way, and that you are always being led? Can you choose YOU? Choose YOU, day by day and watch what unfolds?

Being a high level being, building an empire, and leaving a legacy is a moment to moment decision. It is something that is built behind the scenes. It is built when you are interacting with the world and interacting with *all that is*. When it comes to operating in these high level ways, it comes down to standards. **You are getting what you're available for–Period.** Building an Empire, leaving a legacy, and being Unfuckwithable means you have high standards. **We're talking about standards...*Not boundaries.*** You have transcended beyond boundary setting. You are operating in energetic alignment which means if it's not your vibe... it does not exist in your world. Energetic alignment is this process of naturalization of what is meant for you. You have clear standards of what you are and are not available for. **It's not about boundaries... It's about standards.** The High Level individual knows this and the High Level individual LIVES this.

*Before we even dive deep into the homework of this chapter, take a moment now, take a deep breath, drop into your body, and **set some new standards.*** What are you no longer available for? What are you DECIDING is a new standard for you? You WILL receive in alignment with your elevated standards, you will walk a new walk, and talk a new talk. **Once you implement new standards you literally become allergic to what is not vibrating on that frequency.** It's time to refine and align to your new standards in all areas of your life. Elevation in your faith, empowerment, relationships, confidence, magnetism, your pleasure and your success. It's time to refine your standards. Refinement here means releasing anything that is not on your unique elite level. **Have a clear knowing and standard of what IS aligned with your legacy, with your path...*And what is not.***

A High Level Being is a High Level Being-Period. It's not what you do... it's who you BE. You want more and you have standards for how that will look and feel in your life. **You are focused, dialed in, and devoted to actualizing those standards as natural, normal, and to be expected for you.** This naturalized way of being comes from high level embodiment. Embodied standards, and personal power is you being Unfuckwithable. It's not something that can be tapped into once and then forgotten-it's embodied. Once you learn and integrate these ways of BEING, it's just who you are. **Your energy is attuned, your vibe upgrades, your frequency rises, and everything you desire-desires you.** This embodiment of personal power is not situational. It is NOT circumstantial, or conditional on xyz going your way. It's not dependent on being in a good mood, or having circumstances aligned. **No no my love, this is a way of existing where you are infinitely powerful–*no matter what.*** Being the High Level Being means you are willing to feel it all. Again, *we feel it all to have it all*- there's no shying away from the shadows, no suppressing, and no leaving behind. As your standards rise you WILL feel grief, you will feel spaciousness that can easily feel like emptiness... there is a recalibration period in which your new standards attract the aligned frequencies. **Be fully on the journey... no rushing here.** Be in full honoring of all parts of you. It's about falling in love with all of you and when you do that, you're truly Unfuckwithable.

This is a realm of openness... There are no conditions here.

Your power, your confidence gets to be unwavering. The high level being has a level of certainty in their life, they don't sit, wait and wish. **They create it, they receive, and they have unshakeable faith in it all happening for them.** None of their success is a fluke. it's to be expected-it's certain. You're Unfuckwithable no matter what, you're good no matter what...You know your human/avatar will flow through the inevitable waves of emotions and energy, and you know your soul will lead you. You know that your power and self concept is not dependent on anything outside of You. You also know that you get to have it all. **You begin to expect that incredible things are happening and unfolding for You- no matter what the circumstances appear to be.** Again, the high level being both EMBODIES and OBSERVES their beautiful life. They deep dive into the shadow work, self worth work, and they're willing to embody, and LOVE all parts of themselves. I myself feel things on all levels– the incredible feelings and the painful ones. I integrate all of it, process it, dance, scream, and shake it out. I don't rush any of it. I know it is all medicine and all part of my divine unfolding. Embodiment is messy, raw, and wild. What you do with that embodiment, how you make art of it...**Now that is an articulated, curated, strategic masterpiece.**

Personal Power is being with uncomfortable emotions. Observing them, integrating them and knowing that no matter what kind of mood you're in. No matter how high or low your energy is, and no matter what is happening in your external world–YOU are powerful! The most successful (holistically at that) people in the world have this in common- they KNOW they are powerful. This knowing is unwavering. **This knowing is represented in their standards, their beliefs, thoughts, relationships, actions, and environments.** Let's backtrack now... back to the core belief that it is all happening for you. You are exactly where you need to be. **Everything is unfolding FOR you–it's all adding up.** You are a High Level being, you desire an opulent, expansive, soul fulfilling life. You know you want more. More from a space of GROUNDED wholeness, success that feels fulfilling and supports the collective rise. You desire MORE... More in pure alignment with all that is GOOD for you, your family, your community, and the collective at large. Quick reminder that you are RARE. You are important, and you are here for really big things babe. The practices within this book are leading you and re-coding your consciousness for your highest timeline integration through this high level facilitation. Take a moment and revel in that. *Breathe in. Breathe out. Be proud of yourself. Breathe it in... it's happening now.*

You are ready to meet and align with your Highest Self.
You are ready to dive into the quantum realm...collapse time and create the life of your dreams.
You are here to live your most love filled, pleasure filled and most abundant life.
All this and more in alignment with your divine purpose.
Nothing is off the table, everything is accessible to you.
It's so close– I can see it for you...Can You?

Personal Power is the absolute energy of *ever evolving Holistic Success.* Being Unfuckwithable is a lifestyle. This energy... this embodiment grows and evolves *with You.* When you unlock your personal power and you take on the identity of the CREATOR of your life, magic happens. Better yet, when you take on the identity of the CO-creator. When you are ALSO open to all the co-creators that want to support you... you are literally unstoppable, unshakeable, and limitless AF. The high level individual understands co-creation, they are aware of their *sacred creatrix energy* and their *sacred receptivity energy.* Magnetism (in all areas of life) is a combination of energy and execution, action and alignment, intention and surrender. Holistic Success is next level success in any/all areas of your beautiful life is about knowing when to move, and knowing when to open up to what already is. I personally move fast, I move intentionally and I move strategically. I also rest hard, lean back and open up to the medicine that life is serving me—*The medicine that I can only properly receive when I am in pure trust, surrender and nothingness.* Things workout the best for me when I focus on fun, flow and ease. When I let go of the rush, and when I lock into the truth that there is nothing but abundance. I always have more than enough time, energy, money, and resources to do, be and have what I desire. It always works out better than expected for me. It's always working out for me-even when it seems hard. Even when I can't see that it's adding up. It's all the bridge of incidents and the divine unfolding. I don't have to know the "how", or understand the process. *I simply surrender to it.* **I don't have to do it alone...I am a CO-creator.**

Back to being ALL of You. I personally am the type of woman who dances between Mamba mentality (the ongoing desire for more, better, success, elite levels of being and high fucking standards for my work ethic, gifts and life), AND being the divine feminine goddess who leans back, rests, surrenders and trusts. This dance (that is not always perfect) has truly served me, and the high level elite professional clients who work with Me. This dance between doing and receiving, masculine and feminine energetics, strategy and energy, devotion and discipline making it happen and trust. I am not just a 'believer' in this harmonization of energetics and embodiment...*I have the certainty that this dance is required.* This dance is my alignment. When you are the type of person who is building a regenerative empire, leading a new paradigm, and BEING Unfuckwithable... alignment is required. I am absolutely about wanting something so bad and knowing it's meant for Me. I'm about wanting it so bad that I become obsessed, singularity focused and dialed into the frequency of it. Luckily, and strategically for me... the focus and frequency of everything I want depends on my *alignment.* **This, in turn, depends on my dance between doing and receiving.** It is not aligned to lean back all day and expect things to happen for You. It's also not aligned to hustle your tits off and expect things to happen for You. **There is a deep honoring of the body, the energy system, and the divine timing of it all.** The spacious rest, the ease and the lean back allows divine intervention and timing to shift things FOR You. The action, the doing, the forward movement, and discipline creates the initiation for the universe to respond to. BEING Unfuckwithable is about so much, and a big piece of the Unfuckwithable experience is about having everything you want...but absolutely not at the cost of Your wellbeing. You can want more, strive for more and BUILD more... but the energetics and definition of Unfuckwithableness is based on the very concept that you already ARE whole and complete without any of it. This means you will not contort yourself, disrespect your wellbeing or energetics to have more. The distortion that many high achievers, self developing and spiritual kings and queens fall into...Is the delusion that something is missing until xyz arrives. Nothing is missing. You are whole and complete, AND you get to create and receive more from that fulfilling place of WHOLENESS.

You get to have it all AND you already have it all (feel me?). You can move toward a desire and want it so bad while also feeling so whole and complete as you are. You get to move with desire AND land in the present moment with gratitude and presence. You are whole, complete and worthy as you are AND everything else you desire just gets to AMPLIFY that feeling. Release the obsession over a past or future illusion... nothing is missing my love. And don't deny yourself of feeling what you're feeling, desiring what you're desiring, and moving toward it powerfully. Being **Unfuckwithable** and being a High Level Individual is about landing in the openness of this nuance. Existing within the "Both-And". The LIE is that there are deficits, that something is missing... that there are rights and wrongs, blacks, and whites. *This high level experience is about dropping so deep within your own truth, that the only option is dancing and flowing with all that is.* Honoring the nuances of this unique experience that IS this life. Land into the fullness of this moment and allow your soul given desires to lead you. *Take a breath here. What are your soul desires?* **The very act of connecting regularly to your souls desires, facilitates their Co-creation.**

Do it now, and do it often. The work within this book is enough to allow you the discernment of knowing what your true soul desires are. Discerning what desires are actually true for you. If they are true for You, they are of your highest good. Therefore, they are for the highest good for all. However, if you want to deepen your practice of connecting to your own soul... slow down more, meditate more, sit in stillness more, and connect to your heart more. *Journal more on what is actually a desire of your heart.*

If you want it, you want it, AND it's meant for you. It's meant for you and you get to have it, AND you're powerful enough to know that you are ALREADY whole and complete with or without it. From this grounded and fulfilled state, the desires drop in effortlessly.

Momentum is the formula of manifestation.

Let's talk Momentum. Momentum is a grouping of teachings, transmissions, and practices that channeled through to me in 2022. I ended up coaching on these very teachings and changed the lives of hundreds of people through the principles of momentum. Now, I shall bring them to you. Quick riff on my psychic channel, and how this information comes through to better empower your understanding of how direct, potent, and clear this Momentum teaching is (and all teachings within this book). My work is highly interconnected within the *Dimension of Openness* and channeled from infinite intelligence. I am a higher translator to ALL that is within various dimensions, and I receive downloads both on demand and also randomly throughout my day to day and moment-to-moment existence. I have complete trust in what channels through, and I effortlessly translate it clearly and potently for those who are meant to receive the messages. So, I will give you the process of *Momentum* here in clear terms then throughout the next few paragraphs I will deepen your understanding of the work. *I promise you these Momentum Codes will give you the solid foundation as a high level being to manifest anything you TRULY desire.* Momentum is always building... and once built–this momentum inevitably leads to the "cashing in" of those rewards (desires, manifestations, dreams, goals etc.). *This is the formula.*

The process/formula of Momentum to "Cashing In" goes like this

1. You BE the LEADING ENERGY
2. You integrate high level REFINEMENT (the subtle codes of your alignment AND misalignment)
3. You begin to experience EXCITEMENT (because after steps 1 and 2 there is NO WAY you can't and won't manifest what you desire, SO you have no other option than to be in the frequency of excitement-Yay!)
4. Cash in (aka have all desires manifested)

Alright, now let's deepen this so you can actually live, and integrate this formula into your own life. This is a chapter where you likely will want to take notes in your journal. Let us start with NEWTON'S 1st law of motion, "An object in motion will remain in motion in the determined direction until an OPPOSITE force is applied." Your momentum starts when you set the intention toward what you desire. You begin to act in alignment with what you desire. This is YOU being the LEADING energy. You decide what is TRUE for You. You see your vision, you list, determine your goals and desires and then you move. Your vision (if true for You) is being put into motion. You have been LEADING that direction through your thoughts, beliefs, actions, energetics, and embodiment. For example, if you desire to attract more money into your life, then you become the leading energy–you make it clear that you desire more money. You begin to think and feel like a wealthy person. You begin to align to abundance frequencies, you take action aligned with you attracting, generating, earning and/or receiving more money. This positive momentum is being created from the foundation up, stacked, and to be eventually cashed in. The opposite forces would come in either internally or externally. **For example an internal opposite force could be: limiting beliefs, doubts, and fears from within around scarcity and lack.** An external force in the opposite direction could be: someone hacks your account and robs you of thousands of dollars. **Nonetheless, it is YOUR and ONLY YOUR responsibility to get BACK into alignment... BACK into momentum.** It is important to note that both INTERNAL and EXTERNAL forces can be OPPOSITE or POSITIVE. For example an internal force in the positive direction could be intentional thoughts (which compound into beliefs) around money being a supportive energy and something that is all around and infinitely available. An external force in the positive direction could be walking along the street and finding a $100 dollar bill on the ground. Whether the forces are internal or external, if they are in the positive direction (aka aligned with your intention) then your only job is to say "Thank You, More Please," and start to build on that validation that it's all adding up, it's all aligning and it's all happening for You. If they are 'negative' or forces in the opposite direction-your only job is to get BACK into alignment. It's pretty simple Babe.

When it comes to momentum, YOU are the leading energy and everything is responding to YOU. You have the power. You are the magnet. You are the attractor ,and it is all responding to your alignment (or lack thereof). You being the leading energy means not only are you DECIDING what you want, you are DEVOTING to living in alignment with that desire. Setting the foundation for your momentum to build and compound into stacked and cashed in results requires your intention, embodiment, and aligned action. *This is not a "set it and forget it" situation.* **This is a daily and moment-to-moment devotion to staying on the path.** DO NOT DEVIATE from the path of momentum. If you do deviate, notice it and shift back into your frequency of alignment. This ability to stay in alignment and in the positive direction comes from your foundation of embodiment and awareness which we covered earlier in this chapter. Hold the vibration, hold the frequency, and HOLD the standard. Know that it is inevitable for you. Nothing outside of you shifts your momentum–that's on you. *If something happens externally, it's your JOB to realign and get back on your path.*

Most people require external validation to prove to them that it's "working". **Those who stay focused, stay in their alignment and cultivate an internal sense of knowing are the ones whose momentum turns into stacked and cashed-in results.** Do not seek outside validation. Your job is to build the *Unfuckwithable* KNOWING that your success, goals, dreams, and desires are INEVITABLE for You. Every time you look outside yourself for external validation you lose focus. You leak momentum and your momentum is melting outward vs moving forward. **The important thing is to be so hyper-aware of your INsourced power.** Your insourced power–aka your innate *unfuckwithableness* aka the energy of you deciding that it's all adding up, the energy of you choosing aligned thoughts, building aligned beliefs and taking aligned action. The insourced power is YOU noticing when you deviate from the path. You then do the rewiring, and reprogramming. Start shifting the doubt, fear, and blocks into the pure aligned, positive direction of the path. This focus on insourcing keeps your eyes on your lane and builds an unshakable foundation of personal power. **You are building** momentum from within. **This allows you to be the 1%.** The 1% person who stays IN IT, when the majority of people would unplug or put up a block RIGHT before it's about to manifest. *When you can INSOURCE your power and have a knowing that it is all aligning without any external validation or proof–then, you are UNFUCKWITHABLE.*

The second piece of Momentum is the awareness of your subtle codes of alignment and misalignment. This is the work of getting to know which actions, energetics and embodiments/ways of being actually support your momentum AND what is actually hindering it. *Subtle codes are just that... they're subtle.* They are nuanced, and can be easily overlooked when you are not operating from a High Level space of intentionality in your day to day. When you are operating from a High Level energy of awareness and observation of self you can start to easily discern what feels like an aligned action, energy and embodiment, and what feels misaligned. **The faster you recognize the subtle codes of your misalignment, the faster you can realign and get back on the path of your alignment.**

So babe, slow down... take a deep breath, remember there is MORE wisdom in your pinky toe than anything anyone could ever teach You.

Drop in... drop into your body and breathe.
Where in your life on the path of your desires are you MISaligned?
What needs to be cleaned up and released?
What actions, thoughts and beliefs need refining?
What clutter needs refining? What excess needs refining?
What doubts and fears need upgrading?
Take your time reflecting here, in your body on these truths.
Then once the awareness of the misalignment is clear it is your sole duty to get BACK into your alignment.

This refinement phase as we look at our subtle codes of alignment and misalignment is what I like to call HEALTHY ASSESSMENT ENERGY. Once you are clear on what you want, and you are CONSCIOUSLY aligning toward it, you will have moments of "why isn't it here...yet?" In these moments you are losing focus and looking outside, so first off get back in your lane and secondly healthily assess.

Let's do some healthy assessments now together–This is where you get hyper dialed and honest with yourself...

1. Are you REALLY in alignment?
2. Do you REALLY believe in it happening? (have you actually done the *belief work* to believe your dream life as available..to do the work to believe in your desires as TRUE for you?
3. Have your thoughts, actions and energies REALLY been in a positive direction toward what you are manifesting?

THIS is healthily assessing. From this place we either clean up and refine what needs cleaning up, or we healthily assess that- yes in fact all is aligned, and from that space we KNOW that our desires are inevitably on their way. From this knowing we get to move into EXCITEMENT energy. The energy of, "It can't not happen!!". *Excitement energy is the landing strip for it all to drop in.* When you get to a space of excitement about your desires, you are a welcome mat for all that is aligned. From this excitement space you begin to create safety, neutralization, and naturalization of your desires. They are a guarantee–there is no pressure, no rush, you feel calm, certain yet excited about the unfolding. This excitement energy then yields the- "what's next frequency?" This is the frequency of... "My desires are here, they are a guarantee..." So! What will I do now? What will I do with them? How will I exist in this new reality? How will I exist with more love, happiness, security, health, money, fame, impact, purpose, my dream house, dream car (insert your desire) etc.? The excitement energy IS an energy of naturalization because it inevitably yields the frequency of "what now?" **From this space my love...It is only a matter of 'divine timing' before your desires land.** *Your only job from here is staying in the excitement,* *neutral and naturalized energy of it ALL happening and actualizing NOW.*

When it comes to your Momentum stacking and cashing in– "knowing" is not enough–if anything, knowing is harmful if you do not also know how to embody and integrate that knowing. Being a high level being who actualizes what they desire means that you are LIVING the knowledge. The channel was clear with Me years ago… as I said earlier–the age of KNOWING has shifted into the age of INTEGRATION. The knowledge of what is aligned and is not aligned is integrated into your lived reality. **It is not stacking unless it is TRULY aligned and it is not cashing in until you release what is not aligned.** Read that again. Alignment is a full body and energetic experience, alignment requires your embodiment of it. Example, someone may "know" they have outgrown a certain relationship or way of interacting. They may know that it is no longer aligned BUT so long as they continue to participate in the relationship and that outdated, misaligned, old paradigm way of being… nothing is changing. *Again, knowing is not enough… it is harmful to know something if you are not LIVING in true alignment with that knowing.* Now, when you DO know for certain that you ARE living in alignment the way to shift yourself into the excitement phase of cashing in your desires (and quickly at that) is to consciously NOTICE, take account of and REVEL in all the stacked momentum. **This stacked momentum is all the times you acted, thought, believed, and lived in alignment with that in which you desired.** Give yourself the MASSIVE energetic upgrade of SEEING your success so far and see that it is ALL adding up. Every thought, belief, and action that IS in alignment IS STACKING up and ready to INEVITABLY cash in. *From this space of SELF validation, INsourced personal power–an energy of "I'm fucking PROUD of myself and all that I have done to align to this manifestation." You WILL shift quickly into an energy of CERTAINTY… you WILL KNOW that your desires are guaranteed.* From this energy of certainty you naturally get EXCITED about your desires dropping into your reality because there is NO WAY that they aren't.

You are a HIGH level being building a holistic regenerative empire and leaving a holistic and stunning legacy. *You're on a High Level babe…act accordingly.* You are the leading energy. You are building momentum until initiating your desires into fruition. *You set the frequency–and then you watch the Universe respond.* A life lived with intention has a compounding effect of a legacy left behind. The high level being LEAVES a legacy, no matter what. A high level being transforms the planet, the collective consciousness, and these upgrades penetrate the generations to come. You are consciously and subconsciously building an empire. You are leaving a legacy as you walk the walk and talk the talk through mindful intention. In your boldness, and in your simplicity…In your iconic moves and in your subtle codes of being–you are high level and the world is responding to you accordingly. We are consciously building empires in ALL areas of our lives and leaving a legacy to be remembered and lived on. We are changing how life is lived, and we are elevating our ways of being and those around us into individual truth. **We are CHOOSING life giving energies and regenerative ways of living.** We are building a New Earth and leading a New Paradigm–it starts within, every single time. It's about who we BE behind the scenes, and who we show up as in front of the world. We are elevating the collective consciousness and healing the Earth, one intentional move at a time. *It's an energetic and strategic way of existing, that changes the landscape of all elements of this life.*

For your homework: daily devotionals…In honoring HIGH level energetics, I want you to…

A. Take a breath, a deep breath… drop into your solar plexus (the belly) and hold yourself… connect to your innate power. Connect to your innate high level energetics and breathe. Take three deep breaths and affirm **"I am POWERFUL"** –affirm this until it feels true. Let that integrate.

B. In your journal begin to write out what BEING a high level individual means for You. Naturally write out what comes through. Once you have written out what naturally flows through…

C. Reflect on the following:

1-How do I show up in my relationships as a HIGH level individual?

(ALL important relationships in your life)

2-How do I show up for myself as a HIGH level individual?

(My own self care, wellness, mental health, fitness, nutrition, spirituality, action, energetics etc.)

3-How do I show up in my career/life's work/purpose/business etc as a HIGH level individual?

4-How do I FEEL and EXPRESS my CONFIDENCE as a HIGH level individual?

D. Lastly… in your journal (following some deep intentional breaths), begin to write out:

What you are NO LONGER AVAILABLE FOR? What is NOT aligned with your reality as a HIGH level being? Make a list, reflect and truly recognize why these things/relationships/ways of being/thoughts/
beliefs/actions etc. need to go… now breathe… and make a plan to let them go.

I am so proud of You!

I hope you took your time with this chapter, and with these reflections. This High Level Energetic way of life, is a standard...A foundation of BEING Unfuckwithable...These concepts, teachings, and ways of being, MUST be integrated and TRUE for you, before moving on to the upcoming chapters.

CHAPTER 4

UNAPOLOGETICALLY ICONIC

"A fully expressed, unapologetically beautiful, powerful and abundant woman WILL trigger the shit out of you… Shining light on the aspects of yourself that deserve a whole lotta LOVE.

Lean into the edge ALWAYS. If you're not in full celebration of this type of woman,
be gentle with yourself, get curious and get healing."

This chapter is for the individual who is ready to be *seen* in all of their power:

Unapologetic, Unleashed, Magnetic AF, ICONIC

This BOOK is for the one looking to elevate their confidence in being seen, well known, and fully expressed in their truth. *There is no being **Unfuckwithable** without being Iconic.* **The Icon is doing life their way.** Celebrating themselves, self validating, and learning through experience–every step of the way. **The Icon loves who they are.** This is the essential part of getting to know and love yourself…Being the Icon is about recognizing your rare, unique individuality. The work within this chapter is designed to help you recognize your unique power and own that. This chapter is designed to help you remember that your presence is a blessing to the world. Being the Icon, being **Unfuckwithable** is about operating from your truest, purest essence, and magnetism. Iconic energy is about owning the fact that you are NOT relatable; you aren't normal, and you are not here to be easily understood or defined. You are RARE, unique and you are done trying to fit into the constricting molds of the limited society. **You're fucking done** with self censorship and playing small, you are here to **STAND OUT.** Icons are here to lead in the New Paradigm by inspiring thousands if not millions, with their purest integrity (while continuing to navigate the inevitable edges of being this rare). **Being an Icon means you hold the duality of not being liked or palatable to the masses, while simultaneously expanding and inspiring the others**. Being an Icon is an elevated experience of life that honors ALL of your beingness... and yes, the results are juicy AF.

A little on me, Haley –The ICON of New Paradigm Spirituality. My life (by design), my HIGH level energetics and my Unfuckwithable-ness is based on the concepts of BEING an Icon. I live an Iconic life designed by me, and I want you to do the same– in your own unique way of course. I am a NEW paradigm leader. I am DESIGNING my own life–as opposed to being tempted into borrowed identities, blueprints and yawn ideologies of what's normal. It is now time for YOU to step into your New Paradigm Iconic identity. As an Icon, I don't know anyone doing what I do. I don't know anyone doing it the way I do it. I want you to begin to discover your unique innate truths–what makes YOU Iconic? What makes you unique? What is your ACTUAL truth? (not the latest trend or politically correct way of being)–but what actually makes up–YOU? **In a world of woke robotic assimilation... It is an act of REBELLION to be unapologetically YOU.** You wouldn't have picked up this book, devoted to the work inside and made it this far if you too, weren't the rare Icon that I know you to be. I SEE you. Now it's time for everyone to see you, but first you must see yourself. In order to BE Iconic as your naturalized DEFAULT way of being, there is intentionality required. **It is critical to actually get to know and love yourself.** Iconic energy is PART of being *Unfuckwithable.* An Icon is here to lead the way, do it their way and squeeze all the juice out of this precious life–aka bask in the regards, results and manifestations that God wants to drench them in for being their *truest* self. The Icon KNOWS that this existence is unrepeatable. The Icon recognizes the temporary-ness and the precious-ness of this life. They are here for ALL of it.

Being an Icon is a multifaceted experience, but in simplicity is based on these key principles/processes.

#1 Getting to actually KNOW and LOVE yourself.

#2 Dropping the borrowed identities, stopping the self-censorship and CLAIMING your own truth.

When you decide to live an iconic life—you decide to enter a profound healing journey that cannot be experienced within the cages of mediocre living. **Being an unapologetic Icon is the deepest initiation into self healing and self discovery that there is.** Iconic energy and new paradigms of self and collective leadership requires us to own both our power *and* our vulnerability. **The New Paradigm creates spaciousness for the "both-and" always.** We have well outgrown the illusion of separation—the illusion of right and wrong and the illusions of pedestals and hierarchies. We are working within a much higher level of life here on Earth. Within the dimension of openness in order to BE the Icon living an *Unfuckwithable* gushing-in love life…We must honor the nuance of everything, be willing to see things differently and be willing to be judged. **Your purest expression elicits your deepest healing.** When you express your truest self, you are doing what most people won't do… *you are actually living your truth.* **When you express your authentic truth, and then question it, or be questioned, or trigger someone, or trigger yourself…You are invited IN to a deeper, purer opportunity to self validate and to self heal.** Your fullest expression (be it insights, expression or embodiment) opens you up to the most vulnerable corners of yourself. When you live this way and are courageous enough to show yourself in this way, You open yourself up to the wrath of fear, hate, and misunderstanding that you could have simply avoided through the perpetuation of normalcy and status quo living—but you're not here to play it safe or play it small. This embodiment of your innate TRUTH, opens you up to deepened self awareness. This self awareness is where you get to observe. This observation (when you're devoted to this work) is what leads to your healing, and then allows you to experience the most blissful ascension here on Earth. *Your full embodiment of truth (and the journey of healing that got you there) is what leads you to living a truly FREE experience of this Earthly realm– through wealth, impact, the juiciest experience of love, connection and intimacy.*

An Icon is ever evolving. Icons are devoted to evolution over their lifetime, because they are wise enough to know that this life is *circular* in nature, and we are ALWAYS growing, learning, expressing, healing, and basking in the rewards of this life. **This evolution over a lifetime places you in a smaller grouping of the population.** A smaller grouping of individuals who live differently. This rarity creates polarity– it creates disruption. Not everyone will like it. As an Icon, a lot of people are watching you. A lot of people are celebrating you and, conversely, most likely a lot of people are doubting you. They're being triggered by you and/or hoping to see you fail–DO YOU ANYWAY! And my love, many people are too focused on their own lane to even care about yours (yay for those people!). This knowledge within these pages will help you to simply–Do You! Do it well, and make this life the one that goes down in history. Personally speaking, as a New Paradigm Icon living an unconventional life on display, I have navigated a lot of hate, misunderstanding, and SO many projections. I live this beautiful unapologetically successful and joyful life that I have co-created, and that's triggering for many people. Generally speaking, I receive a lot more love than I do hate (praise the lord). Inevitably though, triggering people is part of being a disruptor in an outdated system. This can come out as projections of hate toward me and my lifestyle, and that's okay!–I truly don't personalize it. By no means is navigating projected hate easy…However, it is also part of this rapid evolution, unrealistic success, Iconic beingness, and living a life by my own design. **I'm more than okay with triggering some good people along the**

way. *(notice I refer a lot in this chapter to the people who are not yet awake–as "good" people…this is because I genuinely know that they in their heart of hearts are doing what they think is right, and they truly mean well. They haven't necessarily awakened to the infinite potential realities that exist, and are not yet aware of the groupthink, woke, brainwashing that they are under–but they ARE good people. I believe all people are born good, and ARE good at their core–conditioning brings out the demons–no doubt about it–but I will continue to refer to all people as **good and ever evolving**).* My mission, my empire, and my legacy is much more powerful. I deeply heal, I radically empower, I awaken, I inspire, and I ALIVEN those who are ready for TRUTH, and high level embodiment. **I focus on the impact I am here to make, and release the projections of the "haters" –I am changing the world profoundly–*and that is where I direct my focus.*** My life's work is part of thousands (soon to be millions) of peoples highest timeline integration through healing and evolution, so if that means I receive a bit of hate along the way–so be it. **My work changes lives and I am devoted to my work no matter what.** Again … if you are not in FULL celebration of a thriving woman–observe it, get curious about it, and heal it. **If you are being triggered, it is simply an invitation for deeper healing.** As an Icon, you will trigger people, and you may even trigger yourself. This is an INVITATION to deepen the love, compassion, and understanding YOU have for you.

Throughout this chapter you will hear me speak a lot about "Woke Robotic Assimilation" and "BEING Iconic." Being Iconic is the exact rebellion to this overarching, old paradigm, pretending to be new– of brainwashing and control…**This is what I call "Woke Robotic Assimilation": Preaching "authenticity" & "individuality" but ~~canceling~~ anyone who *questions* or *opposes* the status quo…** The Icon however is brave enough to speak truth, lead with love, and hold the duality of inspiring many while also shining light on wounded pain points. **This New Paradigm Iconic life is NOT about priding oneself in being** controversial…*But rather knowing that you may be received that way, and walking forward with your truth anyway.* Being an Icon is not about always intentionally going AGAINST the status quo… But rather deepening your internal practice of recognizing what actually feels true for you, and what feels like LOVE and ALIVENESS in your body. Often, inevitably when leading with your innate knowing–the status quo thoughts and belief systems show themselves to be harmful to individuality, and therefore life itself. As an Icon, it is critical to develop a practice of witnessing the mainstream narratives and norms. **Critical thinking and intuitive feeling is essential.** From this witnessing, you can practice dropping into your body to recognize the *integrity and truth* behind the narratives–*or lack thereof.*

There are some fabulous mainstream ideas like "be kind" and "we're all in this together". But is that ACTUALLY being felt, represented and embodied in the mainstream paradigm? It's very *popular* to say "respect individuality" and "be authentic" but only to a certain extent it seems–only when that 'individuality' matches the current wokeness. **These popular phrases ring true until your individuality and authenticity no longer match the trending status quo.** The Icon is in a moment to moment lived, embodied, and observational dance with life. The Icon chooses to lead with their innate essence, individuality, and truth–even if that truth rubs up against the dominant narrative of what is currently acceptable. The dominant narrative within old paradigms may trick you into believing your individuality is celebrated, but there are always conditions. **The old paradigms may package themselves up as "new" and at a first glance seem positive and loving–but pay attention to your intuition, critically analyze with your brilliant mind and actually drop into the felt energy in your body.** You are wise enough to know what is life giving, conscious and of a loving vibration–and what is not. Use discernment, and continue to BE ICONIC.

It's important to know that by living a truly Iconic life…you will trigger a lot of people who prefer the watered down version of you. When you lead from your purest expression–that is LOVE, the robotic assimilation (that is constructed from a much lower vibration and darker intention) constricts, reacts, and attempts to REPRESS you. *Be love anyway. Speak truth anyway. Do you anyway.*

Now my love, take a deep breath, find the spaciousness, and connect to your own heart–your own knowing and allow this all to land. *This has been a wordy few paragraphs AND I trust that you can receive it.* Now let's drop into our breath, bodies and consciousness for a few moments.

Take a few moments to reflect on the times in your life when you had a thought, idea or belief that did NOT match the status quo.

1.How did that feel?
2.Did you choose to express and live in alignment with it, anyway?
3.Feel into the times in your life when you felt like you didn't even know your own truth, your own thoughts or beliefs…because you were conditioned, programmed and wired for so long to adopt ideologies that never actually felt *true* for you.

Breathe into these reflections. Take your time here–it can be uncomfortable to uncover what has been a borrowed identity and ideology, it can be uncomfortable to feel so far away from our own grounded center and it can feel even more uncomfortable to know that in some way shape or form that we have played a role in the illusion...

It is time now my love…
To drop the borrowed identities and belief systems,
and instead live your own unique essence and truth.

Let's talk now about what I call "In-Sourcing". INSOURCING– aka getting to the center of your own being, your own knowing, your inner truths, and grounding into your innate identity. In-sourcing is your sovereignty–your individuality, your gut, your intuition, your self-concept, and your self-trust. **In-sourcing is at** the core of being Iconic and therefore BEING *Unfuckwithable.* The vibe is always coming back to your own center, your own truth, and your own innate being. It's about being **UNFUCKWITHABLE** in your own innate personal power. **Unconditionally SURE of yourself.** You aren't easily pulled out of your lane, and if/when you are pulled off, you are aware of it, and you get your ass back on your highest timeline. *You aren't borrowing identities or belief systems–you are remembering and creating your own.* Iconic and New Paradigm Living isn't about *taking on* ways of thinking and being, to be considered unique...You ARE unique–Period. *So let go of the external optics and validation if you REALLY want to blow the fuck up in the most expansive ways, and be fully free in all areas of your stunning life.* In-sourcing, being Iconic, and being *Unfuckwithable* is about being your innately brilliant self, who is naturally and inevitably unique. I don't want you to think like me, or someone else you may look up to.

I want you to be empowered, and inspired to look within YOU.

My Iconic Life Top Pillars
I can be around powerful fucking people and not get lost in comparison, rather it expands me into MORE.

I can be around "3D/old paradigm" people and not let it stunt my evolution, or fuck with my vision. Rather, I get to bask in the grounding and lessons of it.

I can be around all types of energy without clouding and obstructing my own.

I CAN interact with ALL types of people and not LOSE myself in it.

I can see and hear negative shit, and not make it mean anything about me.

I hold a level of power, certainty, and TRUTH in who I BE wherever I go.

No matter who I am with or where I am existing, I AM my most innately brilliant, stunning, kind, powerful, inspiring, and conscious self.

I set the stage. Not the other way around.

I hold myself in my vulnerability and allow it to free me. I can sit, talk, and hear people who see things COMPLETELY DIFFERENTLY than me, while still holding them in a space of respect, love, and understanding. I don't make it mean anything about me, my timeline, my truth or my power, AND, I don't make it mean anything about THEIR worthiness or value as a human being. **I can get curious about a new perspective or belief without feeling attacked or discredited.** I can be around "triggering" people and not let it fuck with me. I can receive positive and "negative" feedback–receive it with neutrality, openness, and allow it to expand my growth. I can be with the uncomfortable sides and edges of myself. I can amplify my gifts and my power, without worrying that I may be *'too much'*. **I can spend time with friends and family that don't "get me"(my beliefs or views) and I can love the fuck out of them anyway.** I can gush in love and adoration for friends, family and communities who hold wildly different beliefs than me. I can love *them* because I get *me*. "Love thy neighbor" is not conditional on seeing eye to eye on every single topic. I am so aware that this life is mine– in my fullest experience and my fullest expression I live MY soul path. I live my purpose, not through watering myself down and drowning into normalcy–but by existing as ME. I can change the world in a stunning, conscious, and loving way while holding that truth. I understand and embody nuance and duality, while walking my own path. **This life is about SO much more than me AND I am at the center of my own universe.** I can remember that my individuality and unapologetic energy is LOVE… it's not selfish or mindless…It is LIFE GIVING. I know that trusting my own internal compass and then expressing those truths with the world is a GIFT of generosity–not an act of narcissism. **I understand that when I feel free and others feel triggered, that it is not my responsibility– that's on them, not on me.**

This chapter, this book, and my very existence is about being a permission slip for you to do you–your way. Personally, as a healer, psychic channel, and a LEADER, I am walking this walk and leading this energy with absolute certainty that I will expand, empower, AND trigger a lot of people. I will hold myself in all the contrast, polarity, and duality of the realities of living unapologetically Iconic. **I will hold those with love, respect, and understanding who are uncomfortable with witnessing a woman living UNLEASHED.** I will live freely and be fully seen as a disruption to society… AND I will do it ANYWAY. *Take a deep breath gorgeous one–step into this now–YOUR Iconic life. What does that mean for You?* This Iconic life is why you're here. Being seen in that liberation will do a world of GOOD. It's time to own it. It's time to live it. It's time to hold yourself in it and regulate that you are safe in your individuality and ALL of the power that comes with that. The workings within this chapter and throughout this book will open you wider than you've ever expanded before–into new territories of unapologetic and empowered living. *This is why I do what I do, this is why I wrote this book, and this is why I walk this walk, as the Icon of New Paradigm Spirituality.* Life by design created by YOU and for YOU–is a life of guaranteed freedom, wild successes, joyfulness, and it is one where the collective inevitably wins. **Doing what you want from a heart and soul centered space of high level consciousness IS the medicine that heals the world.**

Let's talk about *holding it all* **as the Icon.** Holding duality, holding polarity, and holding the nuance is an inevitable part of BEING Iconic. **Holding the contrast of being the savior and the disruptor.** Duality is what makes this world so expansive and exciting. Duality makes life worth living. Contrast is what makes all that exists…*beautiful.* Let me speak for myself here, let me honor my duality, and let this be the permission slip for YOU to honor yours. *"I'm joyful, fun, loveable AND powerful AF. I'm playful, goofy, flirty AND direct. I'm generous, I'm open, I'm a giver, I'm a healer AND I hold clear standards for putting my needs, wants and energy FIRST. I'm focussed and refined as well as chaotic and wild. I'm welcoming, I'm open, I'm connected AND I intimidate people every day. I'm magnetic, I'm extroverted, I thrive in social situations AND I LOVE, crave and NEED my alone time. I'm independent, self-led, in my* *power... AND I LOVE to be taken care of and led."* Being the Icon, being *Unfuckwithable* and being a high level individual who leads themself. A high level individual who feels into all their edges, properly processes them and THEN embodies the next level. This person plays with duality, dances in the nuance and lovingly lets go of the limitation of holding just one identity. **You didn't come here to be the *easier* version of you...You came here to be the multidimensional, complex fully expressed...You.**

Easier versions of you are just that–they are easy (yawn). They will never hit the same as you being fully unapologetically 'you'. The FULLY expressed 'you' may not be completely understood... and they don't have to be. The FULLY expressed 'You' likely ruffles feathers. **You came here to actually LIVE... not to play dead.** The FULLY expressed 'You' is a WHOLE LOTTA WOMAN!! YEEHAW! Ever evolving, always learning, always growing, and always leading with love. Committed to their highest timeline. Even if that commitment requires more challenging levels of what it means to be...well, YOU. Meeting the deepest darkest, edgiest edges, and the most uncharted territories of YOU is the greatest gift you can give to yourself, and therefore the collective. Be you fully... complex, multidimensional, brilliantly originally–*you*. Your complexities make you magnetic. **You may think the world desires a watered down version of you. You may think replication is a sure fire way to success...But I promise you that doing it YOUR way...doing you, IS your magic.** Your intuitive innate way of being is your fast lane. Being an Icon requires you to stay in your own lane with your head held high, focussed on your empire, life, and legacy. This also means you speak the truth, even when it feels scary. *You aren't here to tell people what they want to hear.* You are here to speak the truth–this is what society needs to hear. You are a New Paradigm Leader paving the way to expand the awareness of those around you of what is possible. **This means YOU go first. Make the bold moves, take the risks, and show the world what is possible.**

On this journey of Iconic living, New Paradigm leading and being Unfuckwithable, you will likely trigger a lot of people's unhealed wounds. **You will embody a *free* energy that they subconsciously dream of experiencing, and your very existence will show them what they're missing.** Your ownership, expression, and lifestyle of freedom will hurt the void that they're experiencing. Your job is *not* to make everyone comfortable. You aren't meant to stay comfortable or be stagnant either. A New Paradigm Leader is here to live life by their own design. This means expanding yourself and your fellow Earthlings, showing them a new way of life that is possible—a life of infinite possibilities, freedom, and overflow. *Anyone triggered by YOUR free-est expression is right on track to their own much needed awakening and personal deepening of their own self mastery.* **We are all innately brilliant, innately conscious, and innately kind. We come into the world this way. Your job is to remember that, and be a stand for others remembering that.** Your fullness will trigger the ones playing small. This is their opportunity to expand, even if it is uncomfortable at first. We are meant to continue evolving and growing. We aren't here to be average and live mediocre lives. **Woke robotic assimilation (when we conform to it) keeps us a species very average and very low vibrational.** We came here to be ALIVE. When we conform to mediocrity we miss our potential—we miss precious moments. *You know* there is a rarity within you, a roar meant to be heard. It's time to own your freest expression, even in the face of resistance. Being the Icon means there are inevitably more eyes on you. You walk forward anyway. **You must know yourself and be a stand for the life you're creating.** Know yourself so you can handle the outrage. You can handle the responsibility of being a mirror for those who are playing small. **Again, Iconic living and BEING Unfuckwithable is NOT for everyone...*But you wouldn't be here reading this chapter if it wasn't for you.*** There has never been a more crucial time to experience alchemy, self mastery, and true freedom in every facet of your life. There has never been a better time to BE Iconic.

Now, let's talk about having more eyes on you. Being an Icon requires you to own the fact that you DO have desires of the Earthly realm, maybe it's fame, recognition, wealth etc... maybe it's not... but let's get clear on what it is. You're not an Icon in hiding...you're an icon on DISPLAY, and this means that you are also open to external projections. **If you are here to make a big difference in the world, get ready to start standing out.** First off, take a deep breath in... Are you ready and devoted to being a leader? To do life your way and know that it will intrigue and repel more and more people? *Breathe into it...You are safe, you are being held, and led here.* **Personal Power is KNOWING you are whole and complete as you are and that everything else is a cherry on top.** However, you are a High Level human and you are here for all the cherries (wink wink). **It is critical when manifesting anything or actualizing your desires that you claim and own the fact that you have those desires.** Own the fact that you WANT it. Most people are too timid to ask for what they want...*the Icon however OWNS it. One of my famous quotes is: "God's not a Fuck Boy, you don't have to play hard to get"...* Babe...OWN IT– *ask and you shall receive.* Part of living as the ICON is unapologetically desiring the desires of your heart AND actually experiencing the desires of your heart. *There is no fawning, no shame, no guilt, no pretending, no shrinking–there is just you living your iconic, impactful and abundant life.*

So if you aren't going all in yet, or you're not at least outwardly expressing that...lets look at where you may be holding yourself back. *Let's look at any potential subconscious fears that you may have about actually LIVING this iconic life.* You consciously may want to be iconic, do you–and do it well, live a life of empowerment and unapologetic expression, you may want fame, more impact, more sales, more clients, more followers, more publicity, more money, more collabs, more more more etc. *You may consciously "want it"–but is your subtle body and subconscious mind fully on board as well? Let's dive in deeper.* First off, it's a beautiful thing to want more. The divine feminine yearning within all of us, is ready to be satisfied with MORE, and we get to give that all to HER. I refer to "Her" as your feminine pleasure body/your inner divine feminine...the part of you with desire. Regardless of your sex, sexuality, gender...no matter how you identify...You have an inner divine feminine and an inner divine masculine. Harmonizing and properly honoring these sacred parts of you will allow you to achieve and receive your desires with so much more ease (more on this in later chapters).

It's time to explore this babe, it's time to own the fact that you desire MORE. It's time to OWN that there may be something (or many things) in the way of that *more* actually manifesting. This chapter on BEING the Icon acts as a container of grounded expression. A container of words, moments, and permission slips for you to remember. **You are supported and celebrated here for wanting more. I am a stand for YOU wanting more and actualizing that more.** Let this be an invitation for you now to meditate on, or journal out those gushing desires. *Take a break here to BE with your desires. Hold your heart, hold your gorgeous body, and claim them now.* Come back to these words–this chapter and these integrations often. Understanding your innate brilliance, observing, and healing. Dig deep into any conscious, subconscious, generational, conditioned, and energetic blocks that would stop you from FULLY being seen in the ways your soul truly desires. This is a process that you get to keep coming back to.

So, the divine feminine within you consciously wants more. CONSIDER...

1. What parts of yourself must be looked at? Are there parts of you that potentially fear this level of expression, this truth spilling out from you, this fame, recognition, money, impact... this new responsibility and new higher level of power?
2. Are there subconscious parts of you that were told "you're greedy for wanting more"? Do you on any level fear having more money, fame, impact, friends, opportunities, love etc etc.
3. Are you on any level fearful of the projections and hate you may receive when you show up unapologetically?

4. Is there anyone in your life who will be specifically triggered by your newfound iconic expression and TRUE power? Will they shame you? Will they reject you? Will they judge you?

Breathe in, it is safe. Hold your heart and exhale…You are safe.

Now, let's talk about the reality of what being an unapologetic and Unfuckwithable Icon looks like in the face of the far to overarching "Cancel Culture." You likely have heard of cancel culture– the ostracizing and attempt to shut down the entirety of an individual for speaking on what is deemed unacceptable to the masses. **My take on cancel culture essentially is this:** *when someone cancels someone else, they are saying, "I can't see you in this expression. I can't love you in this expression because I can't see and love myself in ALL my expressions." Cancel culture is a deep form of hate. Rooted from self hate.* As an Icon you will face the reality of being misunderstood, hated, and deemed problematic in your very existence. Holding, navigating, creating safety in the duality of wanting to be seen more and more AND feeling more and more urges to hide–is critical. This is the ongoing evolution of expansion. As you grow in your unapologetic expression of self, you take up more space, your energetic and physical frequency expand– your "bubble" of power expands. This expansion inevitably has you rub up on other people's bubbles. Rubbing up on other peoples bubbles creates discomfort and creates a larger projection field where those around you, those who are not standing in their own innate power, start to feel your presence as a direct confrontation to those places within themselves where they are playing small. My brilliant, Iconic sister, Jenna Rose has a poem that reads *"I want to be seen, and hide all at once."* The Icon often waivers between wanting more recognition, wanting to be seen and heard…while simultaneously wanting to hide away from all of the projections. This taking up more space can (if we're not observational and intentional) catalyze an old paradigm of external pressure, causing us to constrict, to play small and to keep everyone else comfortable. The Icon expands no matter what.

We must create a world where TRUE uncensored self expression gets to exist. We must stop perpetuating a world where individuals are terrified to speak and live their truth, to conform to the norms within the heavily conditioned society. We must raise and hold up future generations to proudly express their individuality, uniqueness, and rare identity in whatever way feels aligned and true for them. **If someone is uncomfortable with the way another human is expressing themselves, it is the responsibility of the human who is uncomfortable to regulate themselves. Creating safety in themselves and notice what comes up for us is our sacred responsibility– It is NOT the responsibility of the individual in their fullness to dim, shrink, play small or play dead.** We are here to SERVE LIFE–not to perpetuate mediocrity. *We are here to BE ALIVE–not play dead.* If we continue to perpetuate a world where humans are conditioned to being watered down versions of themselves then we are creating a false illusionary society. Normalcy is wildly inauthentic and plainly dangerous for emotional, spiritual, and mental evolution. **Humanity itself is at risk of extinction if we continue to perpetuate robotic assimilation, artificial intelligence, mass group think, only politically correct narratives and false pleasantries as the norm.**

It may be status quo for the masses to preach "authenticity" and "be yourself", but when it ACTUALLY comes down to innate pure unfiltered and uncensored self expression, the hyenas of the world come out to prey. The hyenas will do anything in their power to keep you small. This chapter, these lessons, and these integrations will support you in regulating your nervous system to feel safe in holding the duality of what it truly means to be Iconic. It is your time to be seen, well regarded, well paid, and well known in your zone of genius. We will create safety in you fully owning your beliefs, your life, and unapologetically living your iconic lifestyle. Get ready to stand out. Your expression deserves full exposure and the world needs to see, feel, hear ALL of you. If you haven't yet fully, take the time now to explore and own your soul's desire of publicity, fame, wealth, impact, and influence. If this is not a true desire for you, honor your desire to be seen by those in your world, and be seen in your truth. From this knowing, close your eyes, smile, open your body– pull in your truth. As an Icon you have a lot to teach the world. Your exposure can only be good for the world, the planet, and the collective consciousness. Breathe this in and visualize just HOW GOOD this fame, wealth, and recognition is for you, your community, and of course the collective. **As Icon's we are building fame, wealth, impact, and the influence you desire from a place of integrity.** A place of grounded certainty in yourself–whole and complete with or without any external validation or recognition. Again, being an Icon, at the foundation is about BEING *Unfuckwithable*. Iconic energy at the foundation is about living in a way that is true to you. Iconic living is of HIGH SERVICE to your soul's work, path, purpose, and mission on Earth. **We are here to raise the collective consciousness and lead a new paradigm.** You are here to do just that, within your own innately brilliant and unique way.

In my own unique Iconic New Paradigm, I am able to understand and SO CLEARLY see the controlled narrative. I can spot what type of expression is appropriate, celebrated, and tolerated by the masses. What type of expression is celebrated and therefore controlled by the old outdated fear paradigm that continues to attempt to rule the world. **I can quickly spot low vibrational control techniques.** This is what I call "Woke Robotic Assimilation" also termed "Mass Psychosis". *There are the brain washers and there are the brainwashed.* **Then, there are the ICONS.** The Icons of the NEW Paradigm choose sovereignty and true freedom. Within the controlled narrative and mainstream conditioned society, good people are brainwashed into thinking they are free. *Mass psychosis* has attempted to control the masses into virtue signaling robots, who conveniently agree with the most 'woke' thing that the majority of humans were forced into agreeing upon. **This means that by fully expressing yourself**

as the Icon with unconventional thoughts, ideas, expressions, and ways of being... Your very existence will make the world uncomfortable. Your non-conformity will inevitably attract hate by the very beings who have not *yet* stepped into their bravery–their courage and their OWN unique innate expression. **Your integrity and character will likely be questioned.** Because you are an innately good human being, with a strong consciousness and foundation in love–this questioning could potentially derail you because you so badly want to be liked, accepted and SEEN as a "good person". This questioning will rattle your ego and make you doubt your very authenticity, if you are not completely centered in your truth and grounded in your power. **As an outlier, an unconventional Icon of the new Paradigm you must develop a practice of deepened self awareness, self assessment and self observation.** *Take a deep breath in… and ask yourself, "Who am I, and how do I want to live?"* **As an Icon you must create an ongoing ritual of self regulation, nervous system regulation and physiological optimization so that your body and energy system is STRONG enough to hold you through the edges.**

From this foundation of knowing yourself, cultivated by the practice of coming home to yourself–You CAN powerfully lead a new paradigm and live fully, freely and peacefully as a rare and iconic being. **Breathe it in babe…you are SAFE and it is GOOD for you to deepen your self awareness to bring forth your unique thoughts, beliefs, and ways of being into this world.** Practice this yourself–holding duality and non-binary thinking. For example, you can be insanely inspired and empowered by someone AND not relate completely to them or agree with everything they put out/believe and preach. You can STILL respect and honor them fully as a free thinking, speaking and expressing being. **Practice noticing your own judgements and truly DO THE WORK to clean it up.** Again, the New Paradigm creates spaciousness for the "both-and" –always. **Allow others to empower and inspire you…. BUT you know your ultimate truth.** No one is your savior. You and your connection to your own highest self have the answers. You have your own innate knowledge as a new paradigm leader and you are always connecting back to your truths. **When you do know your ultimate truth and you do trust yourself–you're completely FREE.** You are completely fine with seeing someone you love and look up to say or do something you don't fully align or agree with. You're also neutral to the various ways of being, seeing, thinking, and speaking. You're no longer a shell of a human. You are a strong, empowered, clear and conscious individual who is not often triggered, and if and when you are...you know it's on YOU to clean it up.

You are GOOD at your core. You are kind, conscious, and overflowing with integrity at your core. Woke robotic assimilation is not your truth. **It's time to undo it all.** Love is at the foundation of your most original way of being, way of existing, and way of interacting. Move out of your head, drop into your heart, and live this stunning life fully expressed. ***Take a deep breath babe... you are safe and it is GOOD to be ALL of You.*** You aren't designed to be relatable, you won't always be politically correct, you won't always resonate with everyone, and you absolutely won't be understood by everyone. **Being palatable to the masses is not why you're here.** You are here to live fully expressed–fully you. Your life was never meant to be censored. Your life is meant to be uniquely designed by you, for you. Because you are innately good, innately kind. and innately conscious at your core. Everyone wins when you embody your purest alignment. **Your true essence IS your cleanest frequency.** I've said it before I will say it again...The highest timeline is the path less traveled...but it IS the most beautiful path. ***Staying in your lane isn't a concept to "know"–it's a lifestyle to EMBODY.*** Doing "the work" is not for the faint of heart and being Iconic and bravely leading a new paradigm and paving a new way DOES take work. Living life by your own design is 100% not the norm, not widely accepted or understood by the average person. Luckily, you aren't here to fit in.

You are here to stand out, to build your empire, to leave your legacy, to amplify your impact of love, consciousness, creation and empowerment to the collective. **You are here to have everything you want and more.** You are here to be expanded and surprised with the abundance of the universe. You are here to alchemize, to rise, to master yourself, your emotions, and your ways of being while being completely held and led by ALL that is. You are here to embody and observe your stunning life. *Walking as soul consciousness and experiencing all the pleasure and wealth along the way.* You are here for a stunning life. You are willing to lean into the uncomfortableness to create what it is your soul truly desires. You're ready for it to be aligned, ease, and joy filled in every way. *You are here for all the miracles and of course a lot of "to be expected" success.* I see You, I KNOW You. You are a high level Individual. You are here to live a fully expressed life by design *by you– for you*. The collective inevitably wins.

Now let's take a hot minute together and lock this in.

Deep breaths, land in your sacred body and breathe this in.

Affirm:

"It's time to be famous."

"It's time to be seen."

"It's time to express ALL of me."

"It's time to be paid really well for my charisma and my competence."

"It's time to inspire and impact millions of lives."

"It's time to live fully and completely unapologetically as me."

Let this all sink in, let this feel and BE true in your body. As always babe, bring your own unique flare to these affirmations, take what serves you and leave what doesn't.

Alright, back to business. **Being an Icon REQUIRES a healthy ego and a thriving soul.** Read that again. Some spiritual teachers speak of "killing the ego" but we're not operating in such binary thinking here. We are operating within the dimension of openness babe and there is all the space and room for your ego to show up purposefully and healthily. **A HEALTHY ego (there is no "ego" death here) and a THRIVING soul (your soul takes the driver's seat babe) is the match made in heaven to actualize a life of your dreams.** Iconic living and being Unfuckwithable is about living with the subtleties-life in the nuance. It takes solid recognition of your rareness AND an honoring of the oneness consciousness that connects all of us. Individuality AND union with all that is. Being an Icon requires you to uphold an ever evolving and rising consciousness of love. Your very foundation is integrity, kindness and rock solid values that serve you AND the collective. **When you serve self from a life giving regenerative basis you naturally serve LIFE which serves the collective.** *Let that sink in.* **Your vision, mission, soul path and soul work is foundational in a oneness consciousness AND an awareness of your Iconic rare individuality.** We are connected in oneness AND it is your unique faith, spirituality, souls desires, and ways of being that are authentic to YOU. Your rarity allows you to walk with certainty in your own lane. Build new pathways that regenerate, heal this planet and support those who inhabit it. *Your attention is to be focused INWARD to change the OUTWARD…Feel me?*

When you serve <u>self</u> (from a regenerative foundation)…You serve *LIFE*. When you serve *life*… You naturally serve the collective. I am a stand for unapologetic selfishness-high level individuality. Selfishness is another word I've decided to reclaim. It's a word I've empowered so many new paradigm leaders, healers, and high level individuals in reclaiming. I hope to empower you in reclaiming that word and what it means for you. When you are self giving, self nurturing, self loving, and self caring- you serve life. A law of the planet is that life serves life. When you serve life, you serve the planet. When you serve the planet, you serve the collective. **So, if more humans focused on loving the fuck out of themselves…*There would be no hate,***

fear, separation or scarcity. **Because love yields love, abundance yields abundance and so on.** There would be no scarcity–there would simply be OVERFLOW. When you serve *self* from a place of high consciousness and from a foundation of LOVE... *You inevitably heal the world.* This I KNOW to be true. So, focus on the most indulgent and high integrity service of SELF. Then watch as the world around you elevates, heals, and rises. When you heal yourself you heal the collective. *This is the nuance of the "both-and"...the nuances of life in the subtleties.* **We are in a paradigm where we are deeply honoring the oneness, consciousness, unity, and interconnection of all that exists AND we are honoring our individuality, iconic rareness, individualized path, purpose, and vision here on Earth.**

When you thrive–you support the collective thrive. Start where it counts Babes, and always, always, ALWAYS ground in your own truth. You can be inspired, activated, and in awe of other incredible leaders...but the Icon locks into her own truth. Breathe slowly, deeply, and drop in... *"Who am I?...And how do I want to live?"* The Iconic high level individual exists within the foundation of self trust, self observation, self development, and self honoring. Harmony in all of it. This high level awareness of self, the knowing when to uplevel with the deep honoring of your timeline ensures evolution over a lifetime. THIS is a life to be remembered, a legacy to be left behind. Iconic Unfuckwithable-ness means you know yourself and LOVE yourself. So Queen/King–Do you and do it well.

Some final important notes on BEING the Icon

Fame, impact, and leaving a legacy comes with a set of responsibilities. You are BOLD, confident, and unapologetic. You are loved and magnetic to many, all the while repelling to some. You are constantly navigating dualities–inspiring and expanding while also triggering. Dancing with the temptation to fall back into smallness. Reminding yourself your bigness is safe until it is your reality. **YOU set the stage–not the other way around.** They will get it and roll with you, or they will WANT to get it and celebrate you. They won't get it and they will ignore you, or they will be triggered as fuck and hate on you...DO YOU ANYWAY. You are not easily understood or defined and that's your magic...OWN that. Validate yourself and make your BIGGEST devotion to be understanding yourself. As an Icon you will likely surround yourself with more Icons, big energies, big ideas, unconventional thoughts, and beliefs. You are constantly being expanded into being a living, walking and breathing embodiment of multidimensionality and honoring that in ALL beings. Practice holding duality and non-binary thinking...be alive in the nuance. **Be mindful of how you are either building and leading a new paradigm or perpetuating an old and outdated system.** In your own boldness, as you walk your walk as a stand for what you believe in...Be sure to hold space for the contradictory stances and ways of experiencing life. Be mindful about what paradigms you are perpetuating and practice loving self awareness. I encourage you to change your mind, shift, and choose again often. Allow others to empower you and inspire you, but YOU know your ultimate truth (and if you don't, then that's your work). Time to dig deeper. When you DO know your ultimate truth and you DO trust yourself, you are COMPLETELY fine with seeing someone you love and look up to say or do something you don't fully align or agree with. It doesn't fuck with you. It doesn't shake your understanding of the world and you're able to ground in your OWN truths. **You know in your heart what feels like love—you KNOW what feels right, good, and true in your soul.** You know that your deepest, stripped down purest essence of BEING is your truth and it is something to celebrate. No more borrowed identities. *It's time to be fully...You.*

Remember the attempted mass psychosis and controlled narrative of what TYPE of expression is appropriate, celebrated and tolerated. We call this "woke robotic assimilation ". **Be mindful to not perpetuate old systems disguised as progress.** This mass psychosis has attempted to control you into a virtue signaling robot, who conveniently agrees with the most woke thing that the majority of humans agree on. Be LOVE to all beings, notice your own judgements, clean them up, do the work and BE the walking embodiment of truth. **Remember...*Cancel culture renders you average and mis-informed. The more you subscribe to the predominant narrative, the more you will fall into the illusion of separation.*** The more you will fall into the delusion of "us vs them"... this illusion of separation leads to binary hateful thinking. The average human being has been overwhelmed by conditioning and has not been blessed with the new paradigm 'knowings' that you have. You are here reading this because you are doing life differently, you are choosing to live and honor the nuances AND multidimensionality of this precious life. Be patient and gentle with those who don't 'get it'. Be gracious with yourself when you forget your truth. Most importantly–stay in your OWN lane. **Do not compare yourself to the average human–you are far from average.** VERY few people are willing to align properly and very few people are willing to LIVE out their authentic truth. Send love to all beings, no matter where they are on their journey, with love, truth, and your iconic essence.

Deep breaths in babe...***You are rare, iconic, and worthy of being seen and recognized.*** Make your deepest devotion understanding Self and allow your truest expression radiate from within.

No matter who you are, where you come from, what your story is/was, BE the main character. You've outgrown your limitations. The old programs and paradigms no longer serve you. The conditioning attempted to keep you small, no longer serves you. It's TIME to be at center stage, high level, main character vibes. KNOW what you want: speak it, feel it, and decide to HAVE it. You have a divine assignment here on Earth. A unique purpose and you GET to have a soul fulfilling life where all your desires drop in. In claiming your truth, your desires, and embodying that alignment unapologetically–you are a living breathing rebellion. A rebellion to scarcity, limitation, and fear. Welcome to the realm of conscious fulfillment AND unrelatable opulence. The realm of self leadership, personal power, energetic standards, and ongoing upgrades. All this creation with a big juicy surrender to the inevitable divine Intervention. What a vibe! I'm celebrating you Queen/King for making it this far. What an expansive chapter–one of depth and scope. Now, it's time to devote yourself to this work as a living breathing integrated embodiment. Moment to moment. Evolution over a lifetime. Complete ownership and reclamation of ALL that you are–multidimensionality, **Unfuckwithable,** unapologetic, completely FREE and authentically YOU!

Now! It's time to dive into the homework portion of this chapter.

Important notes to remember and INTEGRATE moving forward:
1.You are in charge of clearing and anchoring into your own energy and your truth
Deep breath.. Hand over heart– "Who am I and how do I want to live?"

2.You must consciously and consistently create SAFETY in being: seen, being the Icon, being WELL PAID, being sought after, being LOVED, being HATED, creating safety in your fullest expression, AND creating safety in *other people's* fullest expression(s).
*This may be tapping over the heart - affirming "I am safe" "it's safe to be seen" "It's safe to be famous", "It's safe to be uncomfortable", "It's safe to be rich/ wealthy", "It's safe to be ALL of me" .
*This may also be lying in bed under the covers and consciously safely recalibrating (it's very critical to create safety for your human self, inner child and fearful parts as you ELEVATE into your next level.

3.CRITICAL FOUNDATION OF BEING THE ICON
The foundation of being Iconic is based on the following 3 pillars. I want to clearly state the 3 pillars and ensure you are aware and conscious of INTEGRATING them.

1st Pillar: Consciousness
2nd Pillar: High Level Embodiment
3rd Pillar: Iconic Essence

These foundational pillars are to ground all of this work.
Come back to them often and ensure you are LIVING in alignment with them.

As part of your homework here, I have written a
Love Letter reminder to You babe...

"It's your path. Your one precious life in this existence.
It's time to own it. BE it. Find You. Understand you. Validate you.
You are the divine expressing itself as human for a little while. A manifestation of God. It's a big fucking deal. Act like it."

The High Level Individual moves...
QUICKLY
STRATEGICALLY
INTENTIONALLY

Make the aligned moves with who you are NOW with what you have NOW and watch it UPGRADE.

Homework / Daily Devotionals:

Before each numbered reflection, take a few deep breaths, close your eyes, and drop into your body.

1."What would Exponential Evolution look like for You?"
*Reconnect here to your true heart desires and how being Iconic and FULLY you will unlock portals and open doors of opportunity for these desires to manifest
2. As an ICON it's not about a "niche down" you get to own the fact that you are multidimensional AND you have the ability and focus to be competent in ALL the expressions of You.
It IS about REFINEMENT. Organization and CLARITY are critical for your human mind/ego–iit also supports your SOUL to refine so you can STAY IN YOUR LANE (focussed on your soul's path VISION and soul's mission.) **This reflection is YOU and your journal–clearly articulating what you do and how you live,**

your offers, services in the world, your life's work as an Icon, how you show up etc. Can you REFINE what this looks and feels like to honor all of yourself *but in a pure and clear way.

3.Baseline Frequency is key when you are a top tier individual like the Icon that you are. **So, this homework is about consciously deciding what your practices, rituals, actions and ways of existing will be that allow you to raise and align your baseline frequency moment to moment to stay TRUE to yourself and your pure, clean energy.** Breathe that in babe and focus on your baseline energy. You are an *Unfuckwithable* human when you are in energetic alignment and your physical body is nourished holistically. Hold this frequency and don't let yourself dip. When you do 'dip'—embody fully and come back to your baseline. All parts of you are welcome. But as the Icon who impacts and influences hundreds, thousands, millions… you are required to hold a grounded energy so you CAN do your soul's work here in service on Earth while feeling GOOD.

4.BE THE FUCKING ICON. IN your journal reflect…**How does the Icon show up, dress, talk, walk, live BTS and in front of the world?** BE THEM NOW. Start practicing more and more full expression. Start witnessing the ego and start seeing other people react to you and practice coming back to your truths in the face of adversity. Practice sharing more from your soul's truth, practice regulating in safety when you are NOT met with unconditional love and understanding. BE the love. BE the validation. BE the evidence FOR YOU and then watch it ALL manifest in alignment for you. GO BE FULLY EXPRESSED!

5.Tonight and over the next few days feel into…**What makes you Iconic? What would your fullest expression look like, feel like BE like? How can you BE ICONIC moment to moment each day? Why are you here (Earth)? Why are you Iconic? Why do you want to be Iconic? What are your dreams and desires around being Iconic?** Let these reflections land and ALWAYS come back to this grounding affirmation and self inquiry "*Who am I and how do I want to live?*"

The last juices that I want to leave you with for this chapter, are some *morning affirmations*...
Lock them in, while you look at your gorgeous self in the mirror each day.

"I surrender to the divine timing of my life."
"I am open to miracles today and always."
"I know it's all unfolding for me."
"I know the universe is always aligning for me."
"I choose inner peace, joy and pleasure today and always."

I celebrate You, Queen/King
for completing this very full, juicy, and expansive chapter.
Come back to this work when it calls You.
FULLY integrate it.

CHAPTER 5

STAY IN YOUR LANE

The versions of you that exist in other people's minds are absolutely none of your business. This chapter is about living a life of alignment, living in your path, not falling into distortion and delusions of other peoples paradigms, timelines and realities. **You are here to walk YOUR path, live YOUR purpose, and leave YOUR legacy.** Every single time you step out of your lane, you are postponing your results from cashing in. You fall out of your alignment, and you procrastinate on igniting your magic. **Staying in your own lane requires focus, dialed attuned, and refined VISION.** It requires you to leave A LOT in the rearview and TRUST and SURRENDER deeper than ever, as you propel forward faster and faster. Staying in your own lane requires you to self validate, to understand self, to release the wonder, and the "what ifs" and the worry that not everyone will celebrate you.

The versions of you that exist in other people's minds are absolutely none of your business. Read it again. Imagine how far ahead you would be if you stopped worrying about what everyone else was thinking about how YOU DO YOU, and focused more on YOU DOING YOU in the DIRECTION of your dreams. The Unfuckwithable being, does not try to fit in, they don't mind being talked about (good or bad), they'd rather be focused on their own lane than get tripped up in someone else's. If they catch themselves wondering if they're too intimidating, too dramatic, too loud, too driven, too clear, too certain, too ambitious, too successful, too focused, too self oriented, too confident etc etc. they must CHECK in with themselves and realign. **They get back in their lane and get back to their VISION.**

This–BEING Unfuckwithable, is life in the FAST lane. Every single successful actor, leader, artist, musician, writer or scholar that you

LOOK UP TO all have one thing in common…they stay in their lane. **They are focussed, determined, and DRIVEN.** There is no time, no space, no availability to look in the rear view when you are in the fast lane. There is no divergence from your lane–it's simply not safe. Unless you are looking to crash–stay in YOUR lane. The fast lane is the FAST lane. I will be treating you like a Formula 1 driver, and holding you to those focussed standards, because I ONLY see you in your highest timeline. So dial IN babe. **There is only room for focussed, attuned, dialed, and refined alignment in this lane.**

So, let's talk about staying in your lane when you could so easily fall off. **There will always be temptation to deviate from the path.** Your ego will get hella loud when your desires are the closest. When you're in your lane, thriving in the richness of the present moment–the euphoria of it AND quickly moving forward to your next and newest desires…things can get wobbly. Your ego can get loud and tempt you to deviate. *Your ego loves its comfort zone, and if you move too fast or rise too high it will attempt to shrink you back down*. Do you crawl back into your comfort zone? O*r do you observe it, see it for what it is, and lean the fuck in to your next evolution?* The reason life by design is the path less traveled is because everyone thinks they want the wealth, the impact, the euphoric joy, the ease… but very few of us are willing to lean into the inevitable painful and scary edges along the way. **Very few people are willing to be devoted to their alignment and STAY in their own lane.** Again, if it were easy… everyone would be doing it. If it were easy, everyone would be LIVING it. Everyone would be billionaires, living wildly free–living healthy and stunning lives. **It's not to say it's not available to all of us–I genuinely believe it is.** You arrived on Earth with INFINITE possibility, and that possibility and potential is begging for your actualization of it. Instead, it comes down to a matter of devotion (more on this later).

Everyone has potential, great potential at that… but not everyone is willing to live up to that reality. It's a matter of who is willing to lean in, to do the work, to stay aligned, and to re-align when we wobble off. **Who are the RARE ones willing to stay on THEIR lane and truly LIVE their highest alignment and actualize their dreams?** *I know it's me, and I know it's you.* It's completely natural to get pulled off your lane once in a while–that's normal, to be expected and part of life as a human. **What IS important however, is how fast you get BACK in your lane.** Your willingness to shift, make the moves, and be bold enough to change it up is the work. Your willingness to evolve, to let go, to surrender, to start over, to execute, to regulate… to trust is your magic. Very few people are aligning in this way. Very few people will realign when they misalign. Very few people are willing to do the work. **Are you willing to be the 1%?** *Are you willing to do the work?*

There comes a point in life when potential just doesn't cut it any more. Potential actually just leads to bitterness (if you aren't properly cultivating that reality). **Potential is just that… it's a potential, until it is ACTUALIZED.** My job is to facilitate you through the work, codes and integrations within these chapters to be the Unfuckwithable being who ACTUALIZES all their potential– and then some. **I am taking you to the furthest corners of yourself, to understand your greatest potential, your truth, and guide you properly, to actually LIVE that way.** The work within this book is designed for you to see yourself the way the creator designed you and empower you to live that truth. A rare percentage of the population will actually REACH their potential (and continue to expand and evolve it)…*luckily–you are rare.* **Your potential is LIMITLESS babe–you wouldn't be reading this if it wasn't.** It's massive devotion walking the path, staying in your own lane, and living a *life by design*. It is RARE to be the one walking with desire AND simultaneously grounding in what IS. To WANT more and KNOW it is readily AVAILABLE (while also honoring divine timing…) and walking with pure gratitude and presence. **Potential is MEANT to be actualized.** So we're going to do that. We're going to devote ourselves to alignment every single day. We will do and BE what it takes. *While of course honoring the ebbs and flows of LIFE in a human body.* We are here to actually HAVE our desires (from a place of holistic wellbeing/wholeness). **I will NOT let you play in the "some day" "one day" energy.** Your potential is to be alchemized, actualized, and MANIFESTED right here, right now. Potential is only as good as its execution. Therefore, KNOWING you have potential, is not enough. **Following through with FOCUS—now that's the juice.** There is no settling here. There is no deviation from the path. **There is only momentum that stacks and inevitably cashes in while you walk your walk and live your truth.** Your massive desires manifest, certainty is embodied and HOLISTIC success is experienced every step of the way. **You have made it this far because you KNOW in every inch of your being, that you are ready to cultivate the LIVED reality of your *infinite potential.***

Alright buckle up babe because I'm giving it to you straight. We're in the fast lane, and we're taking off. These next few paragraphs are full of juice for you to rev up the engine of alignment and allow what you desire, to drop in. Take your time, breathe slowly and receive these codes. **Momentum and FOCUS are the names of the game when it comes to staying in your own lane.** Momentum is always building, stacking and waiting for your soft landing strip to cash in. If it seems like it's taking forever…It is time to mix in some healthy assessment energy. Observe yourself with high level discernment. If the energy is ON, the frequency is CLEAN, the action is aligned and consistent… It just hadn't happened YET. SO KEEP GOING.

Most people are unwilling to hold faith, stay aligned and continue to vibrate on the frequency of alignment. Most people won't keep going—*but you're not most people.* Our brains are programmed for immediate gratification, external validation and instant dopamine hits. The heavily conditioned Matrix (an old paradigm of limitation, control and fear) also perpetuates this disempowerment and addictive state through over stimulation in media and through our devices. Most people don't hold the grounded power strong enough to actually BE Unfuckwithable aka operate in HIGH levels of PERSONAL POWER. This is where you are different, my love. You are RARE, unique, devoted and you are integrating the codes to BE Unfuckwithable. You are here for the long game, the devotional aligned path…it's so much deeper and SO much more rewarding.

When I speak of "staying on your lane" I am speaking of the lane that is YOU, living your best life, on route toward your dreams and desires, and cashing in a tonne of rewards along the way. **You in your lane is the experience of powerfully moving toward your desires and KNOWING that they are iNEVITABLY cashing in–in divine timing.** The important note here is–if you ARE in your alignment and you DO trust that it's all adding up and that your desires are meant for you–it is simply a matter of divine timing. When you unplug from the certainty and wonder why your desires haven't manifested yet–you lose your momentum and you leave your path. When you question why it's "not here yet" instead of focusing on your alignment and focusing on the excitement of it dropping into your reality–you drop the momentum and drop your power. When you get caught up on "taking score" and move into scarcity that your desires haven't landed yet, and that something must be wrong–you block yourself from *having.* When our mind wanders into "fixing" energy we deviate from the path. If you catch yourself in scarcity, and wonder why it's not "here yet", your ego will trick you into thinking there's a problem that needs to be fixed, which just procrastinates you from the actualization of your manifestation. This is where healthy assessment energy is SO critical because you can properly assess if something is off and you can clean it up right away. When you healthily assess, you can also see if everything IS indeed in alignment, and if it is you can get back into your trusting momentum. If all is aligned–that must mean *it just hasn't happened YET, a*nd in that case, you can simply turn your faith and alignment all the way UP.

**Reminder: If the energy is ON, the frequency is CLEAN, the action is consistent and you're living in devotion and alignment with your desire…*It is on its way, and it just hasn't happened YET.* Stay plugged in, stay turned on in desire and let it LAND Babe. The Universe and the mystery of life plays a powerful role in our CO creation and divine timing is real babe.

You are only responsible for your half of the creation–you in your lane, powerfully present while moving forward IS your work.

Now in terms of existing powerfully in your lane, and achieving/receiving the desires of your heart there is a common human error I see…and that is: *shying away from your desires.* The fear of failure…or the fear of success…The fear of going all in. So, if you REALLY want what you say you want…**The biggest question I have for You is, Why are you NOT going ALL IN yet?** If you REALLY want what you say you want, if you REALLY want what you've been building momentum toward then stop unplugging, stop quitting, and stop slowing down JUST as it's about to get good. **No more procrastinating!** Procrastinating can either be you looking around for things to fix OR when you slow down and unplug (lose the excitement and belief) because it's not here *yet*. Notice the times you've done that in the past–unplugged JUST as it was about to manifest for you. It's like this babe…you will never know unless you go all in. *SO GO ALL IN.* On your journey now…ask yourself: What IS my fast lane/what sort of life am I living as I walk my highest path? Who do I need to BE in order to align to the fast lane? What old stories do I need to heal and upgrade to BE this high level focussed version of myself? What do I need to release to stay dialed in MY OWN LANE? Now, focus on continuing to build and move forward with the alignmed energy and action.

This healthy assessment is critical if it feels like your desires are either taking forever, you feel out of alignment or you have lost your focus and intention. Assessment is only for if you really feel like something is off or misaligned. If so–shift it, refine, and upgrade it. Usually, however–for the high level individual (like yourself reading this) it isn't a matter of misalignment (because you have been doing the work for a long time now, you are self aware and you know when you need to uplevel)…**Normally it is simply that momentum is building and hasn't cashed in YET–** *because of divine timing.*

Remember the divine timeline, remember the inevitability of your God given desires, and remember Newton's 1st law of motion. Do you *really* want to unplug by problem solving and falling into an older outdated paradigm of problems that need fixing? OR, do you want to keep building, stacking and cashing in, in the fast lane? **Come home to your truth and to your process.** If it all looks and feels aligned then you're just not giving the momentum enough time to stack and cash in...so KEEP GOING. Keep moving and aligning from a foundation of CERTAINTY and TRUST. If there are tweaks that need to happen, great...make them happen! But don;t stay in fixing mode, procrastination mode or perfectionism mode–get into the FAST LANE where money is magnetized, love is gushing and success is overflowing. Make it happen by shifting, upgrading, refining, releasing what no longer serves your path. Get back to your clean, clear, unobstructed lane.

Mid-Chapter break– I don't want to move forward until you have FULLY integrated these concepts.

Take a deep breath Boo. You're on a powerful journey and this is MONUMENTAL for you.

Healthy Assessment Energy Time - take to your journal or meditate on these...

1. How have you been building momentum?
2. What's your process?
3. Is it aligned? Energetically AND physically?
4. Any sticky energy?
5. Is the frequency clean?
6. Does it feel GOOD? Or is it obligation based?
7. Now once you have gathered your healthy assessment information, you will know if you need to clean up some energetics. OR, if you're ready to get back into alignment NOW and open a soft landing strip of receiving.

Alright, the vibe here is this: We are wildly capable of having everything we want AND we are whole and complete as we are. There's no rush, it's all adding up, the magic is in THIS moment, and we are here. SO, lean back, release the illusion of pressure, scarcity, and any delusions of what needs fixing–FULLY surrender. *It's all on its way babe.* The ego only ever gets loud and impatient to fog your connection to source/soul/spirit. The ego is a beautiful thing when we are aware of it, but it becomes detrimental to our evolution and holistic wellbeing when it begins to run the show. These processes of *Momentum, Focus, Staying in your Lane* etc. are all about FULL integration of your highest timeline in a regulated manner. **This process is about going ALL IN on YOU and YOUR DREAM LIFE.** We allow the upgrades to occur with ease. The process is designed so you can easily tap into your truth on a moment to moment basis–*standing in your truth makes you Unfuckwithable.* This process allows you to witness the lies your wounded ego wants you to believe– observing it and not falling for the lies. Transmute the lies– heal, upgrade, and effortlessly move forward in your purest alignment anyway. Rinse and repeat. Then, of course, CELEBRATE as everything cashes in.

The focus is YOU, dialed in on your lane, and your focus on building momentum, and the FOCUS on the inevitability of your desires dropping in IS what expedites the entire process. Again–FOCUS is the name of the game. The momentum formula and your ability to STAY IN YOUR LANE is literally like clockwork–results GUARANTEED. *As always, the ego is along for the ride– there is no escaping the very thing that makes you human.* So, observe it and see it for what it is. From this empowered spacious place, your *Highest Self* becomes the motivating force and the leading energy. **I promise you, as you walk forward, powerfully in your lane…You will eventually get to the point that when your ego freaks out, you internally get a little excited…Because you KNOW that this means something big and beautiful is coming.** This very ego freakout will tempt you to deviate from your path–this is the exact redirection that STRENGTHENS your alignment and allows the rewards to cash in, in an accelerated fashion. **Your misalignment is always leading you to your alignment**…But you have to choose that, decide that, and clean it up time and time again. **So lean the fuck in, trust yourself, and trust this process.**

Okay, let's switch gears a little bit to explore other potential deviations from your lane that have to do with your external reality and those in it. Let me remind you of your uniqueness and that you are indeed on a higher, faster path for reading this book. When you are on your rise (which is always and ever evolving if you're COMMITTED to evolution over a lifetime), you must be VERY intentional with the environments you exist in– physically and energetically. **Who you surround yourself with, the conversations you participate in, how you exist, how you talk your talk, how you walk your walk, how you LIVE is an essential component to increasing your frequency.** Elevating your frequency in turn results in more manifestations. Who you BE behind the scenes, who you BE in front of the camera/in front of the world, your actual lived, embodied reality is ALWAYS being perpetuated and creating more of *itself.* The thoughts you repeatedly have, the beliefs you were programmed to believe and the beliefs you CHOOSE to perpetuate are what is going to make the difference–you must be intentional. *Your friends and family likely won't get it... and they don't have to.*

We're not playing in the realm of logic. We're not playing in the realm of conditions, limits or sacrifice. We are playing and LIVING in the infinite and limitless realms. Unfortunately the average person has been conditioned to assume that they aren't worthy of living it. **What is possible to a heavily programmed and conditioned mind is nowhere close to what is possible for an Unfuckwithable soul who knows their power.** As you rise there will be misunderstanding. Thriving is not the norm In the outdated paradigm that the majority of the population exists in. There are predominant narratives about those who thrive in all areas of their lives..."Those people are selfish, greedy, unrealistic, or weird". The average person will not celebrate you on your way to the top. They won't believe it until they see it. *They may judge you until you make it, and once you make it–**they will proudly say that they know you.***

The average person is living a limited, boring, conventional life. **It is a powerful reclamation to CHOOSE your own lane, your highest timeline... the fast lane.** You are NOT average, and you cannot lose yourself by attempting to fit in with the masses. Your lane is YOUR lane period. As you stay in your lane you must be intentional about who interacts with your lane. **It is CRITICAL to be HELD in your BIG VISION.** It is necessary to interact and surround yourself with fellow high achievers, old paradigm disruptors, and Icons who rebel by living their own *life by design*. **You have to recognize your lane as clear and unobstructed...AND you must constantly and powerfully clear the lane of any potential obstructions.** The average person is NOT celebrating your TRUEST biggest dreams. Most people won't even LET themselves dream their own dreams and live in their own alignment. Holding a massive vision for yourself and walking that walk is necessary. Most people, however, won't even envision for themselves what is possible...So don't expect them to do it for you. They're not calibrating in the same ways you desire.

The average person does NOT understand their own desires, forget them even remotely thinking anything possible outside of their current existence. They could never grasp your desires, dreams or your vision because they are walking a limited, conditioned, and resistance filled timeline. They likely won't get it and they don't have to. The more you look around for external validation to support, celebrate or cheer you on, the less time you are focused on moving forward in your own lane. **This is where self validation, self celebration, and supporting yourself is key.** Finding environments where your visions are celebrated, considered relatively normal, and those around you genuinely expect you to achieve your desires–those are the environments you need.

One of my favorite quotes by me goes like this, "Just because I am living YOUR dream life, doesn't mean that I am living MY dream life". I am incredibly high achieving, successful, powerful and acutely aware of my gifts, desires, and how available they are to me. **I am always walking with gratitude and I am always walking toward MORE.** I am in my late 20's at this time that I am writing to you, and most people won't accomplish what I have accomplished in my 20's in their entire lifetime. *At my current age, as I'm writing this book, I am living what would be considered a "pipe dream" to many of my peers.* What I have achieved, created, and received is enough to make the average person retire and know that they have made it. **I, on the other hand, have the beginner mindset, the energy of this is incredible...AND I am JUST getting started.**

People who begin comparing themselves to the masses begin to "self handicap" - a term I learned back in my University days in sports psychology (self handicapping is playing small so that you don't have to risk the potential of failure so you play it safe). Or they fall into an illusion of a ceiling, a limit, a reached capacity and there is nothing higher. This is why STAYING in your lane is so critical. **Just because your abilities seem supernatural to some, doesn't mean they are supernatural to you.** You are at a high level, thus it is NATURAL for you to succeed, excel, and operate in a new paradigm of elite success, wellbeing, and lifestyle. So remember babe, just because you're living someone's dream life, doesn't mean it's YOUR dream life. *There is more on the horizon–you do not have to cap yourself.*

You don't have to comply with the norms and standards of success, and assume you've "made it" or that "this is the end of the road for you" because you have achieved some of your desires. There is a lane where infinite evolution exists and you actually experience the ultimate human potential. **A lane where you experience ALL that is infinitely available for you.** There is SO MUCH MORE readily available for you to experience, achieve and receive in this life, and having a beginners mindset will keep you living and moving and basking in the richness of this life. You don't have to limit yourself, and you certainly don't have to fall into the woke robotic assimilation and delusions of woundology by accepting the bare fucking minimum of this life. YOU get to decide (no matter who you are) that there is MORE available AND you get to keep aligning to the ever evolving NEXT evolution of you. *Be grateful, be present, and keep moving forward.*

Keep going and be so fucking grateful for where you are at. **Living a high level life is one thing, but actually celebrating yourself for BEING there...now that is the magical elixir.** Living in YOUR lane as you walk gracefully is about harmonizing gratitude and desire, presence and forward movement. Your lane is the fast lane. **Be real, be kind, but don't even think about dimming your light or capping yourself based on the norms of other slower and busier lanes.** Comparison will fucking burn you–every time. You are paving a way, living a new paradigm therefore your lane is a path that has not been walked before...*There is no blueprint.* When you compare yourself to those walking an average timelinc, living in limitation and compliance to society standards... you slow down and you cut yourself off. **The same thing goes to comparing yourself to those who are seemingly "further ahead than you".**

Take a hot minute here babe, be real with yourself. Have you fallen into comparison? Have you been let down when your best friend found their soulmate and bought their dream home? Or have you settled because you seem to be doing well compared to those around you? Take a deep breath, it's safe, you're okay, you are loved, and you are EXACTLY where you were designed to be at this moment. When you compare yourself to those who are rising alongside you or settling beside you, you cripple your confidence, your trust, and then you question your OWN divine timing and your OWN innate desires. You were uniquely designed–time is an illusion and you are 100% supported. It is a powerful decision to begin to believe that everyone's everyone's success mirrors your inevitable success. It is also in my opinion an even MORE powerful decision to decide to stay in your own lane and focus only on YOUR path. Keep your eyes on YOUR lane, when you look into the next lane...You trip over your feet. Never forget it babe.

The recipe for success looks different for everyone. We are all working out our own unique karmas, our own individual timelines, and our blueprints of success are uniquely ours. The only time I want you looking around on your journey, is to catch the view...To bask in everything you have already created...And then say *"Thank You, More Please,"* as it all continues to get BETTER! I channel a lot on witnessing evidence and validation of your desires unfolding from a very self fulfilled space. I call this DIALLED FOCUS with 360 degree awareness. You are focused on making each moment delicious, while moving forward in alignment with the deliciousness that's inevitably coming next. 360 degree awareness, is you seeing ALL the possible ways in which your desires are manifesting–with the support that holds you, and all the guidance that leads you. Stay in your own lane, but with 360 degree awareness...Or as I like to say *"have your owl head on"*. When you look around with 360 degree awareness, you're not looking for external validation– not seeking or needing. You are simply noticing: all the ways in which it IS indeed happening FOR you now, adding up FOR you now, all the ways you are supported now, and always by *ALL that is.* Staying in your own lane with 360 degree awareness is a way of landing in the NOW, while actively co-creating the future. Life in your own lane is a life of devotion and deep intention and MY GOD the results are beautiful.

Life is tremendously meaningful...Every moment of growth, success, and heartache is FULL of meaning (if you choose it to be). When you live with deep intentionality in your own lane you are in flow with all that is, you feel a constant state of bliss and aliveness. Opening, receiving, achievement, nothingness...*It's all so special.* Every day is a ceremony. Every day has precious lessons. Lean all the way into your own lane, and forget the rest. Embody fully, experience, release–really be ALIVE in your own lane. Really be ALIVE in this one precious and unrepeatable life.

Living with such presence and intention goes hand in hand with living life in your own lane–you are then hyper aware and attuned to everything in your vortex. I choose to live with great intention, and my desire is for you to live with great intention… focussed, present, and ready for the divine unfolding. Open up with refined clarity to what's meant for you–what's TRUE for you. **The rewards inevitably cash in because the focus moment to moment is feeling what you're feeling…fully.** Seeing with a wider, higher perspective, and deeply rooting into your beingness every step of the way. *Naturally, your life will feel deeply fulfilling, and of course you will receive in beautiful ways.* This life in your own lane is life in a different frequency, a higher frequency…where everything is a blessing. A life of true aliveness. No matter the pain, the pleasure or the seemingly mundane, it is all a blessing. The way the sun hits us, the way our partners smile at us, the knowing, the surrender…everything is meaningful. **But you must decide to live that way.**

This process of deep alignment, this journey of life in your OWN lane is one of great intention…AND an awareness that things shift and inevitable release as you upgrade. *As I've said before, "Your standards determine how the world responds to you".* This means what existed in your old paradigm will not likely exist in your new, next or highest paradigm. Every time you deeper align to your truth you are refining. This refinement process is a natural part of living life in the fast lane. **Some things stay as they are, most things elevate, and often–a lot falls away.** Take a deep breath, create safety in your inner being, and trust that it is safe for you to evolve beyond what no longer aligns. NOTHING is moving if nothing is moving… or as they say "nothing changes if nothing changes". Walk bravely toward your desires–live a high level life of bliss, ease and alignment… obstructions no longer exist in your reality. *Being Unfuckwithable is about making moves for you, for your empire, your legacy, and for the collective rise that you contribute to here on Earth.* We are always moving toward the next vision, the next desire, the next feeling, and the next actualization. As we are moving forward in alignment, we are actively refining and releasing what is no longer aligned. *You are getting what you are available for… period.* You are co-creating consciously and subconsciously all day long.

When you LIVE in the fast lane, in YOUR lane, on your soul led path... you are naturalizing more and more alignment, and therefore, more and more desires. More intentional living means you are naturally drawing in more of that goodness. Once you become aware of this, understand this and LIVE this... you cannot go back. *As I love to say, "The more aligned you are... the more you crave alignment".*

As we bring this chapter to a close, I invite you to deepen your awareness of your lane, your path, and your devotion to it. **Stay loyal to your future self.** Stay focused on how you desire to feel now, and where you are headed. This is BEING highly magnetic. This dialed vision with an expansive consciousness allows you to be an active CO creator–consciously manifesting desired realities AND outcomes, all the while you are in a surrendered position to receive. You open up to divine intervention with ease. *Stay in your lane with 360 degree awareness, stay focused on the vision, and open up to life, and all it has to offer.* Your soul chose Earth for the full spectrum of infinite experiences. You are here to be a leading energy, so be self led AND co-create with the DIVINE. This work within this chapter is to inspire a high level of clear, refined, and focused energy aligned to your vision while also leaving a LOT of room for MAGIC. It's time to have it all babe, now let's dive into the homework of this chapter.

Homework / Daily Devotionals ...

Before each numbered reflection, take a few deep breaths, close your eyes, and drop into your body. Then meditate, reflect, and/or journal.

1. What does "Your Lane" mean to You? (what does it look, feel, present like?)
2. How can "Your Lane" become even MORE refined? (what/who can be released? Where can you deepen your focus? Where are you doing too much/leaking your energy/multitasking/being stretched thin? What distractions can you powerfully let go of?)

remember QUALITY over quantity when it comes to refinement. How can you FOCUS more powerfully with less distortions, distractions, and frankly less wasted energy?

3. What subtle obstructions are on your path/your lane that you can DECIDE to clean up NOW, once and for all?
4. When in the past (what patterning) do you have around "veering" or "deviating" from your path? (Ex. comparison of others, fear of success, fear of failure, people pleasing, martyr energy, distraction, addiction, unconscious behaviors etc.)
5. With this clear awareness of past moments of deviation, how can you begin to practice noticing these old outdated misaligned patterns and begin to get back on your lane? (maybe, simply noticing the slip and reminding yourself to get back in "my lane")
6. How quickly could you achieve, receive, and manifest your desires if you stayed devoted to your path? What rewards and benefits would be available to you *sooner* if you stayed on this path?

Here are 3 things you can do right now to live life in your own ICONIC fast lane

1. Stop giving a fuck about how you are being perceived and start living for YOU!!! (dress how you want, talk how you want, take up space, do YOU and do it well Queen).

2. Devote to a path of alignment– start focusing on feeling healthy, happy, clear minded, grateful, and be present for it all.

3. Decide to be all the way "on" or all the way "off"

No more multi-tasking, stretching yourself thin, no more scattered energy–be focused AND be present, You're either resting or you're taking efficient action. You're either socializing or you're taking alone time. **Stop half ass-ing it and you will stop getting half ass results.**

Take some deep breaths Queen/King. I'm celebrating You on your journey, celebrating your commitment, and devotion to staying on your path. We are focused, efficient, dialed in on our desires…AND we are leaving SO much spaciousness for divine intervention to surprise us. Focus IN and open UP. Breathe in focus, exhale surrender.

You've got this!

CHAPTER 6

NEW PARADIGM WEALTH

The quickest way to repel money is by pretending you don't like it.
Money is a NEUTRAL resource that exists to empower you, and amplify your life by design.
The time is NOW to clean up any distortion, scarcity or wounds of separation you may have around it.

This chapter will expand and empower you around all things material wealth, energetic and physical abundance, financial realities and money. Being Unfuckwithable will require you to have an open, loving, and reciprocal relationship with ALL abundance. There is NO separation. **This chapter will absolutely challenge any distortions, illusions, and wounds of separation that you may have around the topic of money.** This chapter will support you in healing and cleaning up a lot of bullshit concepts, programs and beliefs that you borrowed from societal norms, past generations and mainstream fear programming. **This chapter WILL reprogram the old outdated 'wirings and firings' and UPGRADE your consciousness, belief systems, and relationship to and with money— transforming any lack or scarcity into abundance and overflow.** This chapter will completely change your reality of and with money.

I invite you to consciously and lovingly witness all that arises for you throughout this chapter and this work. I invite you to notice it, shift it, and choose again. I invite you to receive this chapter with an open heart and an open mind. **I invite you to over and over again come back to the truth that there is NO**

separation. *All that is*-is connected. We are in the *Dimension of Openness.* **You get to FULLY experience life on Earth, through an evolved, unattached, yet deeply loving relationship with money.** Attracting, generating, and receiving **infinite** amounts of money (insert any resource you desire) from a place of wholeness...*Now THAT is Unfuckwithable.* Again, I am channeling, speaking, and writing TRUTH here for You. I will not be beating around any bushes or sugar coating any codes–I want quick and deep truth integration. Therefore, I will not be procrastinating that truth integration to project your precious ego and past programming around your outdated beliefs around money. I am here to support you in elevating your entire life. Having an abundant, overflowing and devotional relationship to and with abundance is absolutely part of that. So let's dive in.

Frankly, I am fucking done with judgments and wounded projections about money. Money is love. Money is neutral. Money is whatever you make it mean. Money is necessary at this time right now in life on Earth, and within the multiple material paradigms that exist here. Money is even necessary on (and in) many other paradigms that exist in the multiverse. *I am in the business of supporting YOU, that brave, bold being reading this and anyone who experiences my work in having the desires of their heart and having what LIFE desires for them.* **Therefore, educating, empowering and integrating an EVOLVED wealth consciousness into every cell in your body and opening you up to easeful receptivity is a must.** If this is sounding like a vibe... keep reading and don't rush through this chapter. Being Unfuckwithable and money are so deeply interconnected. **Money and spirituality are so deeply interconnected.** You living a life of purpose and fulfillment is so deeply connected to money. Whether you decide to use these teachings and integrations to empower yourself through wealth, abundance and financial liberation or you desire to empower others, or you use this work to empower both–this work will change it all. *Whether you could give two fucks about having, generating, and circulating more money or not... these concepts will deepen your* *understandsing of energy, of life within the Dimension of Openness and EMPOWER you to deepen into the abundance that is ALL already around you.*

I have reclaimed so many words and concepts on my individual and collective ascension, empowerment, and spiritually liberated journey. I've reclaimed how money works for me and the world. I've reclaimed my place in any outdated and old hegemonic structure. I've reclaimed how these illusions used to perpetuate separation and hierarchy. **I have claimed wealth as an all encompassing, interconnected, flowing and circular phenomenon in my life and within the collective consciousness and material reality.** I've reclaimed the words: Icon, Tycoon, RICH, Wealthy, Royal, Elite, Boss Bitch, Bad Bitch and I have completely identified the word *Unfuckwithable*. **Being Unfuckwithable requires an open, receptive, high service, and regenerative relationship with money.** This chapter is about empowering and upgrading you to live freely and abundantly with *all that is.*

I am thrilled to be bringing you evolved wealth consciousness INTEGRATIONS... so that money IS your most devotional support system as you walk your aligned path here on Earth. It's time to be unapologetically IN LOVE with money and let money be unconditionally in love with you. **We're here for a supportive, devotional, trusting, loving, reciprocal and REGULATED relationship with MONEY.** Shame, scarcity, and judgements don't exist in this relationship with money or frankly within the paradigm we are entering together. *So check yourself and your preconditioned judgements at the door babe.* We are operating from a HIGH LEVEL and NUANCED understanding of money as a NATURAL part of you and your stunning life. An extension of your genius and an amplifier to your radiance. *Take a moment now...really be here.* Be here with this work, with these words. How is this feeling in your body? How is this landing in your consciousness? How are your previous beliefs already being challenged, called to a higher perspective OR perhaps even being further validated and confirmed. *Breathe in.*

Breathe out. Take many moments throughout this chapter to re-read, take breaths, journal and really sit with and meditate on these concepts as you deepen in this awakening and soon to be abundantly elevated way of life. Now let's carry on.

The Unfuckwithable being has an evolved consciousness of wealth...Educated and aware of the old paradigms of hegemony, systematic oppression and all the conditioned distortions of the old paradigm(s). Patriarchal and capitalist structures have clouded the TRUTH and you are here to reclaim your connection to money, energy and ALL that exists. *The truth is abundance IS your birthright.* No matter who you are, what your story is/has been up until this point...**Money loves you.** It's here to support you and you get to experience abundance now. The Unfuckwithable being, CHOOSES to open to new realities with money, they CHOOSE to see things differently, and they CHOOSE to exist in an EMPOWERED and overflowing generosity with money...For themself, the collective, the planet, and the Universe at large. **They CHOOSE to use their wealth for regeneration, creativity, healing and expression ALL from a foundation of LOVE.** The Unfuckwithable being KNOWS that money does NOT define them, they KNOW that money is neutral AND they also KNOW that their life is INFINITELY better for having it. **So why NOT have FUCK TONNES of it?!**

I personally identify as extremely spiritual and financially liberated. Wealth, money, abundance, opulence... is deeply connected and intertwined with my alchemy, ascension and life's purpose here on Earth. *I am multidimensional and so are you.* I hope you are already beginning to restructure any old thoughts or deeply embedded beliefs that say "you can't be spiritual, or kind, or a "good" person and also have fuck tonnes of money". Fuck that rhetoric. Fuck that perpetuation of separation. Money is not the root of all evil, money is not good nor bad. **Money is NEUTRAL and it is a resource to support those who choose to hold and work with it.** This is the time where you witness yourself, your judgements or the judgements placed on you about your relationship to and with money. I hope you challenge the old paradigms that have attempted to keep you separate or shame you for wanting more.

Breathe in. Breathe out. You are safe,
supported and held.
Money loves you and you GET to unapologetically
love money... or at least for now... see it is neutral.

Let's talk for a moment about the times in your life when you have fallen into the illusion of separation. When you felt you had to SEEK money as something outside of you. When you felt "less than" for not having "it". When you made your entire identity, life, and purpose about chasing it, earning it or hoarding it. You get the point... *Let's honor that as part of the past, forgive ourselves and release any of it that doesn't feel empowered.* Your soul path here on Earth is SO much bigger than surviving, scraping by, experiencing fear, overwhelm and scarcity with money...It is also SO much bigger than chasing money and putting all your life force energy into "earning" and "achieving it". Those low vibrational states are not necessary. **They are in fact the very opposition to the TRUTH, that life on Earth is an infinite playground of opportunity and abundance.** A reality that you are INNATELY worthy of–a reality that you don't have to 'earn'. *Again, if you're feeling triggered by previous perceived victimization of money... take a moment, breathe it in.* **You are safe.** Money itself is not the one to blame, but rather the old outdated systems and structures of old paradigms that attempted to keep you separate. **Let's choose a new path now.**

It's not about *blaming* these old and outdated systems–*I simply want to educate you on where individual and collective victimization and real/true pain has come from.* Now, rather than clinging onto the blame game, let's choose a new path, and if you do choose to project that anger...properly project it to the capitalistic systems (and not onto money itself). Again–money is ENERGY. I took more Women's Studies and Social Justice courses than I can count on my two hands when I was in

University. I was raised in a highly conscious Liberal family (true liberal to be clear (meaning truly liberated and free) - not woke robotic assimilation liberal). I am beyond educated and aware of the various vectors of oppression within old outdated systems. I am educated in depth on the hegemonic systems that are unfair and absolutely sinister in the distribution of money, power, and resources within the old paradigm...AND BECAUSE OF THAT–I make it my MISSION to empower you in your relationship with money.

Being mad at money is the fastest way to repel it from you and your life. *Money responds to you. Just as love responds to you. Just as opportunities respond to you. Just as ALL energy responds to YOU who is the leading energy.* **The Universe responds to you.** Your vibration sets the standard. **So, it's time to love money–or at the very least, neutralize it.** In order to BE Unfuckwithable, receive money with ease and live a lifestyle of wealth and abundance in a way that feels true for you… you must first understand where you are or have been participating in an old outdated system of oppression, separation, lack, and scarcity. Mainstream media (MSM), hegemonic, and capitalistic structures (school systems, prison systems, government), global industrialisation etc etc are some of the systems I am referring to. *The same systems that oppressed you financially are the same systems that work each day to keep you oppressed.* These systems and the people who believe everything they read, hear or see… have trained your brain to FEAR money, wealth, abundance, more than enoughness, overflow, luxury, opulence, and over the top RICHNESS. There is a very intentional and again–sinister reason for this fear perpetuation when it comes to money. *If you are kept poor, in lack and in fear–you are much easier to control.* **Those, however, who are willing to look beyond, feel within and deepen their own understanding of self, their desires and their INSOURCED knowings, WILL be empowered.** Those who allow their own gut and intuition to be the deciding factor on what energies (like money) are good or bad will be the ones who understand it all as neutral, all connected and become truly free. *I invite you to witness the hierarchical paradigms that have attempted to keep you separate, keep you in a hustling or perceived separation from money–witness them and let them go.*

The truth is... money is NEVER running out. Abundance will exist in some shape or form throughout any and all evolutions of life on Earth and life within the Dimension of Openness. There is more than enough money and abundance for everyone. **Money again is NEVER running out.** *The old outdated systems want you to believe there is scarcity, to ensure that you stay in separation and lack.* To make you bad or wrong for wanting more. Money is here to love and support ALL beings in living their most fulfilling and purpose driven lives on Earth. **Let's start to awaken to money as an infinite resource, a resource that allows you and anyone who desires it to have infinite amounts of it.** Let's talk about ALL beings experiencing overflowing abundance...all of us being RICH. **This experience of money doesn't have to be bad, it doesn't have to be reserved for a small select group of people, and this experience of money GETS to be normal and natural for YOU.**

There are infinite realities available to you that allow money to be a GUARANTEE in your life. *There are SO many abundant, aligned, generous, and unconventional New Paradigms of wealth that exist.* There is a whole world (many worlds actually) that do NOT subscribe to MSM, fear propaganda or even experience any form of scarcity or separation. However, there are STILL (and likely always will be) paradigms of scarcity and separation– hegemonic systems exist for a reason. There will always be a choice to stay in a system that does not support you or the collective ascension into freedom, and the choice to step into a new, higher, freer paradigm. Throughout this chapter I will be showing you the contrast that exists in the New Paradigm vs the old. **You get to choose moment to moment, day after day.** *Which paradigm feels true for you? Which paradigm will you choose?*

I want to invite you into the paradigm I choose, and the paradigm I think will be of highest service to your beautiful life here on Earth– The Dimension of Openness and the New Paradigm of wealth. Welcome to the new paradigm where there is NO separation. **Your soul path is truly so much bigger, than what your mind and consciousness can even GRASP right here, right now.** Within this new paradigm we are not only manifesting our heart's desires, our conscious desires, and everything we KNOW we want…*We are also manifesting that in which LIFE desires for us. Or as we might say–God's Plan.* **There is so much more available.** Your openness and your surrender is what allows this bounty, this abundance to drop in for you. **As we build your understanding of the New Paradigm of wealth, and as we clean up any cloudy distortions in your frequency from the old…we are deepening your connection to your path.** Deepening your connection to the abundance that devotionally and infinitely supports you on this path. *Let's take our time here and notice where any large obstructions or smaller lingering obstructions may be slowing down your ability to live your ultimate TRUTH.* Let's become aware of what may be inhibiting you from receiving the infinite abundance that is so easefully available to you. *Breathe in deeply, open up. Exhale and release any distortion, any lack, any illusion that you are separate from the abundance that is infinitely available…let that shit go.* Your life's path gets to be one of easeful service and easeful receptivity. A life of fulfillment, success, and purpose. One of devotion, and one of pleasure, for YOU, and for ALL involved. Money is a resource that exists to support you in fulfilling this path and your true purpose. **Money loves you and wants to support you.** It's time to let it in.

When you understand money as a neutral INSTRUMENT that you get to love, desire, manifest, earn, receive, share, invest, spend and save… you become MUCH better positioned to actualize your soul's devotional path and purpose. Money is an amplifier…money lets you have and GIVE more. More good is more good. Period. All this being said, King/Queen… it would be a DISSERVICE to you, your path, to the planet, and to the collective, to stay disempowered around money. *Money amplifies your vision, mission, and purpose...*And we are here for a FULL and amplified life. So! It's time to completely heal your relationship to and with money. It's time to release the distortions that were conditioned into your consciousness through robotic assimilation, capitalist, and hegemonic systems.

It's time to experience money as your most devotional support system. A supportive energy you can trust, rely on, and truly ADORE. *This is starting to resonate and feel true for you.* You now understand the power of this instrument and ALL the GOOD that it can amplify in this life. *Are you ready? Are you committed... to an abundant, rich, wealthy and beautiful life full of luxury and service?* It's time for more, more abundance, wealth, prosperity, and financial success. It's time for all thls and MORE in an aligncd, evolved, and REGENERATING way. A way that heals and nourishes your life, the planet, and the collective at large.

The New Paradigm of wealth is extremely circular in nature. Meaning there is a natural flow and a natural rhythm. Money flows...there is a deep connection to the Earth, an openness, and intertwining with the cosmos and a deep honoring of the nature of your human self. Money is connected to you, me, and *all that is*– it is ENERGY. **It is incredibly spiritual to honor your own innate abundance and then use that knowing to actualize more abundance in your material and external world.** There is space and purpose for spirituality, faith and consciousness in becoming rich through remembering your innate abundance. There is action and there is lean back–a coming home to your nature. *Circular and cyclical flow–a deep honoring of your inner divine feminine and divine masculine harmonization.* There is a very intentional integration of both the yearning, the wanting, and then actually *having* of those desires. There is co-creation, manifestation, energetics, and embodiment required for ultimate *luxury receptivity.* *There is sensory opening– sacral and tantric energetics. Devotional and sensual practices to open wider to all that exists for you. There is momentum* *building and cashing in.* There is successful execution and there is *strategic spaciousness*. There is high level embodiment, positioning, and boss execution. There is also deep pleasure and divine feminine codes required within wealth actualization and amplification. ***IN-sourced polarity work–union between your inner dominant and inner submissive.***

Your wanting, creation and receiving of money is so fucking spiritual–if you let it be. **Being dominant in your wanting, and submissive in your receiving.** This New Paradigm of wealth requires mastery of your inner divine feminine and inner divine masculine. Actually living in such flow, ease, and abundance takes DEVOTION (more on this coming). Thrival in life, leadership, love, and of course money requires your focus and intention. We are doing all this money work from an EVOLVED consciousness of wealth. Wealth as LOVE and money as energy, energy as LOVE. Therefore, money as LOVE. Wealth as a holistic, regenerative, and supportive energy to *all that is.* ***Being rich is your divine birthright, and something that allows you to further deepen in your soul's path and true fulfillment***. It's time to have it all–from the most aligned, inherently good and generous space.

> *Money is energy and money is love–don't let anyone tell you otherwise*

As we walk our highest timeline and live life in our new paradigms...we must recognize that all the old and outdated paradigms STILL exist. ***The New Earth is not a material world in which only certain humans exist, but rather a frequency in which only certain humans interact (for now).*** As you live this new paradigm, it is important to have consciousness, awareness, and compassion for those still navigating older, less empowering paradigms. It is also important to recognize that this frequency 'game' is one where we can jump timelines. We can rise higher AND we can fall back. ***We always get to choose which frequency we want to exist in, and therefore what physical*** *reality will experience.* *So we must also have grace and compassion for ourselves at times as we straddle all potential paradigms at once.* **It takes devotion, time and practice to stay in your lane, your paradigm, your frequency.** There will be times when you fall off–and that's okay. This new paradigm of wealth is to be walked powerfully with a humble, yet empowered recognition of our blessings. The blessing to be awakened into a position, where we are *open* to seeing things differently. The blessing to actually want to improve our relationship to money, to love money, to be empowered by money and to experience this new paradigm of wealth. It is a blessing to exist on Earth in an open, curious way. It is a blessing to access this information and receive this facilitation. **It is a blessing to break out of the *Matrix* (as they say)...to release the old paradigms, and have the resources to do so.**

> *There is NO deficiency on Earth. This planet is abundant, ever giving and fertile*

Systematic oppression exists, and has existed for as long as humans have roamed this Earth. Hierarchy, hegemony, power imbalances, and FEAR–the root of all illusions of scarcity–have been perpetuated throughout humanity. This systematic oppression controls a group think/concept in which the greater population tends to get on board with (either proudly, consciously or in more sneaky subconscious ways). **Through conscious and subconscious programming, the belief systems of the population get entrenched with a tonne of fear programming, and then humans ultimately actualize this reality of scarcity in their material world.** *Again–you're NOT most people. You are now AWAKE. Awake to the truth, and empowered to LIVE differently. In this empowerment (in your own authentic way) you will empower others to rise and FREE themselves as well.* **Our thoughts and beliefs create our reality–And this is an incredible super power we have as human beings and as the creators of our lives.** It can also be our greatest detriment as a species. When mainstream messaging is perpetuating thought patterns and beliefs that are riddled with fear, scarcity and delusions of deficiencies—our programming can become extractive and our lives can become disempowered. *Again—you are now awake to these truths, and you are consciously CHOOSING a more life giving and sovereign path.*

There is NO deficiency on Earth.
This planet is abundant, ever giving and fertile.

It is the brainwashing perpetuated by greed that creates distorted realities of lack, scarcity, and fear. Again, it is a blessing to know these truths, to break out of the Matrix (old programming), and to actually LIVE in a New Paradigm. **My intention is that this book enlightens and empowers the world to understand their own sovereignty, innate abundance, and that these teachings liberate the world so we can co-exist within the infinitely abundant planet and universe that is HERE for us.** So that we can exist in a highly consciously reciprocal relationship to the planet—and all who inhabit here, the cosmos and ALL that exists within the *Dimension of Openness.* Take a moment here, breathe into your body, regain awareness of YOUR own truths. Come home to yourself. Arrive to your INNATE truths…not the truths you were conditioned to believe…but what is actually TRUE for YOU. Connect to your unrepeatable and precious body, connect to your infinite soul and spirit and breathe into a higher, freer and more life-giving way.

Ok, now back to loving the fuck out of money. Back to understanding money as an energetic and supportive resource, that continues to evolve and change shape, as a means of exchange here in the Earthly dimension. *A resource—as is sunlight, natural energy, water etc.* Money takes on 'form' to be traded and exchanged to circulate abundance in the material world. **Money itself is never running out—because energy itself is never running out.** There is no reason to hate or fear money— it is simply a resource, a free energy, and a form of infinite exchange within the Earthly realm (and many other cosmic realms as well). If you *do* have displaced anger toward money–it is better directed toward your own healing…And if you can't do that, at the very least, properly displace your anger to those *actually* perpetuating fear paradigms and illusions of scarcity (the systematic oppression I spoke of earlier).

Again… it makes sense to be mad at money when that was the story you were conditioned to believe. The story that only certain people can have it, money is the root of all evil, and that money is something to fear. It is understandable that you would be mad at money when you were programmed your whole life that you are greedy for having it, you are a bad person for wanting it, and that it's running out. *If you believe that conditioned script–I understand your hate toward money.* But, I am here to empower you and I am here to free you from that outdated perspective. At some point in your life, you get to make the decision to become empowered around money. You decide that money is not going anywhere, and you are ready to co-exist with it in a circular, loving, and reciprocal manner. *The point comes when you are ready to see things differently.* You are ready to begin to experience a wildly beautiful, unconventional, and abundant reality with money as a supportive resource in your life. I believe that time is now. Time to reclaim your birthright to abundance. Time to own your desires for MORE. Time to heal the pain the old systems have caused you. **Time to awaken to the truth.** *It's time now my love–to flow with money the same way you flow on the dance floor with a champagne flute in your hand.*

Let it be easy.
Let it be natural.
Let it flow like the air you breathe.

It's time to call money in with ease and receive it with ease. It's time to free yourself from the delusions, distortions, and illusions of the old paradigm. It is time to claim your joy, freedom and abundance and heal the conditioning of the old paradigms that were built on fear and scarcity. **It is time to be FREE.** It's time to shock yourself and everyone around you with the financial, internal and external GLOW UP of this work. *Empower yourself, so you can empower others in this liberated financial reality within the dimension of openness.* Whether you are triggered right now/existing in a lack paradigm with money...Or you are empowered as fuck but desire more of it. I invite you to really soak in the teachings within this chapter. It is my greatest honor to facilitate you in actualizing your desires and breaking free from the outdated paradigms of separation. Let's be free! Take a moment here, check in with yourself–are you feeling open to seeing things differently? Are you ready to be informed, awakened and catapulted into a NEW paradigm of wealth? A new reality of earning, exchanging, and receiving money? *Breathe in. Breathe out. You are safe, it's time to expand.*

Now let's dive deeper in. **Let me start off with full transparency with you–having a loving and elevated relationship with money is a DEVOTION.** Like any relationship it takes work and ongoing dedication. I too have been triggered in the past by other people interacting effortlessly with money. I have wanted more and more of it and I even strangled those true desires because I thought it would be deemed-*greedy.* I have wanted more, owned that I wanted more and STILL wasn't manifesting it. **I have been the *bitter bitch* who played victim and I have been the *boss bitch* who manifested everything she wanted and THEN some**.

I have been empowered AND disempowered by money. I have rewired, rewritten and reprogrammed outdated, misaligned and harmful beliefs and benefited hugely. I have also fallen into illusions of deficiency and scarcity while having MORE than enough. I have amplified and magnified my innate truths. I have refined my wealth energetics to upgrade my *attraction point* to higher levels of wealth and financial abundance. *Higher and more refined levels of receiving–were talking BULLSEYE vibes.* I have practiced shifting from scarcity to abundance. Then shifting abundance into material financial wealth. I have learned how to upgrade and elevate my experience with money to align with my truest lifestyle desires–*and I still too have to devote to this work every day as I continue to evolve on this path.* **The work never ends–it just gets easier and the results just get bigger!**

I want to remind you that you are not alone, no matter what your lived reality has been or currently is with money–you get to shift it. No matter where you came from… no matter who you are…no matter who your parents were/are–*you get to choose empowerment now.* I have experienced all the things around money and all the waves led me here–**I LOVE MONEY and MONEY LOVES ME.** I do a fuck tonne of GOOD with money. I know there are INFINITE AMOUNTS of money. It is NEVER running out. Money exists all around me and is desiring to support me. Money is a beautiful part of my life but it does NOT define me. I am WHOLE and COMPLETE with or without it. I CHOOSE to live the reality where I have WAY more than enough of it–*more money than I know what to do with.* WAY more money than is required to alchemize this precious life while I'm here. I choose a reality where more and more humans awaken to their highest and truest potential. I choose the reality where they allow money to support their desires, dreams, and lifestyle. *I choose a world where all beings are supported by money and all illusions of fear disappear into the abyss.* Until this IS the reality on Earth for ALL beings…I will happily continue to exist in my high vibing, empowered and abundant reality. I choose abundance for me and for those who are ready to step into it now. **I am excited to have you on this path with me.** Outdated paradigms may exist, however I CHOOSE freedom, abundance, and infinite wealth–no matter what. I invite you now to also become unapologetically IN LOVE with money. *I invite you to develop an evolved consciousness of wealth.* To know that money does NOT define you, to know that money IS neutral, AND to know that life is INFINITELY better for having it.

Let's rewire your brain and wealth consciousness

First off–money is a neutral resource that takes on whatever meaning you assign to it. For myself and for those who desire to be expanded, healed, and supported by this work– money is love, fun, and freedom. Earth, this paradigm (and many other planetary and cosmic existences,) require resources and MONEY is a powerful and generative resource. *When it's in the hands of well intentioned and conscious people–money can change the world for the better through education, empowerment and elevated energetics.* When operating in a high level relationship to money, combining the following themes becomes critical: self awareness, emotional intelligence, benevolent consciousness, highest self activation, a connection to aliveness, soul and spirit leadership, nervous system regulation and optimization and of course DEVOTION to integrating the wealth codes that are presented to you in this chapter.

It is important to recognize the difference between humans who are wealthy and perpetuate the illusion of scarcity–from those who are wealthy and aim to empower other humans in becoming independently wealthy as well. Anyone empowering or attempting to empower you in the realm of money and finances is NOT to blame for the capitalist systematic oppression that perpetuates ideologies of fear and separation. The wealthy individuals writing books, sharing podcasts and providing coaching and courses on wealth activation–are to be celebrated and thanked. **Those who share insight on supporting a collective wealth reality are aware of the infinite nature of money as energy and they KNOW that it is never running out.** As you continue to go about your day to day life it will become obvious WHAT and WHO fall into an OLD paradigm of scarcity, and WHAT and WHO fall into a NEW paradigm of infinite abundance consciousness.

Systematic oppression is perpetuated through political tyranny and mainstream media's carefully constructed and perpetuated belief systems of fear and scarcity. These perpetuated fear paradigms are designed to keep the mass population in fear, scarcity and in separation from their sovereignty. This is a hierarchical and tyrannical method to keep people poor, misinformed, and easy to control. *You can begin to* *see how the media, the ever changing economy and the overarching governing principles perpetuate fear, lack, and greed.* They constantly remind us that the planet is going to die, resources are running out, and they create that reality by fluctuating the economy at the flick of a finger to exacerbate the illusion of fear. They also CREATE the very reality of good hard working humans having LESS than optimal and real experienced scarcity through unnecessary inflation. The 'higher-ups' behind the political landscape and MSM do NOT want you to be empowered, financially free or awakened to the confines and illusions of *"The Matrix"*. They don't want you empowered to the truth, because they are still operating from an old system that thrives on greed and separation. *They are not awake to the infinite realms, they live in fear, and they choose to perpetuate that fear and separation to hoard resources for their own benefit.*

If they wanted you to be financially free, healthy and happy they would have created a much more financially empowering society. If they TRULY wanted a thriving society of healthy, happy and badass high earners, they would do so through financial education, empowerment, entrepreneurship, and freedom of expression. Instead—you're fed garbage to attempt to keep your brain, body, and vision limited as fuck. You're instead taught to fear money and anyone who is earning it. You are celebrated and trained to say "they have more money than they know what to do with" or "I don't really care about money" or "more money more problems" or "I don't need more than I have" etc etc. Well, news flash babe—the average person saying these things is the same kind of person who would break their fucking leg to chase down a $20 bill floating in the wind. **You GET to love money.** It's nothing to be ashamed of. You get to WANT MORE. You get to own it. You get to experience it. You get to be empowered by it. **You get to feel safe with it.** You get to understand it as neutral, and as supportive for a fully flourishing life here on Earth.

So... back to *"The Higher-Ups"* their goal of keeping money separate from you. They don't mind being "the bad guys" –they are (or attempt to be) anonymous. **They are the ones perpetuating the old outdated paradigms.** These outdated paradigms can look like hegemonic systems that you likely read about in social sciences or have heard a politician speak on (while perpetuating and exacerbating them themselves–insert eye roll). **These systems and those controlling them absolutely DON'T want you to figure this all out.** They don't want you rich, they don't want you healthy and they don't want you sovereign. They definitely don't want you to have massive dreams for yourself, let alone go after them. They legitimately OWN the MSM, politicians, and the majority of large corporations–and they sure as hell want to be the only ones "at the top". *They will perpetuate illusions of fear and scarcity to attempt to keep the majority of humans under their tyrannical control.* This is where my term "woke robotic assimilation" comes in. Most humans have been TRAINED to be small and stay small–limited, quiet, unseen and unheard. Celebrated for falling into the shadows and being manipulated into mundane ways of existing. You have been trained to be average financially, average in terms of your expression, average in terms of your health, and average in terms of your pleasure. You have been trained to not want more for yourself. Trained to be average in terms of how you look, present and express your individuality on and on and on again.

When you're trained to be average in your wellness, finances, love, and experiences YOU ARE EASY TO CONTROL. Better yet...When you are manipulated through illusions of scarcity (that eventually become reality) through mind control–you ARE controlled. You're poor, sick, and unhappy. You are the opposite of liberated. You are NOT free despite the illusion that says you are. Your experiences and desires are easily limited, you have been trained to aspire to frankly *average ways of being and existing.* Average wants, average needs. Nothing too crazy– nothing that could "take away" from the resources "at the top". It is in the interest of greed, hegemony, and capitalism to keep you in lack. **It is YOUR decision now to break FREE from that illusion.** Important to note–the illusion of greed is embodied under the falsity that one can control the infinite limitless abundance of the multiverse. **You can't control it–it is energy and energy is infinite. We are energetic beings and we are infinite.**

Although truth and love always prevail–there are systems and rulers of these systems attempting to shelter humanity from the truth. Over the years there have been rebellions against capitalism, hegemony, and hierarchy–which is fabulous. Unfortunately, now the present day issue is that the same systems and rulers have disguised themselves as "woke" and "progressive". *These rulers get away with their tyranny and illusions of separation in a much more concealed way.* They figured out that humans are intelligent and resourceful as fuck. They realized that humans are innately good, kind, and CANNOT and WILL NOT be controlled unless the *control* was masked as something that would benefit the greater good–*yikes.* They saw humanity catching on and had to change their strategy. There are a lot of political issues I could include here–but let's keep it about money. The systems and the rulers of these systems came up with a solution through manipulative "education" and mass media that over-stimulates global humanity with problems (that they truly cannot solve) in hopes of debilitating the human race into depressed, anxious keyboard warrior activists. When you inevitably DO figure out that there is MASSIVE disproportion in resources globally– they want you to be so fucking overwhelmed and depressed by it that you turn against anyone who is seemingly wealthy. They have trained you to turn against anyone who is NOT struggling financially because you have now been conditioned that THEY, in their independent wealth are the root of the problem– *yikessssss.* Take a deep breath and really absorb this. **Read it over.** Take your time here. We are deconditioning A LOT of the bull shit that exists within the old paradigm /The Matrix and I know it can be alot to take in.

The outdated systems and the rulers of those systems have you TRAINED to think it is NORMAL to struggle. They have trained you to think it's normal to live in scarcity and in lack. They position you as "better than", *like it's not as bad as they have it in* *"third world countries"* so you can't complain, or try to do better for yourself. It's normal to hustle, to burn out, to budget as the only means for savings, to only experience "freedom" when you retire, to only ever have 'just enough'. It's normal to jump on every sale and promo code that crosses you because money is running out, resources are running out, there's not enough!! (insert eye fucking roll). **You have been trained to be MAD at anyone who has empowered themselves with money.** Trained to be mad at anyone who is no longer controlled by societal illusions and old paradigms of existing. You have been trained and conditioned to struggle, and to be angry at the "lucky" and "privileged" ones who are not in the struggle with you. So babe—your anger is valid, but until you actually understand the system, and you understand who controls it…Your anger will be wrongly projected and wrongly displaced. You have a choice now—will you empower yourself into full financial liberation? Or, will you stay angry and broke? Will you stay mentally and physically unhealthy? Will you stay in the limited, old and outdated paradigm? Or will you enter the *New Paradigm of Wealth?*

You are wise. You are capable. You get to decide now. You get to decide that money is a devotional, supportive energy that exists to support your path, purpose, and dreams. *You get to decide that over and over again—until it's just how you live.* You get to choose to be expanded by those who are thriving with money. Their abundance does NOT take away from yours—so learn from them. Again, the people who are actively empowering your experience of wealth/money/abundance (be it through quantum physics, self development, spirituality, financial literacy, manifestation, energetics of money, investment insights etc etc.).They are *not* the ones who have created and perpetuated the system that's keeping you stuck, small, broke, unhealthy and misinformed. Those teaching and inviting you into the new paradigm of wealth ARE aware of the infinite resources that are available and they are here to amplify that flow. The NEW paradigm of wealth that I speak of—is a paradigm in which *all THAT exists* and *all WHO exist* are empowered equally and equitably by the infinite resources that are here and readily available for us. **Money is NEVER running out.** Money is energy...And energy is infinite. **Abundance is a choice... and it's time to LIVE it.** I am co- creating a reality where abundance is celebrated, cyclical, and shared in flow. A reality where instead of shaming those in their abundance, we celebrate them and learn from them. A reality where instead of judging those who live freely and actually go after their wildest dreams... the average person will instead look at them in awe, admiration, and an openness to seeing things differently. **This new paradigm will–one by one, empower those who have been fed a mainstream notion of scarcity to instead live freely, and abundantly.** Those who were previously brainwashed–will join in this revolution. They will rise in their own wealth and experience of money through shared wisdom, openness and receptivity. The rest of the world may live in scarcity and illusions of lack... but not us. The rest of the world may live in the hustle and the chase... but not us. *THIS is the NEW paradigm of wealth.*

Let's talk about the normalization and celebration of *mediocrity* and *struggle* within the mainstream media, social norms, and conventional society. The average human is *trained* through societal norms and conditioning to LIMIT their dreams. Conditioned to not BE, DO or HAVE "too much". Trained to limit their own desires and to squash any desire in their friends or family when it is "too big" or "too out there". **The normalcy of mediocrity keeps you in captivity... trapped in an illusion of safety.** According to mainstream notions–it's not safe to dream... because what if you fail?! The "groupthink" is to celebrate mediocrity and shame those who step out of the limiting barriers. Shame those who want more. Train the masses to strive for survival...but not for thrival. This is why when you have "big dreams" –be it for love, wealth, impact, fame, athletics, career...you name it. The *average* person can't fathom it. They can't celebrate you in your vision–they can't even see it. They are terrified of even imagining the possibility of it. It's just so much safer to be "realistic", "logical" and to play it safe.

Parents unknowingly will promote their children to have "safe" careers, to go to a standard school, become a teacher or an accountant... something that is deemed successful, but not too risky. The average parent is terrified for their child who wants to be an actress, an entrepreneur or a professional athlete. It's just TOO big. It's just too unrealistic. **The average person is so brainwashed by the groupthink that their capacity to dream is so limited.** *But not you... not you reading this.* You know you are different. You know you want more. Your capacity to dream, to visualize, and to actualize is rare. ***Your capacity to expand is bigger, so you must once and for all stop comparing the size of YOUR vision to the person next to you***. It's time to start witnessing yourself as the rare individual with massive dreams that are actually just a standard, natural, to be expected, and actually quite realistic for you.

The average person can't HOLD YOU in your massive dreams because they haven't even held themself in theirs. One can only see to their capacity of what they deem possible. The average person can't be expected to celebrate your dream when, god forbid, they even allow themselves to dream for their own future. So, it is my duty to remind you of your unique rareness. It is my duty to hold you to your highest standard and to empower you in your highest timeline. I certainly know I'm different, and I know for certain that you are too. It takes radical self and collective awareness to know that you aren't here to walk a familiar path. **You're not here to fit in.** You're not here to be easily understood or defined. ***Most people won't understand your gushing desires–because they have been trained to limit their own.*** Most people won't be able to label you. They won't understand your soul. They won't get it. They can't fathom your drive or ambition. They won't be able to label your unique spirituality or way of *being* in the Earthly realm. They will roll their eyes and wish you were more normal. They won't get it...And they don't have to.

I'm certainly not here to walk the average walk, and neither are you. It is time for you to walk your path, live your mission, and spread your purpose far and wide. It's time to allow money to support all that you are and all you are here to do in your precious time on Earth.

Take a moment here to integrate.
Breathe in. Breathe out.

Money is energy
Money is neutral
Money is love
Money does NOT define you.
Money amplifies your goodness.
So WHY NOT have a FUCK TONNE of it?

I have been working with the consciousness of money for a while now... like anything and everything– it's just energy. I work with the consciousness of money because I have Earthly desires. I have wisdom to share far and wide. I have love I want to give. I have wealth I want to receive. Money is not separate from my spiritual path. **Money is not separate from me at all.** Therefore, in the same way I work with all energies... I work with the energy of money. I devote myself to money the same way I would devote myself to anything I am in a relationship with, *because money is energy.* An energy that is very powerful in the material world. Money is an energy that is powerful in many other paradigms, realms, and worlds that exist within the multidimensional universe that we all exist within. **Money is a resource that has the power to change the world.** To change individual lives, communities, and collective realities. Money massively impacts the physical real world in its actuality AND money also impacts individual perceptions of one's reality. *Money is a fluid, ever evolving, and transformative energetic currency that amplifies whatever vibration you are operating at.* You feel internally abundant–money will show up for you, and represent external abundance. You feel internally scarce–money will show up in your external world, and amplify your perception and experience of scarcity. Money can be used for "good" and money can be used for "evil". **Money is a neutral resource that moves in the direction of the consciousness that it connects to.**

Physical money is a real tool in the material world and not everyone has the same relationship with it. This is where we get to decide what type of relationship we want. If you haven't already–I would be intentional about the environments you exist within, the ways those around you discuss money, and what paradigms they are perpetuating in their own lives. **Choose friendships and environments that live in an abundance consciousness and start to normalize thriving as a natural state of existence–*because it is.*** Building trust and confidence with money takes time and devotion. *Like any relationship, there are seasons, there is healing, and there is alchemy.* An abundance mindset is something to be *remembered.* The consciousness has always existed within you, but over countless years of conditioning you must regain your sovereign relationship to abundance.

You are limitless–you are infinite. Stop playing small around your desires and how money GETS to support you! START aligning with the expansive soul version of you that is SO desiring to be embodied. In my work with clients, I used to hear a lot about, "I'm not worthy" or "I don't feel worthy to have xyz–my response is always the same. It's not a matter of worthiness when it comes to money. **You are worthy because you are–period.** Money has nothing to do with it. It's a matter of: *are you willing to say yes? Willing to open fully? Are you willing to align accordingly and receive?* **Money has nothing to do with your perceived worthiness. I encourage you to fully heal your life, heal your relationship to self, and feel fucking good in your skin because you deserve that**. *But don't get the two twisted–you get to choose abundance now–no matter how much self love and self healing you feel you need to do.*

On some level–ALL people love money. All people want more of it and all people have (or have had) some sort of wounding around it. My personal unapologetic LOVE for the material world and my love for money as a spiritual woman and healer, certainly has a lot of people triggered. *Not everyone gets it.* **Not everyone feels like loving money and being a good person go hand in hand.** Not everyone has evolved into the *Dimension of Openness* where they understand ALL of it as simply–energy. There is no separation. **Money is a divine steward of the physical world, money comes from the same energy that you and I come from–creation.** *Choosing to co-create money into your world, and then choosing to co-create WITH that money is a really powerful act.* **An act of rebellion–to decide that this very 'thing' that has so many people up in arms, fighting over it, scared of it, and hating on anyone 'with' it…Is actually quite simply *something to love.*** Something to unite with and something to enjoy–how radical! The way I speak about money, experience money, and the standards I have around money are quite triggering to those who have not yet overcome their wounding around money or their wounding around simply owning their desires. **I'm neutral about money, money is a standard and no brainer resource to love, interact with and consciously expand in my life.** Money is not required to live a life of purpose, and it is not required to walk your soul path. However, if it is something you desire to utilize, enjoy and experience…Then it IS required for you to heal your shit with money and start to relate to it in a loving manner. For me, living my Unfuckwithable life, one where I am so empowered AND I empower the masses requires big resources. Money is required and I will continue to love the fuck out of it no matter how uncomfortable that may make some people along the way.

I am here to EXPAND you. This work is here to awaken you, heal you and deeply serve you. I am NOT here to stroke your ego, perpetuate any outdated groupthink or "woke robotic assimilation" mindsets that consequently keep you small… **I am here to change your life.** Money may not be required for YOU to live an Unfuckwithable life…But it certainly supports me in mine. *So, as always–take what feels true for you, leave the rest.* If this chapter has you feeling triggered-be gentle with yourself. *Breathe in. Breathe out.* **You are safe, and you are worthy of abundance.**

Your past does not define you. It is safe to flip the script. Your wounding makes sense–Let's heal it. Your stories make sense–Let's rewrite them. Your beliefs make sense– Let's rewire them. Your anger is valid–Let's transmute it. If you are feeling insanely expanded, excited and ready to receive–FUCK YA! Let's keep rolling. Money is not responding to your perceived worthiness. **Money is #1 responding to your VIBRATION, and more importantly #2 responding to your level of PERSONAL POWER.** Personal power is at the very core foundation of what it means to BE Unfuckwithable. Power is the certainty you hold, the level of embodied confidence that you emulate and money LOVES your certainty. Money loves knowing that you have big plans for it, money loves knowing you have PURPOSE. Money is an energy that is responding to movement, momentum, and vibration. Power is the vibration that magnetizes money, love, and opportunity. Money–like all energies, wants to flow. Money wants to live out a purposeful existence AND money craves movement. Money is fluid AND desires to be in the hands of a new paradigm wealthy individual who understands the circular rhythm of abundance consciousness. *Always flowing–never stagnant.* **Let's talk about money and power.** As discussed before–being Unfuckwithable is not a conditional phenomenon. It is not limited by circumstances or conditional on xyz going your way. Being Unfuckwithable is a level of certainty and POWER within yourself (regardless of external conditions) that power is what sets the stage…not the other way around. Being Unfuckwithable means that you are powerful–period. **Again, money LOVES power because money loves this level of certainty.**

Real Talk…
You can be…
Moody and powerful.
Happy and powerful.
Angry and powerful.
Elated and powerful.
Heartbroken and powerful.
Sick and powerful.

Gorgeous and powerful.
Feeling 'off' and powerful.
Excited as fuck and powerful.
Neutral and powerful.
Exhausted and powerful.
In LOVE and powerful.
Lonely and powerful.
...You get the rest.

Power is a CONSTANT. Power is a standard of existence when you are Unfuckwithable. **Power is the Unfuckwithable energy that is CERTAIN, and here on PURPOSE.** You are certain that no matter what is going on you feel powerful. You know it's all unfolding for you–it's all adding up. You know that your desires are on their way–regardless of what your external reality demonstrates. You know it's inevitable. **You know you're powerful no matter what.** You know it's all good. So you release any distortions of lack, scarcity or fear. You drop the hustle. You release the rush and you know there is nothing to control. You are solid, you are Unfuckwithable and money LOVES you. To be clear–again, when I talk about "power", I'm talking about PERSONAL power–the high level kind that is not wavering or circumstantial. Not the false sense of power or conditional power of someone who only feels powerful when they feel superior to something or someone else–not hegemonic power...PERSONAL power. Power comes with devotion. **Power is a level of self trust that takes time and alignment to build.** Power is a combination of self leadership (conscious behavior) and energetics (subconscious frequencies). You cannot experience the benefits and rewards of personal power and the lifestyle of the Unfuckwithable individual when you are straddling the old paradigm. Money is responding to your alignment–how you live, think, act, and believe the majority of the time. You cannot expect to have the ideal reality when you are wobbly in your perception of self. When you are straddling old outdated paradigms through your misaligned action, intentions, and energetics despite KNOWING the truth, the path, and the way forward. Money is a fluid energy that responds to your service and desire. Your giving and receiving. When you can drop the "rules" about money and begin to embody your true innate personal power you will naturally be shown your next step. Your path will unfold with ease and effortlessness because you TRUST yourself. **You KNOW wholeheartedly that you are powerful and NOTHING outside of you can change that.** It's you and you. Money feels that level of power and certainty—so the money flows.

Quick reality check and science class:

Breathe in. Breathe out.
Are you embodied in Personal Power *or* needy forcefulness?
If the latter — it's time to clean it up.

Power Vs Force
In case you didn't know—I have a clinical science degree, and Biomechanics taught me all about this one. Now, as a psychic channel and energy medicine practitioner I see that it is all the same.

Power = ease
Force = suffering

Power = efficient
Force = exhausting

Power VS Force is a phenomenon that has been studied in mechanics, engineering, and human behavior.

The consensus is—power wins.

One of my favorite quotes by me goes like this *"Efforting doesn't yield results… alignment does."*

(more on this in the upcoming *"Art of Receiving"* Chapter)

Efforting and "Force" will keep you pushing and pushing for so much longer than necessary.

Forcing will continuously have you coming out with below-average results over and over again.

Power on the other hand is: potent, efficient and all around YUM – power yields EXPONENTIAL results and takes WAY less energy/effort.

Sometimes as humans, we forget that we are the designers of our lives. We are blinded by limitation and we think the old paradigm is the only way. We forget we are rare. The average person is terrified of their own success. They're terrified to go first. They are terrified to outgrow people, terrified to be seen, terrified to hold new levels of wealth and responsibility, terrified to be sought after, and terrified to be hated. **Reminder–you have your lane and others have theirs.** Your lane is one of ever evolving evolution, desires, success, pleasure, edges, manifestations, love, and gratitude. *Their lane is whatever their lane is.*

Stay in YOUR lane. Stay focused on your goals. Move in alignment with your highest timeline–make moves as your highest self. Remember love, the high level individual moves quickly, strategically, and intentionally. Everything you have learned up to this point in this book gets integrated into your wealth consciousness. Let this be your most successful season of life YET–in all the ways! Let these teachings land deep, and from this moment forward actually LIVE that way. Remember angel–money is a neutral resource–something that GETS to really support you here on Earth. It's also a very significant resource in multiple paradigms actually, and on various planets. **When operating from an evolved consciousness with money–it facilitates a LOT of good, generosity, reciprocity, abundance, healing, nourishment, and so on.** Money is an energy form that is not going anywhere, abundance will always take a tangible form so long as you exist here on Earth. So, you can be mad about it or you can embrace it. **You can resist it or you can allow it.** As you become more and more empowered by money, and you improve your relationship with it...**You heal timelines and you flow abundance throughout the collective.** I'm proud of you. I know this work isn't always easy–but keep going.

My life is a million times better because of money–having money, being the match for money in life, and in my life's

work. I use money, spend money, share money, save money, and invest money. I do all of this from a foundation of love and overflow. Money is a resource here on Earth and it is here to support me. Money is an infinite resource here on Earth, and it is here to support you too. Believe me, I would thrive on a planet that relies solely on hugs as energy exchanges, I would buy brand new cars in exchange for a year of energy work and channeling. I would exchange land for the promise that I would tend to it and honor it. I would THRIVE if planet Earth simply "energy exchanged" for reciprocal contracts and relied on that exchange solely for living abundantly. But– that's not the paradigm we are straddling at this time. Money is a resource and a beautiful one at that. Money is *energy*–as I've said many times before and although it can seem limited by dollars, cents, and now numbers on a screen. If we choose to interact with it simply as *energy*–we begin to enter a *new paradigm* and co-exist on a *New Earth*. **Actually having what you want in divine flow and reciprocity is an available paradigm NOW.** Transferring abundance in loving exchange is an evolved state of consciousness to have with money–and that is a choice that is available NOW. **Let's put it this way–the limited definition and context of money is an illusion, but the function of money is energy–and energy is REAL.** Money is a resource we've collectively agreed on as a marker of 'value'. We've agreed on the illusion of money as we've agreed on the illusion of time. We've agreed that money is an important signifier of wealth, freedom, and power and it allows us to amplify your current state of experiencing life. Now you can be mad about that–or you can embrace that. You can choose to be empowered by the fact that money and time are constructs. You can use this understanding of money and time as energy and begin to play with it–'bend it' if you will. *When you understand time and money as energy, you can effortlessly interact with them as a true creator.*

Now that science and history class have adjourned–let's dive into the ways you can ACTUALLY receive and have MORE. As someone existing within the New Paradigm of wealth–you are ALWAYS available to be paid. Always open, receptive, and magnetic. There are no conditions to your receptivity. There are no rules or limitations. **You are available emotionally, energetically, and physically to be paid–always.** There are various portals open for your receiving. You are a high level strategic individual who has set up these physical portals. You are a high level spiritual individual who has open energetic portals...And you are a high level emotionally intelligent individual who has done the work to clean up any distortions and blocks in your frequency. **There are countless avenues in which money finds you–infinite channels of receiving.** You are in flow with abundance. *Inhale, I receive–Exhale, I give.* We stay open to the magic–open to the flow. **We don't create rules or limitations on when or how we will receive.** You close yourself off to the flow when we rely solely on paychecks, sales, clients, customers, salaries or our hourly wages to be your source of income. YOU are the source–always open, ready, and receptive. **There is no limit to the infinite stream of abundance.** When you place limits on 'what' and 'how' and 'when' you can receive, you stop the very nature of the infinite flow. When you set expectations on how or when money will come, you close yourself off to the magical rhythm that inevitably exists. It's tempting to look ahead and think, "Oh I will be fine because xyz payment is coming in" or "I could never afford that because only xyz payments come in" *Do you see how in both scenarios you are LIMITING yourself?* You are placing constrictions and capping the infinite–you can't cap it babe–it is limitless. Most likely you are setting expectations that are way lower than what is *actually* available to you. **Your human mind likely can't comprehend what is coming, the vastness of what is available, and if you try to control it or set projections for it you will rob yourself of the divine intervention that is waiting for your surrender. Humans have free will–you get what you expect–you get what you believe is possible for you.** When you set income expectations–you likely WILL get them (if you truly believe them to be true for you). I however suggest a much more magical and fluid way of approaching "income goals" – why not ASK to be amazed, surprised and supported financially beyond your wildest dreams? **The Universe wants your openness–not your illusion of control.** Money wants to support you babe–and there is SO much more available than you and your little calculator can add up.

I am *absolutely* here for setting energetic standards. Having an energetic minimum or standard in which you are available to receive. This clear intention allows money to understand where you're at. This clear energetic standard (example–"I am not available for anything less than $10,000/month in my business") would be a form of a clear energetic standard. These standards are different from expectations. **When you set an energetic minimum or standard, you are clearly communicating with money the lifestyle that is required for you.** When you set energetic minimums or baselines, you are communicating clearly that this is a standard of living for you and you are unwilling to drop below it. **I find energetic minimums to be incredibly beneficial–***I do, however, believe they are better set when you clearly communicate that you are leaving room for magic.* I personally, as of recently, am at a place where I'm not even setting minimums anymore. I am fully opening up to pure surrender and allowing. **Full trust that money knows me, loves me, understands my vision, and my desires.** My dream lifestyle will take the lead on fulfilling those desires for me financially. However, if you are just getting comfortable with your relationship to money–setting some energetic standards will be extremely powerful for you. Ensure these standards feel TRUE for you… because as I always say, "you manifest what is TRUE for you".

When you can set your standard and then have zero attachment to how it aligns for you–you are in the flow, babe. When you can maintain your personal power throughout the journey of your manifestations dropping in, through the journey of money landing into your world (without any external validation), you are operating in pure Unfuckwithable-ness. **Remember, money is responding to your POWER and your FREQUENCY.** Self mastery and financial mastery go hand in hand–it has nothing to do with time and EVERYTHING to do with alignment. And… sometimes alignment does take time. *So keep going with this.*

So for those of you who are placing time limitations or constrictions on your money flow–stop it. Stop creating unnecessary resistance. Do your money work, set your standards, and actually surrender to the divine timing of it. It's not about time– it's about alignment… the days of the week and month should really mean fuck all. **Stop being a slave to time.** Stop unplugging when the first few days or weeks of a month in business didn't go the way you anticipated or wanted. Stop allowing the day on the calendar to mean anything about your progress. **You are powerful– and money is responding to that–not to your anxious attachment to the calendar.** Alignment is something that DOES take "time". But when it locks in–it locks in. **Everything is always adding up (hello, Momentum training) so LET IT IN.** If you are here for the new paradigm of wealth, you are devoted to this work, which means you're in this for the long game. You know that YOU are your own source. **So! You can actually trust your divine timing and rest in the nothingness**. You can fully release your inner attention whore, adrenaline junky that needs constant external validation: money is here, your raise is here, clients are here, sales are here.. YAY! You can bask in the NOW and know that it's *all adding up FOR you*. **You can exist presently, joyfully, and openly in the moments in between.** Being in the new paradigm of wealth, means money is a supportive energy and always available to you AND you don't spend your precious fucking life obsessing over it. You are so much more powerful than that, babe. The same way anxious attachment energy isn't the vibe in your intimate relationships…Anxious attachment to money is repelling as fuck! Want it, intend toward it, align with, then just BE it. Be abundant. Be love. Be wealth. Stop chasing it, babe–BE it. **When you release the illusion of pressure and the delusion of deficiency you become much more effortlessly magnetic–Let it in.**

Having limitations around what you can and cannot do BECAUSE of money is a disservice to your very existence.

Living a wildly abundant life is essential in living out your fullest and purest expression and it is available now. **You were not placed here on Earth, in all your divinity, to say no to the things and experience you truly want because there's *"not enough money".*** There is an infinite supply–it's never running out, it WANTS to support you, your path, and your desires. Yes, as we know there ARE old paradigm structures in place that restrict access to the most BASIC levels of financial support AND these very structures are breaking down every single time you choose the new paradigm of wealth! **New portals of abundance OPEN and EXPAND for you, every time you choose the new paradigm of aligned wealth from a higher love consciousness.** If you are in a position to empower yourself, even just a little bit more with money– do that. If you are truly ready to BE Unfuckwithable, then living within this new paradigm of wealth and experiencing money as a supportive resource is the only option. **As we discussed in chapter 4, living your most fully expressed life is the greatest gift you can give the collective...And if you didn't already guess it–money AMPLIFIES your expression!** Money helps, money enhances, and money allows you to expand your gifts in this lifetime. So, wherever you are currently at... simply beginning to see money as a neutral and supportive resource is the best decision you can make today. Deciding that money is here to support you in doing a tonne of good here on Earth, and deciding that money amplifies your purpose and supports your path– is one of the most high service things you can do. *Earn, attract, receive, donate, give, share, invest, save, spend, educate and repeat.*

Since I can remember...I've respected, loved, and desired money. Money was always a supportive resource for me. It allowed me to buy the things I wanted to buy. I was able to use it for generosity and self indulgence. Money is a vibe. I, like any other human, heard conversations about lack, scarcity, the ever shriveling economy, and all the classic lines like, "money doesn't grow on trees" etc. etc. Yet, I chose early on to decide that money loved me and money and I had a good thing going. Money was fun, money amplified my life, and money amplified my current state. Money allowed me to have freedom that a lot of kids my age didn't have. I started consciously relating to money early on through my job. I started working young and started to feel the liberation of money in my hands, in my bank account and started to develop a real understanding and respect for the resource and tool that it was. As a generous, fun, kind, and confident woman, money has always amplified my vibe, and I am insanely grateful for that. Money always felt like no big deal to me. I always used it for positive and joyful experiences. I didn't come from generations of money by any means. I lived well, and my parents provided an extremely abundant life for us...but there was no trust fund or generational wealth to be passed down. **There was simply a consciousness circulating in my home of money as energy, abundance as truth, and gratitude as standard.** Money always felt easy, always more than enough for the things I wanted. **I simply started to identify as an abundant person. I then started to identify as a wealthy person.** I naturally lived this reality and positioned myself in this way to continue to earn, generate, receive, and cash in more and more—no matter what my "job" was or what the "economy" was saying.

Fast forward to University...Spending thousands of dollars on an education only to have a career where crossing six figures annually would be like hitting the fucking jackpot. Nooooo, thank you. **I learned quickly that conforming to those standards would not support the lifestyle I desired.** I quickly realized that I was not the norm and what was realistic to most was boring as fuck to me. I finished my science degree. I worked throughout. **I met incredible mentors who thrived in entrepreneurship and I began to experience the expanded life of new paradigms of existing.** My parents had left behind the constructs of the matrix years ago, my friends were waking up, and my mentors paved the way for me. **I took what resonated and left the rest.** I chose— over and over again the life I wanted to live. *I started to construct new beliefs, new blueprints, formulas unique to me, my gifts, and my desires.* I decided that money would be my most devotional support system, and I would use the resource to fund my dream life. I decided that I would do it my way–a life by design. **Here we are, a few years later in my late 20's as I'm writing you this.** Along my journey as I left the old conventions of "school–job–retire—die", and I bravely stepped into entrepreneurship, I started to see how your beliefs around money create your reality–period.

Being an entrepreneur or a self employed individual will kick your ass into surrender. Entrepreneurship will open you up wider to receive in unrealistic and unfathomable ways…but it will also show you the contrast of scarcity *if you let it.* There is nothing "safe" about living an unconventional life… or choosing a new paradigm of wealth… **but oh my god–if you know it's meant for you…what the fuck are you waiting for?** Dive in. I'm 28 years old, I'm about 2.5 years into being solely self employed, I'm a psychic channel and energy medicine practitioner and by no means am I living a normal life. I'm still relatively young, and new at all this. *Yet here I am…empowered, and empowering you.* There were times in my first year-ish of "business" (moments or days or sometimes months that felt like lifetimes) where I thought I would never make another dollar. *Moments where scarcity felt really real–of course I was way too proud to admit it to anyone at the time…*I was ALWAYS the successful one–but holy fuck was I scared shitless at times. *The innate knowing however–it kept me going.* I knew it was all adding up…despite having zero external validation to prove that to me. I knew that money loved me, that what I was doing was worthy of millions-billions-trillions. I knew money supported me, even when I didn't "see" it. I have to be honest with you–the money showed up fast and in big ways for me–early on–quickly. I didn't struggle or suffer, because **I knew.** I knew that money was energy and I knew that it was always responding to me–period.

There were months when I could NOT see that it was adding up, and ya that was scary. Here I am with big expenses, a high end lifestyle that I was not willing to limit, student loans, car payments, rent at the time, a university degree and a college diploma and all the logical reasons in the world to "get a normal job". I would have been incredible as a doctor, a teacher, a scientist, a physiotherapist... you name it. **Success conventionally had proven to be easy for me since early on.** But I knew I wanted something different. **I wanted freedom.** So I kept believing, trusting, showing up, aligning, doing the work... and it was scary, exhausting, and emotionally draining. **This devotion to money as a supportive energy, this unshakeable belief in my dreams and my gifts was the most EXPANSIVE and challenging thing I had ever done.** The expansion led to edges that required leaning in to, thoughts that required reprogramming, and beliefs that required continuous locking-in. **I did it, and I continue to do it, and I know I am just getting started.** The better it gets–the better it gets. With every edge, there is a new evolution. I truly know that I am just scratching the surface of what is available to me. I will continue to walk this walk in a new paradigm of wealth. I will continue to do this work and devote myself to my relationship with money as I grow and grow and grow. **The same principles of money as a supportive energy supported me when I was making zero dollars and they will support me well into making billions of dollars–the concepts are the concepts, and the truth is the truth.** These truths are universal. I am insanely grateful to have chosen this path–this path of abundance and understanding that exists as energy. It has served me and I know it will serve you.

Again, I am fully aware, well educated and extremely informed of the hegemonic systems that do not allow for equal or equitable distribution of resources. **I am well aware that this world has not set up everyone for success.** As discussed earlier in this chapter–there are countless factors as to why the simple "choice" of an abundance consciousness is not effortless, easy or even possible to some. This is all true...AND I stand by the truth that no matter who you are, where you come from, what your reality has been with money up until this point in your life, you GET TO CHOOSE DIFFERENTLY. The teachings within this chapter, the decision to experience money as energy, and your willingness to step into a new paradigm of wealth and OUT of the old paradigm of scarcity...WILL undoubtedly improve your relationship and LIVED reality with money. **Not everyone is set up the same– we all come to Earth with our karmic ties.** We are all born into varying degrees of suffering. There are truly evil energies that perpetuate the illusion of separation and scarcity–actively disempower certain human beings into true scarcity and poverty. One cannot thrive and be empowered by money, if their basic needs are not met. Because of my understanding of wealth, abundance, and money–this breaks my heart. **I know there is more than enough to go around–I know that money is infinite.** The potential to change lives, save lives, support ALL humans in living fully and abundantly IS available. **One-by-one, as we empower ourselves into the new paradigm of wealth and abundance, we can change the reality of abundance for all.**

This chapter–this book is designed to make YOU Unfuckwithable, so YOU can go on living your life's mission and purpose as an abundant being who naturally empowers others into their own abundance. *Abundance yields abundance.* It starts with our consciousness, our thoughts, beliefs, then our lived realities. Money is an amplifier, a neutral resource, and it can do a fuck tonne of good if we choose it. Having more money in the hands of conscious, generous, and socially innovative people will change the world. **When we step into abundance, we dissipate the illusions of greed, scarcity, and lack.** We create a New Earth and we live in true harmony. **The fact is: when you are overflowing with goodness, It's INEVITABLE that you will share that goodness with the world.** This is the case for my world and those in my world. I know that this will be true for you. What you have learned in this chapter will allow you to empower the collective consciousness and *lived* reality of abundance. The more money circulating in the hands of powerful, kind, and conscious people is a collective WIN. Your internal state is naturally already magnetizing–it's in your power to choose WHAT vibration. **I trust that you will choose to vibrate on the frequency of–abundance.**

I am so proud of you for making it this far. I celebrate you for receiving these wealth codes, opening into new paradigms, being willing to heal and clean up any misalignment or obstructions in your *financial frequency*. **The homework chapter here is going to look a little different.** Stay open and follow along. As always, slow down to breathe, meditate, and journal thoughtfully on what comes up for you.

Pt 1.

1. On a blank sheet of paper (you may need a few), I want you to just 'free write'... 'brain dump'... anything arising for you on the topic of money.
2. Take some time to meditate on your relationship to money. Where are things at? Where can things get better? Communicate freely and honestly with the energy of money as though you were talking to your partner or best friend. Ask for what you want and need, and be willing to do your part.

Pt 2.

This second part of homework is going to be dedicated to meditating on and integrating some statements about money– letting them land into your consciousness and feeling into the truth of them.

-I am ALWAYS available to be PAID. I choose now to open infinite channels of abundance. I will take action to physically open new channels and I will energetically open wider to the channels already open. There are countless channels for money to flow through. Money flows into my bank account. I am available to be paid always, I am available to receive always. No matter what... no matter my mood, my energy or how much "work" I've done– i'm available to receive. I give with ease and I receive with ease. My service is desire based. My receiving is desire based. I give because I want to... not because I need to. I receive because I want to... not because I need to.

-Money is its own frequency. A free energy that moves effortlessly. Money is not conditional to 'work'. I don't have to 'earn' it. I simply have earned it because I exist. Money is energy responding to my alignment. My energy is my currency, my energy is my alignment. I am aligned. I am wealthy. I am free. Money is free, and money loves to find me. Money loves to support me and overflow me. Money is pure and I am open to receiving. Money loves to flow, and I naturally receive the flow. Inhale I receive. Exhale I give.

-Hold a vision of your desires. Knowing where you are heading gives money something to get excited about. Your vision gives money something to respond to, to move toward and to fulfill. Your higher vision gives money something more aligned and higher to respond to. Money wants to see your vision and support you in fulfilling that vision. See your vision now.

-Releasing money is good for me and part of my abundant life. Investing in myself feels good. I find pleasure in spending money on the things and experiences that I adore. Money always replenishes itself. It is safe to release money. Money loves to move and always replaces itself. When I release money on investments that support me and my path I am rewarded. I always receive when I give. I give and receive in harmony. My investments return back to me 10 fold (or more).

-I focus on positioning myself well with money. Improving my relationship with money. Educating myself on money. Cleaning up obstructions with money. Opening a clear and soft landing strip for money to land.

-Ensure you are taking 'strategic spaciousness' - allowing space. Opening up to receive through rest and ease. Ensure you are actually living, resting, having fun, playing, and living life. Taking all the space and time you need. No forcing. Simply allowing. You are powerful. There is no neediness or attachment– simply certainty and openness. How can you open to receive more in your day to day through strategic spaciousness?

Part 3.

Affirmations:

-Affirm: "I focus on my personal 'successful execution'. I focus on being incredible at what I am here to give. I focus on my service. I focus on perfecting my craft. I focus on devotion to my service, devotion to my path. I deliver. I give. I am worthy no matter what AND I focus on becoming a better version of myself daily. I choose to successfully execute in my life, life's work career and livelihood. I want to enhance my reality and I will do my part."

-Affirm: "I have a KNOWING. I know it's all adding up for me. Even when it doesn't look like it's happening–it's happening. The nothingness, the space, the "void" is a nutrient dense part of my receiving season. I trust this season. I allow it. I surrender. Even when it does look like it's happening–I know it's happening. I trust no matter what. It's all adding up, it's ALL happening for me.

-Affirm: "I am the source. I am the leading energy. I lead money. Money responds to me and my desires."

-Affirm: "I trust myself, I trust money, I trust the universe. I trust the timing of everything. I release control. It is safe to be uncomfortable. It is safe to be in the unknown. I release control. I lean into the edges. I trust my knowing. I trust my intuition. I make bold moves courageously. I trust the pull forward. I know I am supported. I know I am led. It is all adding up. I have done my part. I will continue to do my part. I am open to receive. Thank You, More Please".

I am so proud of you and truly so EXCITED for you,
as you embark on your journey of experiencing a
NEW paradigm of wealth.

Enjoy all the abundance.
Remember your innate power and enjoy the ride.

CHAPTER 7

THE EDGE OF EVOLUTION

Something big is coming – Can you feel it?

You're at the edge…About to jump. You're at your climax. About to feel it all. You're so close. Things get wobbly–but you hold onto the feeling. You trust. You surrender. You receive. Most people give up just as it's about to get really fucking good. Most people won't lean in–*but you aren't most people.* You are the one who leans in, the one who says *yes* to life, and everything it has to offer you. You are the one who does not accept the average. You are rare. This life is rare. You may not know where you're going, but you know you're being led. You may not know exactly where you're headed, but you know it's far. **This is the journey–*The Edge of Evolution.***

"Every act of creation is first an act of destruction."
– Pablo Picasso

There is an edge at every evolution that requires you to lean all the way in. All creation is preceded by destruction. The edges of expansion require movement, momentum, and inevitable edges that need your bravery. Moving with the current no matter how rogue, edgy or challenging these waves may be. *The edges become waves when we lean in–when we surrender.* When we begin to allow the inevitable movement, and surrender to it–*versus fighting against it.* In those moments we fall effortlessly in…into our next evolution. *The edge of evolution–an act of overcoming. An act of rising above. An act of surrendering.* **You BURN IT DOWN–the old identity that kept you small, the old limitations that kept you trapped.** There is DESTRUCTION before there is

CREATION. You're not forcing or pushing…yet you are expanding out of the old. Expanding beyond outdated identities, experiences, interactions, and ways of existing. You begin to take up more space–you begin to move differently. **This breakthrough is edgy–but the edge leads to your inevitable evolution.** If it were easy… everyone would be doing it. *If it were the norm to live a life by design–a reality of evolution over a lifetime–everyone would live it.* But it's *not* the norm. *It's not normal to lean into edges and evolve effortlessly, but as you already know… You are far from normal.* You are RARE. Most people aren't willing to lean in and hold themselves through the wobble. Most people can't hold varying degrees of uncertainty. **There are wobbles when you accelerate quickly–*but you CAN handle it.*** You are WILLING to hold it. Willing to hold *more*–from a regulated space of alignment. You are the type of person WILLING to lean in–WILLING to move fast. *Edges, acceleration… evolution. Pure pleasure, wealth, ease, love, connection, and freedom in every way your soul remembers.* The evolution over a lifetime is *why* your soul chose Earth–the edges are simply part of the process. **When you are willing to lean in and release the comforts of mediocrity and go *all the way* in on yourself–you are rewarded.** *Your desires and your life by design manifests.* **There is an edge with every evolution. Will you be the one who leans in?**

Take a moment now and breathe into this spacious thought…
"What would my body do… if it had no mind leading it.
No ego leading it. No plan leading it"

When we honor the desires of the body, we simultaneously honor the desires of the soul. The body is the portal to the spirit's greatest liberation. Devote yourself to honoring the desires of your body and witness how fast things move *for* you. What does your body desire more of? Do that–honor that. When we honor the desires of the body, we make intuitive body based decisions that allow us to live out our soul path. The body is guiding us with ease and in the path of least resistance. The body craves movement, pleasure, and euphoria. **The body craves evolution.** The body knows when it is safe to move. The body holds wisdom. *The body knows when it is safe to lean into the edges–and unfold into its natural evolution.* The mind however will ask you to stay, play small... the mind will choose fear. The mind will attempt to control outcomes through rigid limitations, whereas the body craves expansion. Our job is to retrain the mind, reprogram fear programs, and practice dropping into the intuition of the body. Imagine this–you're at the edge of a pier, it's gorgeous out, you're ready to jump into the warm water–your body wants to go forward–your body pulls you forward–it would only ever be your mind that would stop you. Your body wants the experience–*wants the evolution.* We must create congruence between our mind and body to ensure we feel safe to move. *We must make a practice of dropping into the body, and into the inherent safety of the body– the inherent wisdom of the body.* From this grounded regulated space, we can train the mind to listen to the desires of the body, which are the desires of the soul. **The body whispers, the body longs, the body informs.** *Are you listening?*

> *"There's more wisdom in your pinky toe than in*
> *what any guru could ever tell you"*
> *–Haley Bowler-Cooke*

Your cells hold the knowledge, and your body keeps the score. The work within these chapters is designed to simply lead you HOME to yourself. Leading you home to your essence, your body, your spirit, and your soul. **We are operating from an intelligence *far* beyond logic.** An intelligence that is not controlled by fear or limited by conditioning. *We are operating as the divine.* The soul leads the highest self and the highest self leads the ego. *We are in constant circular communication, with: the soul, the body, and the mind.* The soul leads the way. The soul connects first to the body. The mind tries to run the show...this being said–the mind has a TONNE of power. This is why we must train the mind to open up to new portals. **We must create congruence between**

what our soul wants and what our mind feels safe experiencing. We must communicate safety to the mind so it can rewire fear programming and open up to infinite potential. *When the mind perceives safety, the mind can signal that safety through the nervous system to the body.* Your connection to your own spirit and your connection to your infinite soul *allows* you to steer your precious life here on Earth. We aren't operating from conditioning. We aren't operating from old outdated programs. **We are making moves from an insourced knowing.** We are making moves from the souls' leadership. It is a constant practice of quieting the mind and listening to the body. A constant practice of being informed by a loving consciousness (not a fear based one). *When we do this regularly we begin to change our mind.*

Through proper intentional integration—our unconscious mind and subconscious programs become aligned with the rhythms of the body AND the leadership of the soul. **The edges begin to seem less scary, we lean in further, and then we experience our next evolutions more regularly.** The divine speaks from within us. We are living a life led by the divine—a life of magic: a life of infinite, limitless love, wealth, impact, and alchemy. It may not make logical sense to the masses…because you are operating from an intelligence *far* beyond logic. **When you are attuned to your soul, and you make moves on Earth with the stewardship of a higher love, the decisions you make result in mind-blowing results.** You are operating from an essence that can only be *felt* and *known*. Something so profound—an Intuition that is felt far and wide in your body and in your cosmic consciousness. This highest self leadership is not something the logical mind can comprehend. **We are operating from a higher knowing…an essence that is vast, infinite, and BOUNDLESS.** We are operating from a consciousness larger than your physical being—*yet you feel these 'knowings' deep inside of you.* **The desires, the invisible strings leading you forward are something that can only be KNOWN—not taught.**

*Divine information is only known by the infinite
soul that led you here.
Breathe in. Breathe out. Can you trust it?*

When it comes to leaning into the edges of our evolution, we must cultivate Unfuckwithable self leadership and self belief. No human in their right mind would lean into the uncomfortable edges if they didn't KNOW in their core that they would later experience the euphoric evolution–the results. Again, your capacity to know something deep within you and visualize beyond what your mind's eye can see is YOUR superpower. **Your internal compass is yours and yours only.** You are rare–and your knowing of what is possible for you is on a much higher level. *Most people won't see your dreams as guaranteed...because most people can't even imagine their own dreams for themselves.* Those around you will be tempted to talk you out of your wildest dreams. People will encourage you to stay in hiding–to stay small. Most people won't encourage you to lean into the edges. **Most people won't expand beyond their *own* comfort zones–so they can't be expected to celebrate you as you move beyond yours.** Most people will not lean into their own edges, so don't expect them to cheer you on for leaning into yours. This is where YOUR Unfuckwithable self belief and self leadership comes in. You have to validate yourself. You have to celebrate yourself. You have to comfort yourself. You have to HOLD yourself. Hold yourself in the highs, the lows, and everything in between. Hold yourself in your vulnerability–hold yourself in your own power. **No one can meet you where they haven't yet met themselves.** So YOU must meet yourself there. Lead yourself, and consciously be *led* by the divine. Allowing yourself to be led by the invisible string that pulls you ahead–led by the soul leadership that KNOWS something bigger, better, and more aligned is calling you forward. When it comes to a *life by design* and leaning into the edges of evolution that get you there...

You must protect and cherish your path. Those around you (unless they too walk their highest timeline) likely will not get it or

---

see it as possible. You can only love as deeply as you love yourself. You can only see as deeply as you see yourself. **Therefore, you can only be seen, loved, and held at the levels in which the one seeing you sees themselves.** Release the need for them to *"get it"* and make understanding YOUR truth your only job. **It can feel like a lonely path when you walk your highest timeline.** It really is a rare thing to wake up to the simulation, and wake up to the distortions, and CHOOSE a better way. It is rare to CHOOSE alchemy, freedom, and soul alignment. It can feel lonely, but I promise you–you're not alone. **There is an entire cosmic, energetic, angelic, and physical universe of divinity supporting you–celebrating you and leading you forward.** I am cheering you on. But most importantly YOU must cheer yourself on. **There's nothing more fulfilling and satisfying as being met with external validation and understanding–but that is always just the cherry on top.** You must first meet yourself. Fill yourself up. LOVE ON YOURSELF. Forgive yourself. Be completely fascinated in the wonder and the beauty of YOU. Validate yourself every step of the way. **Hold yourself as you lean into the edges, and be proud of yourself as you bask in the rewards of your evolution.** This is the work you have to do. This work makes it easier to lean into those inevitable edges. This work makes the discomfort bearable. This work makes it all worth it. This work makes it feel truly like a no brainer–a simple step of the process. **You happily lean into the challenges because you know deep in your core that there is a guaranteed evolution awaiting you.**

As you rise on your journey, as you continue to heal at deeper levels, as you expand into new paradigms of higher alignment and desired realities–you *will* meet resistance. **The resistance is only ever an invitation to go deeper.** Deeper into your alignment of your highest self. An invitation to deepen your self observation. An invitation to deepen your certainty in the paradigm you *choose*. An invitation into deeper conviction in your path– *in your truth*. **Resistance is a *gift* when we decide that it is.** Resistance strengthens us, builds our resilience, and aligns us to higher levels of receiving. When we decide that resistance is just an opportunity to align deeper with our desires and with our dream life–**we are rewarded.**

Resistance when manifesting is often 1 of 3 things ...

1. **The Universe may be redirecting you.** Giving you whispers of something better. Something more aligned. It gets uncomfortable because you are MEANT to move.
2. **Your "ego" is clinging to a safer / older / outdated, and therefore misaligned paradigm.**
3. **An invitation to go even deeper in your self awareness, self leadership and recalibration to the certainty of the paradigm you choose.** Deeper conviction in the paradigm in which you LIVE the life of your dreams. You are being asked to stand more firmly in your power, your decision, your truth.

It is important to note that manifestation is natural and it is meant to be easy. If you're truly in alignment it should feel flowy and easeful. The edges and resistance should *not* derail you. When aligned, you will move through them with power and conviction. If you ARE facing a lot of resistance (resistance that is not easy to move through), then you are likely being asked to step back. You are likely being invited into a new path. *Do less, lean back, surrender more, and trust the unfolding.* If resistance keeps showing up on your path and you are following *your* plan, then the universe may be showing you a better, easier way. The resistance may be evidence that there is a faster, smoother path... one that can only be reached with true surrender. **Your plan is great babe... but the universe's plan is *always* better.** Be clear and aligned in your action toward your desires, lean into the challenging edges as they arise, trust the path, surrender to resistance and keep going.

Your expansion and growth evolves with you, and with every new growth spurt, there can be discomfort. As you rise into more alignment, wealth, love, and success, you will continue to be "tested". You will continue to be expanded. These "tests" are simply an invitation to dive deeper into your self awareness and personal truth. An invitation, to deepen your conviction in your decisions, to elevate your self worth, your path, and your truth. **This "resistance" is an opportunity to choose again or to choose more powerfully.** An invitation to calibrate higher and more powerfully to the paradigm chosen. These invitations WILL present themself to you as you *rise*. ***Again, the resistance is a blessing–an invitation to surrender deeper.*** An opportunity to rise higher and higher. Trust it. When you notice the edges, the resistance, the "tests", lean in deeper. Walk bravely toward what you *know* is meant for you.

Your ego will get hella loud when your desires are the closest. Do you crawl back into safe keeping? Or do you observe it, see it for what it is, and lean the fuck in to your next evolution? **The reason *life by design* is the path less traveled is because everyone wants the freedom, happiness, wealth, impact, and ease...but very few people are willing to lean into the inevitable painful and scary edges.** Few people are willing to lean into the edges that lead to the inevitable evolution. Again...if it were easy, then everyone would be doing it. Everyone would be billionaires, alongside their soul mates, living wildly free and stunning lives. *It's not to say it's not available to all humans–it is.* **It is infinitely available.** But not everyone is willing to claim it. Your thrival does not take away from the next person's *thrival.* **It's not a matter of availability...It's a matter of who is willing to lean in.** It's a matter of who is willing to do the work, to stay aligned, and to re-align when they wobble off. I say to my clients all the time– "it's fine if you get pulled off your lane once in a while... what's important is how fast you get back on". So few people are willing to shift, to make moves, to change it up, and to evolve. So few of us (the human race that is) are willing to let go, to release control, to release old outdated patterns, and to start over. **So few are willing to properly and successfully execute, to regulate the new ways of existing, and to *actually* trust the process.**

But you're not most people.

***Personally... My ego is the loudest when my desires are the
closest.*** The contrast is real. When my desires are closest–I'm
beyond aligned, AND YET I feel the oscillation of conflicting
thoughts. My certainty, openness, and flow with life is on point,
AND YET I get loud moments of doubt. **My foundations shake,
and I am forced into a truer and deeper surrender.** I am at the
point now on my journey where resistance and edges are neutral
to me, if anything they're more exciting than dreadful. **I get a little
excited when I feel my ego freakouts bubbling to the surface–
I know change is coming.** This knowing allows me to ride the
waves of the *ego freak out* and let my higher self calmly steer the
ship. **I am constantly reminding myself and my clients that
there is a fine line between anxiety and excitement.** Often, as
you are about to leap into a new paradigm the confines of the old
and outdated paradigm start to encroach. Fear creeps in. You are
being shown contrast wherever you look. "Tests" will show up for
you. The inevitable edges–before your evolution.

**The ego gets loud right before a manifestation manifests
because it is the final cry for mediocrity.** The final attempt to
stay stagnant, small, and to stay in environments that you've far
outgrown. The ego gets loud to fog your connection point to
source. The ego gets loud to cloud your connection to your own
soul and spirit. **This is a perfectly designed function of the ego.**
This is your fear response kicking in–your survival mechanisms at
work. The NEW PARADIGM where you are heading is unknown,
it's scary and the ego has no conception of how to survive the
newness. **We repeat the cycles not because they were serving
us–but because they are familiar.** The brain loves familiarity. It
takes much more conscious intention, alignment, and devotion to
step into a new paradigm than it does to stay in an old, outdated
one. **The ego is here to survive–not thrive.** It is the soul that
craves thrival, and luckily–the soul is the one in the driver's seat.
**The soul must ensure the passenger (ego) feels safe,
regulated and heard as they move...*but the soul drives.***

Stepping into new power is unfamiliar. Rising up and into new levels is scary. The ego will do anything it can to stay where it is. *The mind will attempt to prove itself right so that it can stay where it is–because... survival.* The ego will begin to visualize realities that prove the old paradigm is "right". Your brain is constantly working to prove itself right, constantly looking for evidence that validates its CURRENT belief system. Continuously attempting to prove, amplify, and strengthen evidence that SUPPORTS pre-programmed thoughts, beliefs, and behaviors. **Again–this is a normal function of the brain that we GET to use to our benefit.** This feature of the brain can be INCREDIBLE if we are running high vibe, conscious, confident, and highest self actualization programs. This can also be DEBILITATING if we're running old, low self worth, mis-aligned, lack, and fear based programming. If we are attempting to *quantum leap* into a new paradigm, then this feature of familiarity can be challenging to move beyond. Challenging because you don't *yet* have the material external validation that you *will* be safe and supported. **This is where belief work, visualization, and nervous system regulation is number one.** This is why it is imperative to consciously AND subconsciously reprogram your brain. To know that there are subconscious programs running that are trying to keep you stuck and instead *choose* to expand beyond them. **This is where you have the power to create congruence between what the soul desires, and what the mind perceives as safe and as possible.**

When you are close to your new paradigm, the old programs try their hardest to be heard. These are the moments when your external world starts to *show you* contrast or contradicting 'evidence' of what your soul has been guiding you toward. For example... you know in your heart of hearts, in the deepest depths of your soul that you are *meant* to leave your 9-5 job and start your own soul aligned business. You are just building up the courage to do it. You've set the plan into motion, you've taken the aligned action, you are energetically attuned–you feel powerful as fuck. Then all of a sudden, you start to have people approach you telling you about the "instability of the economy", you see articles everywhere talking about how "only 2% of new business survive their first year", your partner comes home that day and empties all their fear and doubts onto you etc etc. **Your external reality is showing up in contrast.** Your ego wants to cling to this 'evidence' as 'signs' that you should stay stagnant, stay where you are, and maybe justtttt maybe open your business up next year. **Your SOUL if you listen closely enough however... will lead you, show you, validate you to TRUST your intuition and know you WILL be supported.**

Remember, the subconscious mind keeps you safe and stuck and repeating patterns if those are the programs you are used to running. **The brain loves familiarity, and will attempt to create external projections based on the internal fear programming.** In order to expand into new paradigms, you must work with the subconscious mind and begin to reprogram it. The ego is only concerned with the perceived success of "survival". If you have survived your old paradigms and programming–your ego is happy and your subconscious mind will continue to run programs that yield the same results. You survived your old life...despite the mundane, pain, trauma, cyclical toxicity, limiting beliefs etc. etc. **You survived, so your ego is content.** Your ego's perception is, "ok this is safe, let's stay here, let's repeat these patterns". Your ego is terrified of the new paradigms, new realities, new cycles– scared of the unknown (even if the unknown is the best thing that could ever happen to you). Stepping into new power is unfamiliar and as we know– the ego LOVES familiarity. Your ego will keep you powerless before becoming fully liberated and empowered because it is perceived as SAFE. **So–to overcome this–to move beyond this limitation we must get our egoic mind on board with us.** Familiarity is a sure fire way to get your ego on board with your new paradigm and next level reality. **Therefore, the unknown must become familiar to your ego, in order for the ego to allow itself to happily exist there.** The ego must begin to feel comfortable in the new paradigm and then from there expand into the next and new territory. We do this over and over again as we walk our highest path. *This is what we call "evolution over a*

---

lifetime". A lifetime of leaning into edges, surrendering to resistance, allowing your knowing of what's next, and what is meant for you to lead the way.

The ego is a beautiful thing…but not when it runs the show. Observe it. See it for what it is, so you can then make the moves as your highest self time after time. *Eventually you will get to the point where your ego freaks out and you actually find yourself getting a little excited.* **You will know that this means something big and beautiful is coming.** So lean the fuck in babe, trust yourself, and trust the process. We aren't here to "kill" the ego… the ego is not going anywhere. **We are not escaping it, so let's learn to coexist lovingly with it.** Let's learn to familiarize ourselves with our next desired reality and new paradigms so we can feel comfortable on this ascension journey. This is the process of integration—integrating your highest timeline in a regulated manner to allow upgrades to happen with ease. **Ease and regulation is necessary, so that your ego and human body can feel supported.** When you are in conscious awareness of this natural process and function of your ego, then you can easily tap into your truth, witness the lies your wounded ego wants you to believe to be able to powerfully move forward in your purest alignment. This is the process of evolution over a lifetime. The process of leaning into edges and basking in the results—over and over and over again. New levels and fuck tonnes of celebration— it's like clockwork. **As always…the vibe is we are wildly capable of having everything we want AND we are whole and complete as we are right now.** There's no rush—no need for pressure. There are no illusions of deficiency here. We are whole and complete. It's all adding up. The magic is in this moment here. Lean back and surrender babe…it's on its way.

Now, let's talk about the edges of uncertainty. I personally am blessed to be at a stage in my life where uncertainty feels like sexy, yummy foreplay. The unknown now feels like I'm blindfolded, in full surrender, and excited for what's next. However, it wasn't always like that. Uncertainty used to feel extremely unsafe and unsettling in my nervous system. I really loved control and wanted to know what was next–every step of the way. Which to be fair, is a normal response for most human beings (especially if you have experienced trauma and dysregulation in your life). The egoic mind CRAVES control, and always wants to know what's next. High achieving, ambitious individuals also often want to know what's next. We love planning ahead, casting our next level projections, and micromanaging every step of the way. There was a time when I LOVED control and was TERRIFIED of the unknown. Regardless of how 'normal' it is to fear the unknown... **the normalcy of it does NOT make it optimal.** It's not optimal to live in fear of the unknown. *If you fear the unknown–you essentially fear life.* Life on Earth in itself is an inevitable experience of existing within the unknown. **If you fear the unknown then you will spend a lot of your life in resistance.**

Surrender and allowing is actually our NATURE, whereas control is a learned and conditioned illusion. It is natural (not nurture/conditioning, but our true nature) to surrender. **To surrender, is to trust that we are supported and to trust that the path will align ahead for our greatest unfolding.** We aren't meant to know what's next. **We as human beings are actually designed to be co creators...Therefore surrendering to life and the divine plan.** Yet here we all are–riddled with conditioning, borrowed programming, and fuck tonnes of fear. So, how can we begin to create safety in the unknown and start to experience the curiosities of it over the anxieties? **First thing is to be totally loving and accepting of the fearful feelings that are arising.** The fact is–you feel uncertain, fearful, and you're not fully in trust– *yet.* That's okay babe–again...that's normal. But we're not here to be normal... we are here to thrive. **So, as the fear arises, embody it fully–feel it in your bones. Shake it out, scream it out, dance it out... let the fear LIVE.** As I always say, "the high level individual EMBODIES and OBSERVES their stunning life." We are not going to deny the feelings as they come up–*even the most uncomfortable ones deserve embodiment.*

We cannot free ourselves when we bypass what is presently true for us. The fear that arises in the experience of the unknown (or even in the potential fear of the upcoming unknown) is a very real experience. *Pretending you aren't scared is a disservice to your very existence.* As I love to say, "fake trust is like a fake orgasm…nobody wins", so don't fake it. You're scared, you're not fully in trust, and that makes sense. Feel it. It's totally normal and I have absolutely been there many times prior to or directly after taking "leaps of faith", being in the "void" or simply just existing as an entrepreneur living an unconventional life. **Before you can surrender to the unknown you must first experience the *very real* emotions of scarcity and horror as you release the reigns of control.** So feel it all so you can be free of the entanglement. Process the emotions by feeling them fully, then allow them to be released from your system.

Once you've felt, processed, and released the misaligned energies and emotions—you can move forward. Once you've let the emotions of lack, distrust, anxiousness, scarcity and fear LIVE by naming the fears, allowing the fear to have a voice and be heard…THEN you can move forward. **From this integrated space you can begin to ground yourself.** You can begin to regulate, and then OPTIMIZE. You begin to heal your root chakra (the energy center that is terrified right now based on future circumstances that are not actually true). Your root chakra is concerned with your safety and security, and this is the part of the body that thrives in groundedness. So take some deep breaths, lie down in a child's pose, and remind yourself how strong, safe and secure you are. Remind yourself of your inherent safety. Remind yourself that it always works out for you. Remind yourself that you are always supported. **Affirm: "I am safe, I am safe, I am safe".** Then, wholeheartedly breathe into that—feel that as true in your system. Once you have "calmed down" your root chakra, and you have come back into your inherent safety and groundedness…THEN you can POWERFULLY move forward. We don't skip steps here—we operate from alignment, which means deep honoring of ourselves through each step on the journey. **There is no optimization without regulation first.**

When we are processing the fearful edges of our inevitable evolution, we MUST come back to our inherent safety. This means coming home to ourselves and back to the truth. Coming back to the true reality that is love, wellbeing, vitality, and insourced empowerment. We come back to the fullness, richness, and support of this *NOW* moment. **Right here, right now–you are secure and you are supported.** In this moment, all your needs are met. Any distortion of lack, fear, anxiety or worry is an ILLUSION. Any deviation from this *NOW moment,* this *PERFECT* moment, is you clinging to an illusion. **Leaving the present moment for worry, for worst case scenario thinking, for scarcity or for anxiety is a lie.** It's a deviation from your truth, your path, and your very existence as a divine being in human form. **Abandonment of the present moment is an abandonment of yourself.** I want to program your brain here to understand: A) the power of dropping into the safety and pleasure of the present moment, and B) the deviation and distortion that occurs when you attempt to escape it. Your brain now is beginning to understand how UNNECESSARY it is to worry. How ILLOGICAL it is to fear the unknown. **Your brain is now realizing that there is inherent safety, security, and SUCCESS in your surrender to the unknown.** Your brain understands that so long as you are held within the container of your human body, you are held, supported, and inherently SAFE. *It is safe to expand, safe to grow, safe to evolve, and safe to bloom into more.*

When you understand and embody your inherent safety you stay in your lane. You stay on your path, and in your truth, and you trust–wholeheartedly trust. You then flow with the *"nothingness"*. You flow with the *momentum*. You flow when the desires drop in, and you are powerful and certain in the "void". **The unknown starts to feel like a curious moment of expansion and growth.** You begin to get excited about what is coming…and even when it hasn't happened yet... you know it's on its way. *You hold the knowing that "even though it hasn't happened yet, doesn't mean it's not happening".* You find great pleasure in the inbetween. **You feel safe and regulated in the space between wanting and having.** You find openness, creativity, and expression in the moments leading up to it. You find joy in the "clim(b)ax" –as I like to call it. The climb up...the journey to the top. The process of aligning and the celebration of having. **You decide to enjoy the climb to your inevitable climax.** The great orgasmic sensation of cashing in your desires and cashing in your next level is as delicious as the journey that it takes to get there. **There is no separation, because you understand the great unfolding as divinely orchestrated.** You truly trust. You truly surrender. *This my love, is mastering the edges of your evolution.*

We always hear these statements: "abundance yields abundance", "jump and the net appears", "just trust", and "it's all happening for you". **These concepts are truer than true.** However, our energetic and physical systems cannot and WILL NOT believe them to be true–if we are not in a state of inherent safety. If your nervous system is not regulated, your mind is spinning and your physiology is in a fear/survival response–then you do not feel inherently safe. No amount of true statements or affirmations will integrate until they feel true for us–until we are open, regulated and SAFE enough to integrate them. This is why the actual embodiment of our feelings as they arise, is crucial for the natural processing and detoxification process. It's really difficult to believe these positive, true statements, when your brain is running a "lack" program. It is impossible to feel the truth in the new expanded reality when your ego is attached to old and outdated programs. That's why when the thoughts/feelings do arise (as they will–you're human) you must fully feel, embody, and integrate them to properly process. You must process in order for your "scared parts" of yourself to know they are being heard. Again, we are not "killing" the ego–we are working with it in union. We are working alongside the ego and all of the wounded, and scared parts that exist within us. Reassurance, validation, consistent reminders, and physical support (through breath and body work) will encourage the ego to feel and know it is supported as you leap forward into your highest timeline.

Once you have created an internal experience of safety in your physical, emotional, and energetic systems, you can begin to use mantras and positive affirmations to reprogram the brain. Once you are properly regulated, you can begin to open new portals within your consciousness. Once you are grounded you can open up to receiving. Once you are optimized you can affirm and integrate the TRUE statements in alignment with your desires and dreams.

Mantras are designed to support you through times of uncertainty or throughout the space in between receiving/cashing in your desires. They are also powerful in re-affirming and amplifying what you already know to be true. You must be in a state of homeostasis for your body to properly program the true statements.
So...*Breathe in...Breathe out.* Affirm the following, and repeat as needed.

Affirm: *Just because it hasn't happened yet, doesn't mean it's not happening.*

Affirm: *It always works out for me, better than I even expected.*

Affirm: *Love, money, resources, and support is always there for me, I welcome more and more of it.*

Important note–Mantras don't work unless your body is regulated, open, and receptive. They also don't work if you don't believe them. So– regulate yourself through the practices listed before and pick mantras/affirmations that you believe in–mantras that feel *true* for you.

As you begin to feel empowered, curious, and excited through the edges of your evolution...Here are some important notes to further integrate into your consciousness.

1. ***Actually FEEL what arises within you.*** Feel into whatever emotions come up, embody, process, and integrate them to create a regulated system where you have actually processed and released what is not serving you.

2. **Don't pretend you aren't terrified or scared shitless at times.** You're a human making MASSIVE leaps of faith each day being the rare individual that lives an Unfuckwithable and Iconic life by design. It's not for the faint of heart. You're brave AND you're allowed to be simultaneously scared at times. You're allowed to feel doubt at times AND still make *moves* toward your dreams. You are allowed to feel uncertainty AND still drop into your deepest knowing of certainty from your highest self. You can experience the very real human emotions of scarcity, anxiety, fear, and lack AND still manifest all the desires of your heart.

3. **"Nothing changes if nothing changes"** –This is your tough love reminder that YOU are responsible for your happiness. You must feel into your highest sense of being and KNOW when enough is enough. Your comfort zone is NOT the space in which you evolve and grow from. You must take a survey of your life and KNOW when it's time to make a move. You must trust the knowing and lean into the edges of your next evolution.

As I have said many times before, it takes a rare human to walk their highest timeline. It takes a rare human to live a life by their own design. It takes a rare human to move toward their desires, to stay in their lane, AND stay open and receptive to divine intervention as they go. It takes a rare human to speak truth, when their truth challenges the status quo. New paradigm leaders are the trendsetters–they don't comply or subscribe to current trends. They ARE the trend–they are ART embodied. They don't submit to the standard ways of thinking, believing, or living. **They trust in something bigger.** They go after what they desire courageously and they believe in something MORE. **As you bravely walk this new paradigm and New Earth timeline, you challenge the norms around you.** You bravely lean into edges when the masses shy away. **You disrupt the illusion with your TRUTH.** These high level frequencies in which you begin to embody are potent and powerful. The level of certainty and self leadership required is at an all time high. Push back can be stronger than ever as you break into new paradigms. Once you are regulated in your next and new paradigm, you can only interact with "like frequencies" –meaning the contrasting energies, people, and experiences don't really show up in your new reality. The new paradigm, once regulated, is full of alignment, and as we know, "alignment yields alignment". When the edges do arise, we can confidently know we are at an edge of our next evolution. This means we are at a new beginning and a new standard is being set. **We have the choice to courageously lean in…or stay put.** I KNOW that you are here to continue to lean in–I know this because you are reading this book.

**Stay in your lane and remind yourself
of YOUR ultimate truth.**
*Breathe in. Breathe out. Find your center,
and ground in with this powerful question.*
Who am I? And how do I want to live?

This life is unrepeatable–it's all happening now. Who do you want to be as you walk this Earth? Who will you be? How can you be more ALIVE? –When the mass psychosis tempts you into submission. When the outside noise is loud, when the sinister forces of mind control are at its all time high. When fear attempts to rule your world, when doubt overwhelms your system, and when your ego internalizes the external projections…Who will you be? You are invited to a *deeper* awareness of self in these moments–a deeper awareness of self, right here, right now. You are invited to step into a new edge to explore and a new clim(b)ax to bravely journey forward. **You are being invited into a deeper awareness of your consciousness, and you are invited to powerfully embody your TRUTH.** As we evolve over a lifetime there is no escaping our ego, and there is no escaping the readily available option–that is fear. **You are always presented with a choice….Stay? Or EVOLVE?** In order to evolve gracefully and in a regulated manner you must consciously work *with* your ego. *As you know, a thriving soul and a healthy ego are required now, more than ever.* Something I have mastered and I invite you on the journey to master as well– is cultivating an ongoing healthy relationship with my soul, my highest self, and my ego. Having a healthy ego and a THRIVING soul is something I commit to master through ongoing devotion to: communication, safe held space, conscious programming, support, and intentional regulation. I consciously commune with my soul and spirit. I commune with my ego, and most importantly, I consciously commune with my *highest self* (who I consider the boss of my ego and the assistant to my soul). I have a healthy ego who is aware and in charge of both my strengths and my fears within the material world. I have a healthy soul who is *heard and amplified* through a life filled with freedom and led by desire. **I honor *all* parts of myself because there is no separation–we are in union, together.**

Breathe this in, let's make it safe. Let's regulate this next step.
It's time to walk your walk.
It's time to devote yourself to your truth.
It's time to surrender to your path.
It's time to align and be rewarded, in bigger ways
than you could ever imagine.
Welcome to the New Earth

Remember my love, the high level individual moves quickly, strategically, and intentionally. Your intuition guides your action. You are only available for the infinite path–always in alignment. **You CAN hold it all.** You know and live in alignment with the *dimension of openness.* There is no separation. You have surrendered to *"The Edge of Evolution".* **You have normalized and naturalized exponential evolution.** You have regulated the edges and are confident stepping out of your comfort zone. You are aware that with every positive transformation, you will inevitably face discomfort. You trust in the aligned action that calls you forward. You feel comfortable leaning back and receiving. **You KNOW how powerful you are.** You are unconditionally powerful–powerful no matter what. You're a high level individual and you act accordingly. You open fully– to the infinite and limitless realms of abundance. You are ready to move fast. **You desire evolution–now.** You are always rising. Your desires are inevitable. You walk forward in alignment–refined, certain, and open. *You don't know exactly what's next but you know it feels so right.* You don't have full clarity yet, but you HOLD the vision. You don't know what it is yet...but you want it. *You may not know where you're going–but you know you're being led.* One thing you do know for certain is–you want MORE. You know it's meant for you. You know you're ready. You trust yourself and you LEAN IN.

You are at your edge of evolution– can you feel the shift?

Freedom in every single way, is something that is available to all of us. We have to want it, ask for it, and then choose it–again and again. **The high level individual is in an ongoing state of choosing–love over fear, growth over stagnancy.** You CHOOSE to live your dream life. You recalibrate, moment to moment with constant inquiry: "What would my highest self do?", "What bold move would my higher self make", "Who do I want to be?", and " How do I want to live?". *Much like being Unfuckwithable, the "Edge of Evolution" is a lifestyle.* One of wellbeing, growth, luxury, wealth, ease, and pleasure. But also one of discomfort, expansion and breaking open at times. Constantly leaning in, accelerating, landing, and receiving–edge after edge after edge. *Know that the edges get smoother and they become flowier as you become more fluid in your expansion.* The lifestyle is a choice, and the journey is as delish as the destination. No matter how bumpy or tumultuous the ride is, you are embodied in the adventure of it all.

Our bodies are a lot like the Earth

and our souls like the cosmos

It's time to free them both

This life is available to everyone...but it's not for everyone.
How intensely do you want freedom? How much freedom do you want? How passionate are you about having ALL types of freedom? Ex: time freedom, financial freedom, location freedom, freedom in your wellness, freedom of the mind, and freedom of your body. True sovereignty. True liberation. Freedom...moment to moment. A life of bliss–one that you have carefully curated, created, and designed. How serious are you about it? How devoted are you? **I choose this life**. More and more of us are choosing this life. YOU are choosing this life. *THIS is the New Earth–an ongoing decision to live the life our soul remembered.* It's time to reclaim your spirit. It's time to liberate yourself here on Earth THROUGH your body portal. There are no limits. Your next paradigm is here now. *The time is right now–it's waiting for you.* It's time. Claim it. **The New Earth is here and it requires your ongoing devotion.** Hold this frequency, even when it seems like nothing is happening. Stay aligned, even when misalignment is happening. Stay grounded, even when things begin to wobble. Stay in your lane, even when everything in your reality (perceived or real) is trying to pull you off. Lean into the discomfort, when comfort tempts you into stagnancy. Fully embody the pain when your triggers show up, and properly process. Choose freedom, even when the masses choose compliance. **CHOOSE to BE Unfuckwithable in a world where most have forgotten their power, and LIFT the others up with your overflowing empowerment.** I would be lying to you if I said it was easy. None of this is easy...AND yet, I wouldn't trade this way of life for anything.

I, myself, live a life of ease, abundance, success, pleasure, and joy...because I am ongoingly willing to lean in. **There are many edges to this life, and I smooth those edges with proper integration, regulation and optimization.** Edges show up as difficult conversations, many magic darks, untethering, and loss. **Often, as I rise to new levels I am saying goodbye to the old outdated paradigms and all that came with it.** I am saying goodbye to the old ways of being, interacting, and relating. As

New Paradigm Leaders we are being called to deepen our integrity and our understanding of truth. The motto for me has been "nothing conditional and everything limitless". I don't want to engage in conditional love, transactional relationships, limited abundance or surface level anything! It's not that I can't handle these things or that I get triggered by them... I just simply desire MORE. These lower vibrational things don't nourish my soul, therefore I'm not available for them. **Again...it's not about boundaries–it's about standards.** When I raise my frequency– my standards elevate. **I naturally release what is no longer aligned with my new elevated standards, and that IS edgy.** When you courageously walk toward your next and highest timeline, you can effortlessly block out the noise of fear and the temptation of stagnancy. *It isn't easy–but it is worth it.* You move with MAIN CHARACTER ENERGY. Constantly self inquiring– "What would my Highest Self do?", then you do that. You TRUST the unfolding. *The edge is the place to be when you are living a life by design–one of evolution and rich experience.* **The edge is the place to be, because it means you're on the verge of your next MASSIVE expansion.**

It's inevitable that you will receive, achieve, and create everything you desire. You're high level after all. The speed in which you evolve has to do with your willingness to lean in. Your openness to the journey, your bravery to lean into the edges will dictate the speed of your evolution. As we've covered, edges can feel scary and so uncertain. Yet, they inevitably flow into the most expansion, ease, and success. *We're talking about the mind blowing success that you could never have even imagined.* YOU living your highest timeline is truly a GIFT to the collective consciousness. It's a gift to this planet and to the universe at large. You have been empowered with knowledge and integrations. You have been leading yourself, doing the inner work, taking the aligned action, and embodying your higher self. You've been leading yourself *and* allowing yourself to be led. **Now you are ready to have and hold it.** The edge of evolution is often the step that most people shy away from. They aren't interested in bravely moving forward. They don't want to fully say goodbye to their old paradigm. They aren't willing to make the edits, tiny micro shifts or refinements. They resist surrendering to the process. Now, as I've said before... you are NOT most people. You KNOW something is coming. You KNOW you are destined for *so much more.* **You are ready to take off.**

Breathe in. Breathe out. Are you available for the shift?
Are you ready for the evolution?

As we lean into the edges...We are making art out of uncertainty. Turning the void, the unknown, the in between... into pure GOLD. It all feels so close and you're so ready. You're ready to embody this work fully. *You're ready to feel it all to have it all.* I can now assure you–that you are ready. You have done the work. **This chapter (once integrated and embodied) is an ACCELERATOR to your evolution.** You are no longer a slave to a system. You ARE the creator...the designer of your life. The *Edge of Evolution* is a lifestyle, a devotion...a way of BEING. The edges, the evolution...it's non-stop. **You can't stop it...you can only accelerate it.** Now my love–you have the tools to accelerate. The acceleration keeps getting faster, more regulated and more easeful. This life is available to everyone, but only a select few at this time on Earth, will step up and claim this space. *We are paving a new way.* Creating a world where everyone experiences bliss, ultimate wellbeing, and infinite success. This ascension is a process and a lifestyle for the brave and courageous. *We are paving new pathways, so that one day ALL beings can coexist in a true reality of freedom and sovereignty.* One day we can all unite in unconditional love, support and alchemy.

For now we focus on our path and our path only.
Some will choose alchemy–others will choose mediocrity.
It's always a choice, and the choice is available to You.
It's time to choose to live an extraordinary life.

You're at the edge, about to jump. You're at your climax. About to feel it all. You're so close. Then things get wobbly. You hold onto the feeling. You trust, you surrender, and inevitably–you receive. **You are rewarded over and over again with pure pleasure and the experience of YOUR version of success.** Because you are WILLING to lean in, WILLING to move fast, and hold on through the wobble. You are WILLING to hold MORE from a regulated space of alignment. You call in, actualize, and receive– MORE…from a foundation of wholeness. You say YES to LIFE, and everything life has to offer you! **Your baseline frequency is an aligned and empowered state.** You trust and surrender to the infinite bounty. *There is an invisible string pulling you forward–you know you're being led.* **You aren't concerned with the details because you TRUST the unfolding.** This is the journey. *You are at your EDGE of Evolution.*

Something big is coming…Can you feel it?

You lean the fuck in. There is nothing easy about navigating THIS world and creating a NEW one. But you do it anyway. You powerfully and courageously move forward with enjoyment of the NOW. ***You understand the natural death and rebirth cycles of growth and expansion.*** The many edges become familiar–less and less scary. You rise to new levels. You release the old identities–the loss of the old ways of being, interacting, and relating. ***If you've read this far, I know you are capable–I know this is YOU.*** As new paradigm leaders, we are being called to deepen our integrity and our understanding of *truth.* We are required to actually walk the walk–required to actually INTEGRATE and EMBODY the teachings and universal wisdom. **Knowing isn't enough anymore. We must LIVE it to actualize the change we want to see in this world, and bask in the bounty of our rewards.**

I want to invite you in again on my mantra, my vibe and the WHY of my devotion to a life by design. I want to invite you in on the reason I am willing to lean into my own edges time and time again on this journey. ***The vibe is this "nothing conditional and everything limitless."*** I NEVER want to experience an illusion of a limit or a cap. I DON'T want an average life. I want to FEEL the richness of this experience. I want ALL OF IT–in its fullness. **I want to squeeze every last drip and drop of juice out of this experience in this unrepeatable precious body.** I want to land fully in, and receive the bounty available on this EVER evolving precious Earth plane. I want ALL OF IT indulgently, and in the highest form of reciprocity, respect and honoring. **I want to let my very existence be one so FULL OF LOVE and high vibrational energy, that I heal the timelines who came before me and the generations to come.**

I'm not here to be limited, and neither are you. Being Unfuckwithable is a standard of existence. It's not that we can't handle the mundane, it's not that mediocrity "triggers" us...*it's simply that we desire more.* We know it's available, therefore it only makes sense to call it in. **It only makes sense to have it.** We decide it, claim it, and walk in alignment with it. **Mediocrity doesn't nourish the soul, so we're not available for it.** As I've said many times over..."it's not about boundaries...it's about standards." Our standard of living are simply much higher than the average individual. Our standards are on new levels and we continuously evolve and raise those standards as we grow. **We cash in the aligned results over and over again, and we leave our positive and enlightened impact on the world as we go.** This journey is a dance between ourselves and the preciousness of this life. *So cheers my love, cheers to living life by our own design! Cheers to You! And cheers to the New Paradigm!*

Now let us dive into the homework portion of this chapter. As always, take your time, re-read, and integrate the wisdom within this chapter as needed. Breathe it all in slowly and stay present. Come back to the wisdom and practices of this chapter as you continue to evolve on your journey and come up to new edges.

This was a VERY high level and high quality chapter—lots of codes. Lots to practice and LOTS to begin integrating into your life.

Homework / Daily Devotionals:

Before each numbered reflection, take a few deep breaths, close your eyes, and drop into your body.

1. Drop into the reality of your life. This life here on Earth. Drop in to your experiences up until this moment. When have YOU been faced with an *edge* that had the potential to lead to your next evolution? Journal, meditate, and reflect on those times in the past and be *really* honest with yourself...Were you brave? Did you lean in? How did that bravery turn out for you? Was evolution there for you? Or did you succumb to fear? Did you fall into stagnancy? Honestly reflect and just begin to feel CLEAR and aware of what those past edges were for you so you can powerfully move through the next ones. Observe the experienced or potential benefits of leaning in. Reflect on the regrets of fear, and fawning instead. When you are clear on who you've been and how you moved through edges in the past—you empower yourself to upgrade in the future.

2. Start to reflect on your own truth. Reflect on your own patterns, systems, and strategies for walking with courage. How do you normally move bravely toward your desires? (even when fear arises) How do you choose bravery in the face of fear? How do you normally face adversity, challenges, and scary moments in your life? With this awareness, I invite you to breathe in and open up to new ways of being. More high level, refined, and powerful ways of walking with self leadership through the difficult moments in your life. Open up, inhale and receive the wisdom now from your guides. Receive the messages from your intuition, and your highest self. Exhale and trust

that you are being supported and guided always. Repeat and integrate this breathwork and meditation prompt as needed/desired.

Reflect and Integrate the following statements:

1. Those in the top 1% are there because they don't move like the masses–they are rare, and so am I.
2. I don't rush the process–I trust the unfolding.
3. Imagine how far ahead you would be (3-6 months from now) if you devoted NOW to your highest self.
4. How far ahead would you be if you stopped avoiding the things you *know* you need to do?
5. How far ahead would you be if you actually allowed your intuition to be heard and honored?
6. The universe moves for you when you decide–I know this, so I powerfully CHOOSE a higher path.
7. Your desires are ready and waiting for YOU to decide and move.
8. God doesn't need your readiness…God needs your devotion and commitment.
9. Nothing changes if nothing changes.
10. Your next level exists within the *edges* of your next evolution–lean IN.

I am so proud of You, I know this work isn't "easy" but I promise you… It is worth it.

Cheers to You Babe!
Cheers to your New Earth and your New Paradigm!

CHAPTER 8

DEVOTION

Dripping in desire

Open and ready

Fully receptive

Devotion

When we lead ourselves, deepen our alignment, lean into the edges of our inevitable evolution, and operate from devotion— everything we desire is guaranteed. *Better yet, everything life desires for us…is guaranteed.* I am so excited to bring you the intimate workings of this chapter. This chapter is all about "Devotion", which is what I consider to be our *"most innate attraction point".* **The sensuality of this life is why we're here.** Your soul *chose* earth to experience the infinite textures. *To feel the range of what it feels like to live life on Earth.* I want you to think (and feel) back to when you were just a little one, fresh to Earth, just starting to feel your way around. Just beginning to understand the processes of *all that is.* You were starting to understand how "life works". You had desires, wants, and needs. ***You almost immediately started to understand that being supported in actualizing those desires was not only helpful, it was necessary.*** The co-creative element of asking and receiving felt good, it felt nourishing…it was natural. You started to build evidence for the process: having a desire, asking for the support, and then having what you wanted. *A positive feedback loop, and a positive and natural cycle to be programmed into your consciousness.* Your parents and caregivers tend to be the supportive beings in your process. *So, naturally—you devote yourself to your parents, caregivers, and teachers.* In some way they become the source of you having what you want and need in life.

You start to aspire to rise, to be better, to shine, and to give to them. In return, you are validated, supported and you desire and naturally expect–to receive. You want to be seen, understood, and cared for. You also want to see and understand those around you. Those who are close to you, those who support you, those who you are attracted to, and those who you love. *As we grow and evolve, we continue to be "children of the divine".* **Our nature as co-creators (where we act, are supported and then receive) doesn't change just because we become adults.** Our nature is our nature–period. Many adults are conditioned OUT of their co creative nature, and tricked into the forcing, seeking and "doing it all alone" rhetoric of the illusion of separation that tends to dominate society. *The work now is about reminding you of your nature, and validating your true desire to give and receive reciprocally.* The work within this chapter is designed to positively reinforce your nature. *The nature that authentically wants to devote to what it wants, and to also devote to something that feels supportive to you.*

Devotion is a real primal instinct...true human nature, and a process of giving and receiving. Devotion is the commitment of yourself to your desires. *Devotion is an unwavering decision to serve and receive in alignment with your ongoing evolution.* Devotion involves your willingness to ask and receive in full trust. To be supported infinitely, while simultaneously doing your part. Devotion is a deeply receptive, self nourishing, self indulgent, and self loving act. Devotion is also a selfless commitment and generosity *of yourself* for your faith, your lover(s), your family, and your collective community. Devotion is this primal internal yearning for more. This *"no matter what"* energy of devotional service naturally and effortlessly actualizes MORE. *More devotion, means more receptivity, which means more desires drop in.* Devotion is this commitment to your path, your purpose, and your soul's desires. Devotion is a standard of alignment. Alignment with your karmic incarnation, your work and your journey here on Earth. **Devotion is this unequivocal energy of give and surrender.** Devotion is the steward of your life path. Devoted to living your truth and receiving the very real and true desires that both your soul and "human" hold in this incarnation. Devotion is an embodied state that keeps you aligned to the pulse of life, step by step on your journey. Devotion is an embodiment of absolutes–an energy of no matter what. *This embodiment of absolute certainty, and commitment is devotional–and HIGHLY magnetic.*

A few years ago I powerfully decided to be a devotee to this life. A devotee to source. A devotee to my Man/my lover. A devotee to my relationships. A devotee to my clients. A devotee to my life's work, my purpose. A devotee to *all that is. I decided I wanted to give it my all, and receive it all.* **I decided I wanted to go all in.** That feeling of loving harder, giving more, trusting deeper, and opening wider to all that this life has for me. I decided to be an active co-creator, I decided that I didn't want to play it cool anymore. I didn't want to act like I didn't care, act like I didn't want it. I decided to unapologetically claim and declare my juiciest and biggest desires out loud, and with the world. **I decided that ALL IN energy was the only energy I was available for.** This devotee archetype, this lover, this giver, this overflow… it's been the most regenerative archetype I could have ever chosen. It's an embodiment of "I have so much to give, AND I also want to receive more, I want it all". It's an energy of "I KNOW I am whole, complete, and fucking divine as I am… AND there is more here for me, and so I will devote myself to having it". I decided that I will align, and devote myself to living it. I powerfully decided to be a LOVER in my life. *To fall in love with life–truly.* To play and dance with source, to ask for miracles, and drop to my knees in submission. *I would do my work and then surrender to having it.* I decided to say fuck it, and drop the old constricted masculine archetypes that I was conditioned into embodying as a "successful business owner". I decided to get raw, real, and NAKED with my ultimate truth. The boring rules, rigid constrictions and processes didn;t feel true for me so I let them go–I chose to be free. I decided that devoting myself to this life by design was the only option, and that there was no way in hell that I would push or force myself there. *I decided that my devotion to my path would be the most regenerative and fulfilling path that there ever was.*

The transition from feeling like I had to do it all alone, to feeling like I was supported and could safely surrender was by no means an easy transition. Honestly, I still catch myself falling into old paradigms and cycles of forcing and extractive independence. *Now– allowing is the vibe, and surrender is the frequency I have upgraded into.* Being devotional is this beautiful space of giving and receiving. Devotion is this certainty and knowing that your dream life is here and available no matter what…*AND you are devoted to being a steward of that lived reality.* You are receiving and experiencing this life AND you are aligned with the work that is involved and required to create it. **Devotion is this energy of surrendering to God's plan.** Trusting in a higher plan and surrendering to divine intervention. Devotion to your faith, the universe, and the architect of all life. In religion they call it "obedience", in my personal spirituality–I call it *"devotion"*. I am devoted to source, I am devoted to life. I am devoted to my highest self. **I am devoted to what I know in my soul is meant for me.** This devotion to a higher timeline is uncomfortable at first, but the very nature of devotion allows me to do it anyway. This devotion allows me to move beyond fear, and to *"do it scared"*.

Devotion keeps you submissive to your lane, while simultaneously dominant in your vision. You know it's all happening and unfolding for you–you are willing to properly align moment to moment to moment. Knowing that you are supported and living in that way is a conscious choice– it takes immense bravery. There really is no other option than to keep going, and so you do. **This lifestyle takes healing, it takes trusting, and it takes surrender.** To know that it is all adding up, and happening for you. To know that it is safe to keep going, to continue to align and to trust before you *see* the evidence. To believe in something beyond what your physical eyes can see…is devotion to your highest path. To trust that you're not alone is a devotion to source.

This devotion is the most magnetic attraction point, because it demonstrates the highest form of belief that there is. If there is anything that we have understood and determined after years and years of studying the human brain, the human psyche and quantum physics–it is that we understand that one's beliefs create their reality. When you operate in an energy and essence of devotion–you are communicating the highest level of belief. **When you communicate such powerful self belief–you become a naturalized match to the desires of your heart.**

Speaking as a woman who has built a tonne of success in an older paradigm of living, and a tonne of egoic satisfaction in my extractive independence... I can assure you it is not easy to choose a new paradigm of trust and surrender. My very success for many years was built on control. My "old" paradigm was still very vibrant, alive and successful...However, it feels old and outdated to me now. *I MUCH prefer my untethered, surrendered, and flowy way of living and devotion to my life's work.*

Formerly, I built success by making a tonne of moves alone, hustling, feeling like I had to be independent, unwavering drive, and a willingness to succeed *no matter what.* The "no matter what" energy wasn't aligned in the way it's aligned now. The "no matter what" energy was based on extraction–not life giving regeneration. No matter how hard I made it, no matter how much work was involved, how much sleep, rest, and self care was discarded...I was willing to make it happen. I focused no matter how extractive it would be...I was committed. *I was committed to MY plan–NOT God's plan, and there is nuance in that differentiation.* My plan left little to no room for divine intervention. My plan was much more constricted, capped, and frankly unsustainable. My plan was not the highest calling. My plan was not of highest service to myself, the collective or the planet. My plan was not life giving–my plan was extractive. There was no room for devotion...no room for surrender. My plan was consistent yes... but it was NOT devotional. Important nuance–a devotional life is a life of HIGH service to ALL involved. NOT a life of achieving your desires at the expense of your wellbeing…*devotional living is NOT a life of sacrifice.*

Now, I devote myself to God's plan. I devote myself to what the universe has in store for me. I willingly submit and surrender to what my body is asking of me, what my soul needs of me and where source leads me. God's plan, and my devotion to it is so much more open, fluid, and regenerative. As I've said before, "life serves life". When I was so committed and consistent to "my plan", I was operating in extractive ways that did not serve life. Burn out, hustling, forcing, and pressure were far too common to me. God's plan however—is LIFE giving. *God's plan leaves room for the magic, because let's be real—it's all magic.* **The illusion that we are in control and can create a master plan to achieve all of our success will ALWAYS be conditional.** Our microcosmic mind will ALWAYS come up with a limited potential reality. *It is in our surrender to a higher plan, that we experience the infinite realms of receiving and achieving.* **We're never really in control.** The illusion is that we are. Our success IS indeed—SO available…AND there is so MUCH MORE success available to us when we *actually* surrender. When we choose devotion to a higher plan, we simultaneously open ourselves up to divine intervention, angelic, and energetic support that we could never even imagine in our confined human brains. ***When we get out of our own way— we open up to the infinite experience that is so available.*** Devotion is a letting go, with FULL trust and certainty, that you WILL be caught. Letting go, and simultaneously KNOWING that you WILL be held and supported. *You will be led and facilitated into a life beyond your wildest dreams.*

I have personally done the work to completely untether from my old and outdated paradigms. I have untethered from the old systems of hustle culture, burnout, pressure, and forcing energy in both life and my life's work. I have DONE the work…AND WARNING, OMG DOES IT EVER CREEP IN!! The old outdated systems are so pervasive. Hustle culture, toxic capitalism, toxic masculinity, extractive industrialism, illusions of pressure, distortions of scarcity and lack, the illusion of time and money running out...it ALL CREEPS IN. *As I spoke about a few chapters back–it's not about never being pulled off your lane, it's not about never misaligning...It's a matter of how fast you can come back to your lane and back to your alignment.* Devotion to a higher calling, a more soul, and intuitively led life is just that–a devotion. **A great amount of commitment is involved.** Aligned consistency and true surrender to the path– meaning you devote yourself to realigning when you deviate from the path and you catch yourself when you veer out of your lane. I, as many other high level individuals, feel the real raw challenge and tenderness involved with letting go.

Letting go of the illusion of control is probably the hardest piece for high achievers–feel me? We are so ambitious, so clear on our desires, feel so aligned to success that the very thought of surrendering and letting go feels like you're giving up. Letting go of the reins feels like a fast track to failure. It doesn't feel safe to let go because we have been programmed to control. Controlling outcomes and having tight grips on our plans is a way of being that is celebrated in older paradigms, and in the mainstream brainwashed society. **Not only is it celebrated, it simply feels like a safer solution.** We have been conditioned in such an overarching fear paradigm that our nervous systems are not primed for surrender–they are primed to control and constrict. It doesn't feel safe to surrender in our lives and in our businesses, because the old paradigm has programmed you to fear the unknown. Letting go of control is such unknown territory. We have strived for success and we have positioned ourselves to experience conventional success based on old paradigm principles. These are the principles of burnout, hustle culture, and lone wolf tendencies. **This perpetuated illusion of separation makes it nearly impossible to find comfort in devotional surrender.** This is where the reprogramming comes in. This is where you get to TRANSFORM and EXIST in a new paradigm. *A paradigm of open surrender, and a life beyond your wildest dreams.*

When we operate in control and become rigidly stubborn in "our plan"... we block the magic of divine intervention. When we block the divine—our receptivity gets cloudy. Blockages obstruct, and our overall system closes off. "Our plan" is conditional to external circumstances going "our way". The devotional path, when we surrender to a higher plan however–is unconditional. There is no cap. **There are no conditions.** There are infinite potentials. For simplicity's sake, let's put it this way– you can control circumstances to become a high 6 figure earner, you can even control outcomes to become a millionaire. However, when it comes to billions and beyond…when it comes to unconventional success and infinite abundance, there is a higher level of surrender involved. Our human minds can't calculate the "how" of infinite realities. Because our human minds aren't really in control of the greater universe and diving timing of it all. When we open ourselves up to divine intervention, and we devote ourselves to the path, we are then blessed and surprised with infinite blessings and unconventional mind blowing success!

The same goes for love. We can *plan* to meet the "perfect person", fall in love, and have all circumstances go according to plan… and we very well may find a nice place holder. But when it comes to finding your TRUE soulmate, you are completely out of control. *Circumstances rearrange FOR you two to meet, and you must simply surrender to the unfolding of the love story. You can likely go ahead and insert your own personal experiences of where it was just SO MUCH BETTER when you got the fuck out of the way and surrendered to God's plan.* When you loosened your grip on the reins…when you let go a little and more magic came in. Unexpected miracles showed up for you and you were rewarded through trusting and surrender. *Our ego craves control, so feeling out of control can feel like failure.* Leaning into surrender, asking for help, praying in devotion for answers, and guidance feels like failure to our conditions controlling minds. But in reality is actually the deepest alignment to a life beyond your wildest dreams. When you let go and surrender to the devotional path, you are awakening your purest magnetism. ***Again, devotion is your most innate attraction point because it is you in true flow with life and all that exists here.***

You arrived on Earth from a place of devotional surrender. **You had no control, yet here you are.** Devotion is a state of surrender to the path. Devotion is your most innate attraction point and your most innate way of being. *This innate nature of devotional surrender, is the aligned frequency of life itself.* When you attune to the pulse of life, you open up naturally to all that life has to offer. When you no longer resist the waves, you are able to experience the beauty of the vastness. Devotion is such a profound knowing and trust in *what is.* I often say that flow is something you respond to and fluidity is something you embody. *The truth is... there is always flow existing around you, but you can only experience the ease and beauty of the flow when you embody the fluidity.* There is nothing to fix. It's joyful, easeful, graceful, pleasureful, scary, painful, sad, expansive, tumultuous, then it's neutral again...*and so it is.* If you're a high level, spiritual leader, on this self developing journey you are actually MEANT to feel it all. The back and forth between ease, bliss, certainty, trust...then the fear, sadness, confusion, and the sense of feeling lost. You are experiencing all edges of yourself. Some edges feel juicy and delicious. Other edges feel constricting, painful and heavy. *There is no right and wrong when we are on the devotional path... it all just is.* When you are on the devotional path, you are existing in fluidity. You are responding to the flow, and you begin to experience the juiciness of life—a full experience of this stunning life. *Devotion is not only full surrender to "what is"—it's also a clear knowing of what's coming.* Your devotion is unwavering, unshakeable UNFUCKWITHABLE. An embodied energy of, "of course it's all happening for me".

Quick moment of integration for the times when
the waves feel scary, the neutrality feels like
nothingness, and the depths feel heavy...

What to do with this?

First and foremost OBSERVE it

Q: (who is observing?)

A: Your highest self is.

In this observation...You become the witness. You begin to healthily separate yourself from the control of the emotion. You then can safely and intentionally–drop in and embody the feels. *You aren't drowning in the flow, you are riding the waves of it.* You can embody it, accept it and then LOVE the fuck out of it.

I promise you it's all adding up.

The universe is shifting FOR You.

Lean in to whatever edge or pleasure you experience.

BE with what's in front of you, asking to be experienced, now.

This is devotion to the path.
No matter what, you will ride the wave. You will feel it all,
and you will come out on the other side–
with strength, lessons and rewards.

This chapter will empower you to feel full safety and security in the unknown. Integrating safety and security in the experience of all emotions. From the wildest fear, to the seemingly mundane nothingness, to the elation of euphoria. You get to ride the waves through ALL emotions. *Specifically, we are honing in on mastering creating certainty and ease in the unknown.* We are empowering your soul and human body through powerfully navigating the uncertainty and destabilization experienced when you are "in the void". The uncomfortableness of the inevitable in between moments of manifestation. This chapter will empower and open you up to the juiciest transmissions, to bring not only peace and safety to these "uncomfortable" emotions...*you will even learn how to bring pleasure to them.* The devotional path is this handing over of control. A deep sense of surrender. *An experience and embodiment of being taken care of.* Luxury receptivity, openness, and allowing...while also feeling the most powerful you've ever felt. There is a huge difference between *power and control.* There is a huge difference *between power and force.* Within the embodiment of devotion–you become the most fucking powerful creator that there is WHILE also experiencing the most ease. We will dive into divine feminine and masculine harmonization and polarity teachings. *You will become empowered to be a powerful creator AND a powerful receiver of this beautiful life.* We will completely harmonize your inner divine femme and inner divine masc. Innate attraction points and magnetism at an all time high. *So! It's time to align through Devotion.*

There's being in the "void", then there's loving the fuck out of EVERY moment of your beautiful life. There's a life of pressure and control, then there's a life of experience and surrender. There's wanting something…then there's having it. You are here because you are ready to experience unconventional mind blowing results internally and externally on your journey here on Earth. *I want you to open up to this truth– your essence is way too stunning to be limited.* I want you to see yourself in your fullest expression, and be SEEN there. This means going for everything you desire–becoming the best version of you on that journey, and basking in the inevitable success along the way. *Thank You, More Please*, is the vibe. *You get to want your wildest desires and you get to live your wildest dreams.* It is the DEVOTION to this timeline that will allow the journey to feel as delicious as the destination. *Because guess what… there is no destination.* There's just you loving the fuck out of your stunning life. Devotion allows you to experience results and rewards on the path. The devotional path is waiting for you. It is for the brave to claim it, devote to it, and for the brave to live their dream lives. *Throughout our time together as we move through this chapter, I encourage you to start opening up to a more fluid way of life. Remember, fluidity is a choice because the flow is inevitable.* There is flow happening all around us, and it's your job to embody the fluidity to experience the magic of that flow. There will be contrast, AND the contrast gets to be perceived as STUNNING. The contrast is necessary in living a FULLY experienced and expressed life on Earth. Devotion is our most innate attraction point, because this embodiment shows your highest self, source, and you as the architect and co-creator of your life that YOU believe in yourself. ***Devotion demonstrates that you trust the timing of your life, you choose your highest timeline, and you believe in miracles… and as always you will get what you believe to be true for you.***

Since I began leaning into devotion (in all areas of life), I have been continuously amazed by the tangible and intangible manifestations actualized from this way of BEING. Devotion in love, devotion in my life's work and devotion to source. It's been a path of ongoing, expected and unexpected, joyous miracles. I have never felt so ALIVE. I have never felt so certain. *I have a lust for life, like never before.* A lust for life that is so alluring to everything I desire. There is no more chasing or forcing. *There is simply existing.* Wider openings, more portals and unobstructed pathways. More channels and tunnels to allow all that I desire to both desire me, and FIND me. **I am devoted to devotion.** Devotion is the way I move through each day. I am actually awake to the miracles that are always cashing in for me. Aware of the beauty in everything that surrounds me. Open and receptive. I am in awe of the magic of this life. I make the devotional decision to flirt my way through each day. Focussing deeply on the pleasure within each moment. **Devotion is not a matter of efforting, forcing or pushing…but rather a matter of surrender, alignment, and allowing.** And still…the old patterns creep in. The patterns of rush, hustle and future pacing come whispering in from time to time. I share this to remind you that a devotional path does not mean you will not be tested. I can promise you that you WILL be called to higher levels of commitment. *The path is DEVOTIONAL, because devotion is required.*

Devotion is your most innate attraction point–a frequency of certainty. The Universe LOVES certainty, so does love, and so does money. *Devotion is that "no matter what" mentality, a mentality that is highly magnetic to everything you desire AND magnetic to everything life desires FOR you.* Magnetism is a paradigm of MORE. More can be overwhelming to a dysregulated system. It can be scary to embody your innate attraction point of ease, surrender, and trust. It can feel like A LOT. To all of a sudden be cashing in manifestation after manifestation–having to hold it all while feeling grounded and balanced with heightened levels of power and frequency. *It can feel like everything is happening all at once–because it is.* There is an integration period that is required when you walk the devotional path. Again, you must create safety in your new found way of life. The life of ease, allowing, effortlessness, and embodied certainty. You must regulate that this elevated way of life is safe. **You must normalize it, in order to continue to evolve it.** Devotional living is a life of purpose that is unique to you and your path. It is SO special when you find your community and soul fam of devotees… the ones deeply devoting to their own unique life by design. The ones who walk their walk, and wholeheartedly celebrate YOU in walking yours. This is fucking fabulous AND you must first and foremost hold yourself in the safety, validation and ongoing celebration of this life you have chosen. There will always be the option to fall into a more mundane way of living, a more conventional lifestyle. When you firmly and powerfully hold yourself in devotion to your path–the temptation of smallness disappears. We are always straddling two paradigms, the old and the new. In this life of ever evolving evolution and growth…what was once the ceiling is now the floor. **The OLD is always evolving, because the NEW is always upgrading.** Read that again babe, and let that sink in.

As you continuously expand your capacities, you are required to continue to rise. This is why it is called "evolution over a lifetime". *There is no final destination…it just keeps getting better.* This constant evolution is what makes what was once a *new expanded paradigm, an old and outdated one*…Get it? What was once new, expansive, aligned, and exciting…can quickly become old, limiting, and outdated. *We move FAST in the fast lane.* This devotional path is about owning what's TRUE NOW. As you rise, you will be asked to own and reclaim the biggest, edgiest, most vulnerable sides of yourself. When you claim these tender and expansive edges–you devote yourself deeper to your path, and expand more powerfully into new and higher realms. As the waves get bigger, your flow state gets more attuned to the higher levels of possibility. **Desires get juicier and surrender becomes required–more and more.** You are SHOWING yourself fully to life when you ask for what you desire, and you shamelessly walk toward it. Your embodiment becomes more sensual and material. Your most magnetic points are discovered. You are fully awakened and activated through the most vulnerable and sensual embodiments. **With more expansive visions and desires, bigger surrender is required.** Surrender is the embodiment, and devotional feminine trust IS the archetype. **Your willingness to surrender is your ability to receive.** Breathe in…breathe out, and open up my love–it's all here for you. *It's time to come ALIVE.*

Take a moment here, pause. Drop into your sacred body. Connect down to your sacral chakra (below the belly button and down into your sacred womb space). Connect to your body. Touch, feel, and worship. There is openness here. Healing and expansion available. Soft landing strips for your desires to drop in. Can you become more embodied? More sensual. More grounded now. Here and now. Breathe in. Connect. In devotion to your gorgeous self and all that is.

Devotional living is one of the highest forms of existence. You are truly living like a soul having a human experience. So not only are you leaning into edges, evolving over a lifetime, and being fucking iconic doing it, you are creating certainty in the uncertain. You are not only finding comfort in the unknown…you're finding PLEASURE in it. THIS is sexy, yummy devotion. **You don't just accept the unknown…you begin to love the fuck out of it.** Always knowing what's next actually puts the brakes on your pleasure experience. Think about your pleasure experience in the bedroom…if you knew everything your partner was about to do, where they would touch, the tempo, the pressure, the depths…*would it feel as good?* **There is PLEASURE in the unknown, if you allow it.** Devotion is about being *all in* on your juiciest desires no matter what–even when they are "in the void".

You get to decide that the void is the sexiest foreplay of your life. Or you can be miserable about it–the choice is yours, babe. When you are flirting with your desires, when your desires tease you, when they're so close you could touch them...but not "here" yet...*that gets to be the sexiest sexual tension of your life.* You can be stressed about it, or you can allow yourself to fold into the playfulness of it. ***There is no waiting in a life of devotion.*** When your desires feel far away but you know they're coming...*you're all in.* When your desires are in your vortex, when they're so close and you know it... *you're all in.* When they are actually IN your lived reality...*you're all in.* **You are always ALIVE in the great unfolding. It is all happening now. There is only the aliveness, experience, and pleasure in the unfolding.** *Every single moment on the journey gets to feel really important, and really monumental in the great unfolding of your beautiful life.* **It's happening NOW.** You fully feel your desires in the foreplay phase. You fully feel them when they're in your palm. And you fully feel them when they are completely nowhere to be seen. **You STILL feel them.**

This devotional "all in" energy IS what keeps you in the frequency and vibration of actualization. Being all in while in the "void" essentially means... it's all adding up. **Anything that happens...is happening FOR you!** This is easier said than done. Staying in that leading and receptive energy is not for the faint of heart. This is where your devotion comes in. *Your decision to be all in on this life.* **Wanting what you want, holding the vibration of wanting, AND *having it* simultaneously isn't easy.** The concepts of "it's all adding up" seem light, attractive, and easy to comprehend. But it's the true trust, surrender, and belief required, that is often what is hardest. *Don't worry love, this entire chapter is designed to integrate your devotional, trusting, and surrendered embodiment, so you can actually HAVE your desires.* Have them from a devotional, trusting and completely untethered space. ***We will transmute any moments of fear, scarcity, lack, and doubt... into dripping desire, mystery, enticement, and excitement.***

We covered the edges in the last chapter–this work now is about turning the pain of the edges into pleasure. The unknown GETS to be a delicious season on your journey–one that you don't want to rush through. It becomes a curious, exciting invitation into deeper pleasure and surrendered opening. *The Devotional Unfuckwithable vibe of–What if it just keeps getting better?!* (insert heart eyes and drooling face). What if you had this constant knowing, that allowed you to drop fully into the pleasure of the clim(b)ax. This full body smile and excited vibration, knowing that it's all adding up. A deep and held feeling of safety in the moments in between. *Knowing that Source is up to something…Knowing that God has a plan… AND fully trusting that the universe is supporting you. You're not meant to know all the details babe, because this life is going to be the most luxurious, abundant, and vibey surprise birthday party that's ever been thrown in your name AND it just keeps getting better!* Your spirit loves mystery. *Breathe in. Breathe out.* It's safe to be in the unknown. **Always knowing what's next isn't actually the most fun… and it's definitely not the most sexy.** Knowing every move the Universe is making, is like knowing every detail about your dream wedding engagement. Or knowing every detail of your surprise weekend getaway. It's like knowing exactly where your lover is going to kiss you next, or knowing what every wrapped gift is underneath the Christmas tree–knowing all of that is BORING, and it robs you of the excitement of life! **The unknown creates the full experience.** As a former manifestation and success control freak…take it from me… the devotional, surrendered path is SO MUCH BETTER.

I am literally GUSHING in excitement for you to begin to practice Devotion in your own life, and begin to feel into the immediate rewards. To experience the feeling of certainty, and moving forward in alignment with that certainty–no matter what. I'm excited for you to fully TRUST and KNOW that you are supported endlessly. You will immediately feel the sense of excitement, pleasure and safety in the moments that used to feel scary. You will then see and experience ALL the biggest shifts in awareness and then physical reality from: love, pleasure, money, impact, manifestation, purpose and evolution. Through the various integrations, teachings, and embodied upgrades that you will experience moving through this chapter you will begin to encode your true nature as a *devotee* to this life. *A devotee to your body, your highest self and your spirit. A devotee for the higher love and the higher purpose that leads you forward.* . I invite you now as you read this presently…to breathe slowly, and allow these truths to penetrate you. Integrate these codes in your system, and open portals of remembering and *"aha's"* within you. **Absorb these truths and the openings that they provide you, trust and lean back as you are led to all the inevitable miracles of this life.**

You came here to experience all of life's textures.
Certainty is beautiful. Knowing is powerful.
But can you experience these frequencies amidst the unknown?
Can you experience the sexiness of the divine unfolding?
Divine intervention… Is just that, it's divine.
It's occurring from a "felt" realm.
It's not something we can SEE. It's only something we can feel.
Feeling into certainty amidst the unknown IS
your ultimate power.
Devotion to your desires before they manifest.
Devotion to the journey. Devotion to the path.
Experiencing the void as enticing. Mystery. Excitement.
This is the frequency of innate magnetism.
We're never really in control. We must be open to divine
intervention.
We surrender to that divinity.
The manifestations come down to alignment– always.
The path is the path is the path.
Detours and roadblocks included …
These winding roads GET to be part of the divine unfolding.
Who you become on the path is the key.
How you navigate the turns and blocks is your magic.
I often say–divine timing is when you DECIDE you're ready.
With that contrast– if you're not ready to RECEIVE it now…The
universe will GET you ready.

Trust the journey, and practice leaning into as much pleasure on that journey as possible.
The journey is the foreplay.
The "Destination" (lol) is the sexiest sex ever.
There's no destination by the way…
There is just a devotional path.
Life by design…And evolution over a lifetime.

Over the remainder of this chapter and beyond, into "The Art of Receiving" chapter, you will hear me talk a lot about "divine feminine" and "divine masculine" energetics. I will dive into their embodiments, as well as the concepts of "polarity". Connect now to your sacral chakra, bring your hands down to your womb space and connect to the creative forces that brought *you* here. *Connect to your own internal creative forces, recognize now that you are not separate from the architect of this life.* **You are connected to the *wonder* of it all.** Breathe into your body and open up, become more receptive, lean into the allowing. *What whispers are present for you? What messages from your body, intuition, spirit guides or your highest self? What information is leading you? Can you trust it?* Don't rush here, breathe into this. BE here with this. Pay attention to the impulses. Trust the messages. *Allow your innate creativity, your connection to the sensuality, creation and actualization of this life land now.*

The above practice of dropping within the body, opening up, receiving in the nothingness is an example of how connected we are—we can choose at any time—to attune deeper. Dropping into the physical body, touching the sacral womb space and basking in the stillness of the sacral chakra connection, would be an example of a feminine energy practice. *It is the divine feminine and the divine masculine working in harmony that exist as the devotee.* **This feminine embodiment is stunning and intensely powerful, when embodied within the safety of your own innate masculine container.** Your inner masculine is the activator and decision maker that creates the safe and explorative spaces for your inner feminine to unwind and receive (more on this later). This conversation around harmony is important as it is what creates a regenerative devotional life. The harmony ensures that instead of blind obedience we are operating from an insourced connection to our truth. The harmony ensures that instead of blindly hustling via extractive commitment—that we are attuning to the frequencies and needs of the body. **This harmony ensures that your devotion is LIFE GIVING, and in service of your unique PURPOSE and ALIVENESS.**

As a high level, ambitious, Unfuckwithable, spiritual being...your harmonization of both "yin" and "yang" energies is required. Yin being the feminine, the ease and allowing. Yang being the masculine, the action and the containment. This Yin energy, the surrender, the allowing, and the divine feminine reclamation is often the most unfamiliar to embody for high achieving and heavily conditioned humans. Most of conventional society (and the systems I spoke of in earlier chapters) have entrenched conditioning based on depriving, denying, and shaming the feminine energies within ALL of us. **Over the last many decades, the divine feminine has been the energy that has been abolished.** Many forces and structures have been perpetuated to strip humans of their innate NATURE as attuned, in flow and aligned beings. **Your divine feminine is deeply connected to *all that is,* and HIGHLY magnetic to pleasure, miracles, abundance and joy.** This feminine energy has been either suppressed, repressed or even obliterated in many of us through societal conditioning within the extractive culture—specifically in North American capitalistic societies. **The sinister forces at work have been and are TERRIFIED of the POWER of the divine feminine—and have and will do anything they can to captate and abolish it.** Your divine feminine may feel uncomfortable to embody and reclaim at first...but it IS your most MAGNETIC and INNATE energy to embody. **There are magnetic poles within you...and wealth and pleasure codes UNLOCK and open up the portals to your magnet when you come home to your divine feminine nature.** This divine feminine nature and these magnetic codes are discovered through these sexy, sensual, and devotional embodiments. Your inner ability to surrender, trust, lean back and receive is within your very NATURE. **It requires an undoing, a remembering and a becoming.** It is uncomfortable and unfamiliar at first, but once you have surrendered into it–*it feels like coming home.*

My intentional harmonization between yin and yang energies is both the FOUNDATION and CONTAINER of my ever evolving success. For me personally, operating as a high level woman living in alignment and walking my highest timeline looks like a divine harmony between my masculine and feminine energies. **I have harmonized my divine masculine and feminine within.** It's something I continue to nurture and evolve moment to moment, so I can live a wildly stunning life–so I can SERVE from the most grounded and supportive space, and so I can receive in ever evolving and expanding ways. *My life is infinitely better because of this harmonization and this union within myself.*

This harmonization for me means living both FREELY and with FOCUSSED intention. I create spaces and environments for my divine feminine/my yin to play and receive. My masculine energy holds space/creates the container for my feminine energy to exist within. *My feminine is free to be WILD within the security of my divine masculine container.* Expansion and pleasure within the safety of my protective, aligned, and intentional held environments. My harmonization is what allows me to have a *"When In Rome"* mindset–an explorative, adventurous way of life, AND a knowing that I am protected. An innate KNOWING that everything I experience in this life is fundamentally supportive to my path and purpose. I try it all, I do it all. *I live in devotion to the aliveness, to life itself and to the experiences that are positioned in front of me.* I immerse myself in life and I do it with such high level intention and within safe and held containers. My divine masculine is always leading me, holding me, and realigning my divine feminine with my path and center. My divine feminine is always creating and opening up into the beauty of moments. She is living fully and presently knowing that she's always taken care of. M**y divine feminine plays without fear, she knows she is guided and supported.** We are always playing in this balance. *When we are in FLOW with our polarities we get to experience more.* The vibe for me is, *"what does my divine feminine need from me today?"* How can I create containers of space for my divine feminine to receive through my divine masculine's stoic action? **This ongoing awareness of the union within myself is what opens me up to MORE, time and time again.** *A devotional life of RICH experience, while simultaneously walking my purpose and my path.*

The highest form of existing, which is Devotion, is only possible within the held space and consciousness of the inner divine masculine. Your divine masculine LOVES to nurture your divine feminine, and your divine feminine loves to be nurtured. *All this nurture from a state of overflow of course.* When you nurture your inner divine feminine, your inner divine masculine is energized to give and your divine feminine is open to receive. **There is an equal exchange of purpose, service, and receiving going on within your internal state–union within self.** This high level reciprocity within your own union of your own internal feminine and masculine is where the deepest healing and actualization lies. *This high level devotional dance between service and receptivity within your own system is the image in which the universe mirrors.* *Meaning–if you embody mutual giving and receiving with your yin and yang/your inner fem and masc–the universe can effortlessly show you in your material world the same high level of reciprocity.*

There is a win-win exchange occurring within SELF that expedites external and material validation and support. **When your divine masculine takes care of your divine feminine–you develop the deepest sense of trust within yourself.** Your divine femme loves to feel free, to play, to dance, and to know she's taken care of. Your divine masculine loves to create safe spaces for her to fully explore and experience all the textures of life. This combination of action and lean back, this dance, this flow is self leadership fully embodied. **Within your internal system you have this profound INSOURCED sense of self leadership and self trust.** *This self trust and union is what creates an ability to surrender to the divine unfolding of your life. If you trust that you are connected to "all that is", and you trust yourself, you can effortlessly trust the infinite supportive energy of "all that is".*

There is no devotion without trust. Surrendering to divine timing, divine intervention, and ultimately to God's plan, is nearly impossible without trust. **Trust and surrender go hand in hand.** *There is no surrendering without trust, and there is no walking a devotional path without surrendering to the divine plan.* Living a devotional life, means you *actually* trust therefore you can *actually* surrender. When I say trust... *I mean you actually trust.* You aren't gripping the reins of life. You aren't controlling outcomes. You aren't manipulating circumstances. You aren't giving up when the current external realities don't appear to be favorable. **Trust means you trust no matter what.** Surrender means you surrender no matter what. Devotion means you are devoted no matter what. There is no room for control freak tendencies and constriction when you are walking a devotional path. *There is no control when you are CHOOSING a life of infinite miracles that continue to expand, evolve and get better over a lifetime.* **Trust is required.** One of my famous quotes is this *"Fake trust is like a fake orgasm…nobody wins".* I see so many people early on their journey faking trust, faking belief, and ultimately lying to themselves that they trust in the unfolding. This is where you rob yourself of your edges. *You bypass the very real stage in which you DON'T actually trust, is you bypassing the truth and embodiment of your real emotions.* **There is a reason we lean into the edges of our evolution before we embody our devotion–we have to first face the fear and the horror of the unknown before we can begin to trust and consciously devote ourselves to it.** When you are faking trust, you are never fully leaning into the edge of distrust. *Distrust being the shadow or the contrast of what you desire.* When you deny yourself contrast, you deny yourself truth and you limit your experience on Earth. When you fake trust and belief, you rob yourself of your range, your multidimensionality, and the true emotional processing that is required for your evolution. **Again–fake trust is like a fake orgasm–nobody wins.** I've certainly faked orgasms before and I have absolutely faked trust. *I have personally left both in the past and I encourage you to do the same.*

The BIGGEST breakthroughs I've ever had, were always in the moments that I bravely DECIDED to fully lean into the very UNCOMFORTABLE feelings that were VERY REAL at the time. When I embodied the most painful emotions. **When I actually went there–I was rewarded...every time.** When I went there–I bursted through and I came out on the other side with strength, resilience, perspective and true self TRUST. When I actually admitted to myself that I was scared, when I named that fear and looked it dead in the eye. When I powerfully OWNED the present truth that I didn't trust or didn't believe xyz was manifesting...When I admitted that I didn't trust God, the Universe, my lover, myself...when I actually *OWNED* that. **I opened myself up to the greatest receiving. I opened the floodgates to the deepest honesty, healing, intimacy, and pleasure available.** Faking trust robs you of healing. When you can communicate with God, the Universe, your highest self, your lover...whomever that you DON'T trust and you actually drop to your knees and beg for a sign, ask for support, beg to be shown and fully devotionally surrender–you WILL receive. It's not fucking comfortable...*most people won't ever be true to themselves in this way. Most people are terrified of their true vulnerabilities.* But you're not most people. **When you actually fully own your truth and the fears that come with it–you will crack yourself open, you will BURST into your next evolution. When you willingly accept and embody what you're ACTUALLY feeling, you are in position to investigate it and ACTUALLY heal it.** This by the way, is a deeply nourishing feminine embodiment practice, to fully feel the feels. The rawest emotions. The fetal position melt downs. The primal screams. **The wildest and RAWEST details of yourself**

are MEANT to be expressed. God can hold it. Your highest self can hold it. The UNIVERSE can hold it. Your inner divine masculine can hold it. And if you're lucky, your lover/partner/healer/friend/parent... can hold it. When you actually allow yourself to feel the fullness of the distrust, the doubt, the fear, the worry and you actually embody it... it SHIFTS it HEALS it ASCENDS RAPIDLY.

In contrast—when you fake it...you stay where you are, stagnant, bypassed and barely brushing the surface of your truth and potential. So along the lines of fake trust being like a fake orgasm (a reality far too common in this world), you are simply procrastinating the true YUMMINESS of what is available. **When you fake an orgasm, you procrastinate a real orgasm from actualizing in your body, and you procrastinate the depth in your partnership to evolve and become reciprocally pleasurable.** *Similarly...when you fake TRUST, you procrastinate the experience of REAL trust.* You become stagnant and STUCK in this in-between, conditional, and limited reality where you ROB yourself of your edges and delicious details. But when you ACTUALLY embody the truth and the raw emotions that you DON'T FUCKING TRUST, you're SCARED AS FUCK, and you NEED GOD TO SHOW YOU A SIGN...I PROMISE YOU that your experience of this truth—will actualize momentum, results, rewards and an overall cathartic release of euphoria. Then...you will heal and you will actually trust. With all this being said, an important piece to recognize is that trust is NOT a tactic. **Trust is not a strategy that you can just turn on.** *You cannot fake it—therefore, you cannot force yourself into trust.* **Trust is something you surrender into.** There comes a point on your journey, where devotional living looks like continuing to move forward in alignment with AND without trust. When you move without trust you are PRAYING TO BE SHOWN. When you move WITH trust you are WITNESSING AND ACTUALIZING THE RESULTS...*regardless—keep moving.*

Now, let's layer on these concepts. Another one of my absolute favourite quotes it this *"God isn't a fuck boy... you don't have to play hard to get."* Essentially meaning–you don't have to pretend you don't want what you really want. You don;t have to pretend you're uninterested, in the name of "detachment". **You get to loudly and proudly want what you want, and want it so bad that it hurts.** You get to BE hungry... *just don't STAY hungry.* Feel me? Detachment –just like trust is NOT a tactic, it's not something you can fake. *Detachment rather, is something that you evolve into.* When you fully trust, you CAN detach... you CAN surrender. You don't have to pretend you don't want what you want...becasue again– God is NOT a fuck boy, and neither is the universe...*So–Ask and you shall receive.* Go through the process of wanting what you want. Set your intentions. You can set them and forget them or you can set them and be obsessed as fuck about them. Regardless...they're on their way.

Your desires want your readiness AND your commitment. Your readiness AND your devotion is required. You can want what you want, become obsessed with having it, and simultaneously know that you're powerful on your own, you are fulfilled, whole and complete–with or without it. Understand now that it's ON IT'S WAY, because you ACTUALLY trust...you can longingly detach while continuing to want and love it. **Thats option one–and it's a great fucking option.** Another option is this: want what you want– want it so badly, become obsessed, forget that you are whole and complete with or without it. Your needy attachment to it will likely repel it if your attachment screams "I'm not good enough until I have it". That's option 2 and it's by no means an optimal option and yet one I know we've all experienced on some level, and you can absolutely continue to experience it. **It may take a while to actually have what you want with option 2–but it WILL eventually lead you to a place of surrender.** The last option could look like this: You set an intention, you lovingly detach because you trust, you know that it's not really up to you anyway (as there is a much higher plan), and you carry on living in alignment with feeling good and naturally being the match. **Now that...option 3 is expert fucking level.** You may find yourself there right away, or it may take years. **Regardless, I hope you**

understand that your trust is what leads you to detachment/surrender and your detachment/surrender is what leads to your actual manifestation.

You can want something so badly and simultaneously be detached/in surrender AND you can't and won't properly detach unless you actually trust/surrender... Got it? Got it.

Devotional energy is sexy, alluring, and magnetic to our desires. This devotional energy includes both wanting AND surrendering. Let us begin to understand how frequency and energy work in magnetism of our desires– in a nuanced yet simple way. First important note: we are made up of the same ENERGY that our desires are made up of–all that exists is existing within a physical AND energetic plane. Now, think of this sexy, integral, intelligent, and kind man who communicates to you that he loves you, wants you, adores you, AND he simultaneously lives his own life. This man does his own thing, and feels confident, powerful, whole and complete with or without you–that's a vibe, right? (insert your own description of a desirable human being into that example). Now... imagine this sexy, intelligent and kind man who communicates that he loves you, wants you, adores you and YET he is personally incapable of feeling any sort of happiness, or exuding any sort of power or confidence until YOU show up for him 100% of the time–creepy and repelling...right? These two examples show us the difference between attachment and detachment. These examples show us what is alluring, attractive and magnetic VS what is creepy, unattractive and repelling in energy and embodiment. To want something and to be clear in your wanting is SEXY if you are also lovingly detached and whole and complete on your own. To want something from a place of neediness and control is on the creepy repelling side...it's not the vibe.

The same dynamics of energetic magnetism OR energetic repellent goes for ALL energy. Our desires WANT to be wanted (they are alive and energetic vibrations after all). **They WANT your clear communication that they ARE desired by**

you...they WANT your conscious intention. BUT energy loves fluidity–energy is always flowing...therefore, your desires DO NOT want to be controlled. Your desires don't want to feel trapped, because you cannot trap energy. Your desires don't want to feel the PRESSURE of being your only source of power, happiness or pleasure–that is a lot of repelling high pressure energy that the innate FREE energy is not congruent with. Pressure repels. Control repels. **Loving detachment MAGNETISES.** You in your devotional wanting AND your innate fullness, whole, and complete embodiment IS the most alluring, attractive, and magnetic frequency there is. YOU ARE THE SOURCE, BABE. **You don't NEED anything to fill you–you are whole and complete as you are.**

Devotion is a sexy wanting AND a sexy release. An alluring desire, an alluring sense of innate wholeness, with an alluring certainty that it is ALL happening–yum! You in your embodied full trust in yourself, your guides, and in the universe that it is all happening FOR you. There is no need to control–you get to surrender. Devotion is your most innate attraction point because it is this nuanced embodiment and energetic frequency of, "I want you AND I know I'm good no matter what AND I know I've got you"...wink wink - sexy, sexy, yes. **You are whole and complete– period.** No more fake trust. No more acting like you don't want what you want. No more bypassing the real, raw truth AND in that truth taking yourself back home to your INNER source of personal power. Letting your edges lead you back to your center of grounded confidence. Your edges and raw truths are the gateway back to YOU. We are operating at a high level here. **We are living in the land of nuance, the land of the "both-and" where: A. We KNOW what we want B. We are honest when we don't feel like we can have it and C. We let the truth of that edge take us home to our innate wholeness and INSOURCED personal power.**

Being Unfuckwithable is an all encompassing identity, and it is time to FULLY embrace –ALL of it. The universe wants to see your hunger. The universe wants to see and feel your desire. The universe wants to see your raw emotion. The universe wants you to break open into a point of surrender. The universe wants to see you ask for its support…Ask to be shown, ask to receive. The universe can hold all of you and the universe WANTS to hold all of you. All this…all the while KNOWING you are whole, complete, and worthy as fuck…*as you are. **"Devotional Wanting" leads to "Devotional Having". The REAL RAW TRUTH of your 'wanting' is LIFE GIVING, and as you already know…life serves life ALL day long.** Your TRUTH is life giving, and therefore HIGHLY magnetic to your desires. Your authentic expression, emotions, energy, and embodiment of what you are really feeling is what the New Earth needs. Truth is the foundation of all connection, all creation and all healing. It's time for the real and raw truth to prevail.

So, let's own what's true for us—now and always. When you love something, you can't stop talking about it, thinking about it, feeling into it, believing it, wanting it, desiring it, creating it… you can't stop, so don;t stop. THAT is devotional wanting. You are willing to do anything for it. *This is highly magnetic…because it's real.* **The only thing that would turn this *obsession* into a REPELLANT is if you fell into the illusion of separation—which is a LIE.** The illusion that WITHOUT "it" (whatever it is) you are not complete. If you fall into illusion you leave the truth, you leave the dimension of openness and you leave the New Earth. If you fall into the lie that IS *separation*—you change frequency— from KNOWING, TRUSTING and DEVOTION—to *lack, separatism and scarcity.* So be aware and intentional that your WANTING is in alignment with your understanding of SELF as already whole, complete and divinely interconnected with ALL that exists. *Personally, the only thing that actually fulfills me, satisfies me, and nourishes me…is the truth.* I LOVE seeing someone want something so bad and aligning to that something all the livelong day. I fucking LOVE to see it…SO LONG AS they ALSO know that they are innately connected and already in union with what their wanting because they SEE themselves as connected within the Dimension of Openness and divinely worthy of their desires.

Honesty, openness, real, raw–connection…Gorgeous truths, ugly truths, healing truths, painful truths. ALL OF IT. I want all of it. So does the Universe, So does God, so does your highest self, so does the infinite creator of all that exists here on Earth. Your truth is an unapologetic and BRAVE expression of love. **Meeting an uncomfortable truth with openness, understanding, and non-judgment is the HIGHEST form of unconditional love that there is.** It is LIFE GIVING. The truth is what unites us, the truth is what heals us and the truth is what ascends us. I have personally had my heart broken over dishonesty and I fucking refuse to participate in any more illusions. **Truth IS life giving and the truth–no matter how painful or vulnerable it may be–IS the answer.** When we fully and openly wear our hearts on our sleeves and walk courageously toward our desires we are ALIVE. We are involved fully and presently with LIFE. **The truth opens us up to the infinite realms of giving and receiving, and the TRUTH is a core foundation of DEVOTION.**

Here are some of my guiding principles that govern all connections in my life. My relationship to humans, desires, experiences, money, energy–whatever I am relating to I hold these governing truths and beliefs:

1. It's all energy–it's all vibrating–it's all in flow
2. Love expands, fear constricts
3. Truth heals, lies bypass
4.Everything is connected
5.We are alive in lief NOW–it's all happening now
6.No matter how uncomfortable is it–if it is TRUE for me–it must be embodied, experienced and expressed

TRUTH is the portal to healing, and LOVE
is the portal to ascension

As we walk our highest timelines we are co creating a New Paradigm for all and a New Earth to rise and thrive. We are consciously choosing love, choosing truth, choosing a higher way of thinking, believing and existing in this world. I am personally unavailable for lies, dishonesty, and frankly anything BUT the real, raw truth in ANY area of my life. This world NEEDS our aliveness. This world needs energies that give LIFE. **This world NEEDS our true, present engagement with ALL that is.** This means holding more–more edges, more discomfort, more pain AND of course more love, more joy, more wealth, more pleasure, more aliveness and more success. **It doesn't have to be perfect, it doesn't have to look good, it just has to be fucking real.** If it's not real… it no longer exists in our highest and new paradigm. As we upgrade, people and experiences upgrade with us…or they don't–they either rise, or they fall off. **Once you've tasted the TRUTH–you become allergic to anything else.** When you've experienced the moments that feel like, *"FUCK YESSSSS…THIS… THIS RIGHT HERE… THIS IS LIFE GIVING, THIS IS WHAT I CAME TO EARTH FOR!!!"* …After moments like that, relationships like that, experiences like that, and opportunities like THAT…the distorted, distracted and deviated energies don't fly. The mundane conversations just simply don't cut it anymore. Gossip, fakeness, illusions, and lies…quickly become REPELLING. **You essentially become "allergic" to fake energy…no longer fooled by the illusion.** This is because these low frequency, lies and distortions are NOT MEANT to exist in your highest timeline. *They are no longer meant to be experienced by you, they don't match your new higher and purer frequency.*

Those who are comfortable with the truth, can hold more–more pain and of course WAY more pleasure. **When you live in true devotion and you can HOLD it all–you are rewarded.** You can sit with someone in their heartbreak AND in their euphoria. Their edges don't scare you–because you have and are willing to continue to face yours. THIS is devotional living, devotion to truth, devotion to aliveness and devotion to what's REAL. Once your standards are really fucking high, you DON'T, you WON'T, and you CAN'T settle. Again…you are now allergic to the illusion…and that is a really fucking goof thing. Devotion is real–plain and simple. My devotional life means this: I don't do transactional relationships, I don't do conditional relationships because I don't operate in that false reality anymore. Every single relationship in my life (energetics, money, friendship, family or intimate) has upgraded to a high and TRUE vibration of unity. My devotional lifestyle requires TRUTH, and therefore every relationship has been required to upgrade to that TRUTH. **Devotion is holding a high energetic standard and therefore–a high level material reality.** If it's not real–it's not part of your devotional reality. If it's not real it's not a part of your highest timeline.

"The more aligned you are, the more you CRAVE alignment"

As we rise in power, devotion and congruence with our truth– we experience more and more alignment. We are required to BE in alignment, and in turn we hold ourselves to the standard of it. More and more alignment in everything you do and everything/one you interact with. *The more aligned you are–the more you CRAVE alignment.* When you are walking in truth, devotion and alignment it is OBVIOUS and rather JARRING when you experience misalignment. AS we discussed in previous chapters–when you live in the fast lane–any deviation from that lane is a fucking shakeup. Devotional life is NOT a life in cruise control–rather, this is a life of great intention. Meaning–when you deviate from your path/alignment you WILL experience the consequence. Your deviation becomes more obvious to you the more aligned you are–your deviation will present itself through more intense feelings of misalignment when you deviate from the path. It's like, if you never watch violent movies you will be JARRED by the violence that you see, it will feel destabilizing and upsetting (again–this is a healthy and life giving response to misalignment).

The same goes for any misaligned energies that you interact with–if they are not "of the same vibration", and you are really aligned/in the "fast lane" …you WILL feel the clashing of paradigms and the misalignment will be OBVIOUS to you. For me it's like this: I can SO CLEARLY feel and read energy, I keep my energy top tier, clean and high vibrational…so, when I experience someone who is in a very dark, low or fake energy it is JARRING to me–I see it so clearly their misalignment is OBVIOUS to me. Because I am not distracted or under any spell of mind control (like a lot of the population is)–I can SEE so clearly when someone is under that spell. It's like running into a brick wall…when your energy is HIGH and pure, and you run into someone who is so LOW and distracted–it's like you're not even in the same paradigm (because well…you're not). Or when you are so focused and intentional about being ALIVE, and you meet someone who is SO conditioned by their devices, when you speak to them it's like they have lost the light in their own eyes. **You are SO MUCH MORE aware of the subtle energies when you are in presence and alignment on your devotional path.** When you are in your ALIGNED lane–anything that is NOT of the same vibration, coherence or congruence WILL feel destabilizing. *Unfortunately, most people will go through their entire lives not even noticing these subtle energies of vibration–but again…YOU are NOT most people.*

Now before we wrap up this chapter and dive into the homework…I want to give you a little more back story on just how much I ADORE the lifestyle of devotion. **The act of devotion for me–changed the game in ALL areas of my life.** Here's a little look inside my love life: I have loved every evolution of Mitch (my man) and he has loved every evolution of me. Mitch is my soulmate in this incarnation. We've been ride or die since blackberries and Skype… lol. We have folded into one another deeper than imaginable. Our love story far exceeds anything I've ever seen on TV, or in any movie. We have had a tonne of behind the scenes pain and heartbreak– we've navigated these as we leaned deeper into our edges…alone and together. We have experienced the false realities of distortion and we have chosen over and over again to be TRUE to one another. We have consciously chosen a life of devotion to our shared legacy in this life together. We constantly choose open, and honest communication even in the face of pain and discomfort. We have deeply expansive magic and aliveness AND vulnerable tenderness within our relationship. We have the deepest sense of respect for one another in union and we have solid independence and sovereignty to our own truths. We have a fire sex life, and we have a strong cuddle game. We get dolled up and hit the town, and we know how to rest hard and hermit at home. Our love embodies unconditional love, growth, and evolution over a lifetime.

Mitch has told me that, *"It's a constant game of catch up trying to understand me"* ...and he is devoted to that understanding day after day. I have loved every evolution of Mitch and he has loved every evolution of me. **The biggest shift that I have felt in our love has been through my personal surrender into devotion.** Devotional giving. Devotional receiving. **Devotion at its core is our most innate attraction point.** My personal alignment journey, and surrender to devotional living happened not only in my life's work, but massively in my personal life. In a conscious release of the old ways of being–this alpha woman who did it all alone (despite fully having the support that I was unwilling to receive) transformed into this embodiment of a surrendered devotee. In order to fully let love in and to experience the evolution over a lifetime of true intimacy and connection with Mitch I HAD to release control and let my guard down. **I had to accept support–** *the support that is always infinitely available be it materially or energetically.* **I had to know that I am not only the creator, but I am the CO creator in life and in love.** I needed to know and TRUST that I could surrender, to know that I could trust, and that I was not alone in the life I was creating. In both life and love I had to CHOOSE the devotional path of reciprocal giving and receiving.

I went from *Miss Independent* to *Miss Devotee,* and I have to tell you–I like my devotional lifestyle so much better. I am a high level woman who now FULLY surrenders. I do my part and then I lean back. I'm an ambitious woman, devoted to her path who also practices opening fully to what life and love has to give her. I have devoted myself to surrender. After years of conditioning that I had to hustle, after a broken heart and lots of psychological and physiological constriction, after losing and regaining trust–I CHOSE to surrender. **Now, I devote myself to moving with my**

innate feminine being-ness. I devote myself to my *Goddess Codes*, while simultaneously allowing my drive and ambition to lead. I take action potently and when it feels the most aligned. I lean more into surrender, I practice the art of doing less, and I embody *The Art of Receiving* (coming at you next chapter-wink wink). I decided that if and when I do "hustle"– I will feel really good about it, my work ethic will BE life giving. I decided to bask in the aliveness and momentum of action taking–but never out of the illusion of pressure or "not enoughness". I intentionally make moves…I take action–but never from a place of scarcity or lack, but rather from a place of creativity and aliveness. *I operate in regenerative action NOT extractive production.* Devotion in life, love, and wealth has changed everything for me. Manifesting the tangible and the intangible has never felt SO GOOD! I am more alive than ever: in love, purpose, path, and service. I can shamelessly declare my wants and needs, while simultaneously releasing the control and pressure to make it all happen. **I know I'm not alone.**

As we come to the end of another juicy and full chapter…
I want to lock in these important points. As you read through the remainder of this chapter, really drop in. Really be present, and really devote yourself to this work. Devote yourself to understanding and integrating these words. Let this chapter imprint on you. *Let it be lived, felt, and experienced–fully.*

Breathe in. Breathe out. Open up. Receive.
I'm not alone, and neither are you, Babe.
I invite you to open into this divine receptivity in a life of
DEVOTION.
Supported in having it all.
Surrendered to the path.

You were designed perfectly. Your wanting is sacred. Your detachment is sacred. You get to have it all. **Having it all and feeling fucking good while doing it…It comes down to devotion.** Devotion to your highest timeline–a timeline of infinite possibility. Devotion to surrender. **You ACTUALLY trust the unfolding.** No oppressed timelines. No rushed timelines. No forced timelines. No pressure...*ONLY you and your Highest Timeline.* Devotion is nuanced–an individual dance. This harmonization looks different on all of us...***Ultimately, it feels like leading yourself, while allowing yourself to be led.*** Devotion IS your most innate attraction point. Devotion is a harmonizing of your divine femme and masc. Devotion is a lifestyle, a path and a journey to integrate, and further evolve. ***Devotional living evolves with you.*** You embody ease, certainty, and pure alignment in manifestation. You give and receive in harmony. Your yin and yang are balanced and you are a powerful *CO* creator in this life.

Devotion is created through harmonizing your Unfuckwithableness, going after your juiciest desires, elevating your alignment, taking the potent necessary action, dropping fully into surrender, and trusting in the timing of it all. Being so whole and complete AND deeply desiring more.
Owning it. Claiming it. Receiving it.

Reflect, journal and meditate on the following:
Breathe in. Breathe out.

1. What are you devoted to?
2. What is your devotional path?
3. What is your PURPOSE here on Earth?
4. Are you devoted to it?
5. What desires are you devoted to?
6. What service are you devoted to?
7. **Are you devoted no matter what?**

Remember–when you TRUST yourself you can TRUST the divine unfolding of this life.
Now, I want you to begin to understand your yin and yang as parts of yourself...parts that are in a sacred union. They require intimacy, communication, and reciprocal support to thrive. Your

yin is like your inner child or your divine femme–your yang is like your inner conscious parent or your divine masc. This all being said…reflect on the following. **How can you deeply support yourself–WITHIN yourself?**

1. What does my inner child need from my conscious parent?
2. What does my human need from my soul?
3. What does my divine feminine need from my divine masculine?

*in these dynamics you're flowing between setting safe containers, taking aligned action, and having the space to trust, surrender and receive

Reflect on the following in your journal or in a quiet meditative seat…

1. What will "Leading yourself while allowing yourself to be led" look like for you on your journey?
2. What will "being more submissive" or surrendering more look like for you on your journey?

You lead yourself and allow yourself to be led.

DRIPPING in desire
Open and Ready

Fully Receptive

DEVOTION

Take all the time you need to do the belief work, trust work, and surrender work required to ensure you *actually* trust the unfolding of your *life by design.* **Clean up any control tactics. Clean up the pressure. Clean up the conditions and barricades that you have placed on your desires.** *Clean up the rush..and actually lean in to surrender.*
Breathe in. Breathe out.

Devotion to this life…

It's ALL unfolding
p e r f e c t l y.

The "work" is actually trusting and knowing that,

Loving reminder ...

Wherever you are is where you're meant to be.
It's all adding up.
It's all unfolding for you.

*Enjoy the space between where you **are and** where you **want** to be.*

*This space then becomes... where you **want** to be...*

*and that **is** magnetism.*

We are never really in control…

How are you going to respond to the shifts?

You asked for Divine Intervention ...

Now it's time to open up to it.

Receive it fully.

Move with it.

Trust the unfolding.

When moments get difficult– lean further in

Lead with Love.

When moments feel light and full of pleasure–lean further in

Lead with Love.

I promise You… the universe doesn't fuck up.

It's all adding up.

It's all happening FOR You.

CHAPTER 9

THE ART OF RECEIVING

Every inch of you was designed for pleasure.

Efforting does not equate to results, Babe–alignment does. Our very nature as humans with an inner divine feminine is to MAGNETIZE that in which we desire through *beingness.* The *Art of Receiving* is a set of pleasure and wealth codes that have integrated into my consciousness and have been utilized to support countless individuals who have come into my world. *In this chapter–I bring these codes to you.* Your nature is a state of homeostasis, a state of ease…a state of wellbeing. I will use the term, "your nature" as a means of describing what is NATURAL for you. What is a natural way or state of being–the path of least resistance *is* your nature. **Your nature is service and receptivity in harmony.** Your nature is *flow.* You are your most magnetic self when you focus on your *beingness.* Your magnetism exists in your *ripe fullness.* Your innate fertility, openness, and vitality *is* the attractor…to all in which you desire. **Your nature is *being* the co-creator…both creating AND *receiving* the bounty of this life.** No matter who you are or how you identify–you have an innate divine feminine. You have a nature that is open and receptive to co-create with the universe. ***Efforting isn't required.*** Your very nature *gets* to be a state of *"allowing".*

Efforting doesn't yield results…Alignment does.

There are laws of receptivity, laws of the universe, and laws of energy. These laws are scientifically proven in the study of quantum physics. All of us (on some level) can relate to moments in our life where we felt incredibly magnetic. Things just fell into place…times when it all just felt—easy. That magnetism was based in our beingess NOT in our 'efforting' or producing. We can all relate to times when we felt unstoppable, open, flowy, receptive to our desires, and it didn't feel *hard*. *Ease is our nature.* **Efforting and producing is an old outdated construct…a wound and illusion of separation.** *It's meant to be easy.* The only "hard work" is the undoing, deconditioning, and reprogramming of the old outdated cycles. There are moments of edges—yes. Growth occurs outside of the comfort zone, afterall. There is ongoing devotion, and devotion takes work. But the overall energy of true alchemy, ascension, pleasure, and receptivity exists in the frequency of *ease*. Of course there are edges to your evolution, but the actual moments of receptivity (where you actually receive what you want) exist in the state of ease. The baseline frequency of the Unfuckwithable, Iconic, and High Level Individual is an energy of **doing less and having more.** When it comes to the *Art of Receiving*…your only job is to open up. Open up and surrender. **Allow the desires that are already circulating in your vortex…to land.** I will talk about what I call "soft landing strips" later in this chapter. For now just be here with Me… Receive this moment—breathe in, breathe out…open up. **Get 1% more receptive.** We are about to dive into the very foundation of *receptivity* and that is…*pleasure*. But first, a little back story on the "why" of *"The Art of Receiving"*…

My life transformed when I actually integrated these codes and naturally embodied this way of being. **I began existing as the woman who *desired* to be so well taken care of, AND the woman who knew that she *would be*.** No conditions, no rules, no limits or capacities as to how this would look. I just decided. I have abundant desires, I have standards of receiving and I decided that the universe would respond to me with full support. *I decided that life chose me, so I'm going to choose me.* I decided that efforting, swimming upstream, and trying *hard* was not the answer. I decided that my unique gifts, my individual nature, my inner truths, and personal power would be the embodied frequency in which everything would respond to…*not* my productivity. I decided that I would be supported infinitely by all the supportive energies that circulate me (and yes they circulate you too). I decided that I would be supported by these energies while I built my empire of joy, wealth, and basked in the infinite possibility–all this, in my purest alignment. **I held onto the truth that I am a woman who is powerful as fuck…AND I don't have to do it all alone.** I am bold, brave and courageous. I am powerfully aligned in my action AND I am a woman who deeply desires to be supported. **I decided that *I am supported* and would begin to see life through that lens.** Supported by love, money, and supported by source consciousness. **"*All that is*" exists to support me and I exist to support *all that is*.** There is *no separation,* and my receptivity is simply the acknowledgment of that. My life is now a walk of *"Thank You More Please"* energy…I catch myself daily, smiling REALLY big to myself, as I live and experience a reality that is so *fluid.* So abundant–so full. I live a reality where I know I am supported. I live a reality of overflowing love, pleasure, joy, and wealth. Not long ago, this reality would have been just a visualization–now it is my material reality. And…it just keeps getting better.

I want to talk to you a little bit about my journey getting *"here"*. **The journey that created Me, *the queen of Unfuckwithable action AND receptivity.*** If you picked up this book in the first place you are likely a *high achieving Bad Ass* as well. Willing to take action, willing to leap, and open to trusting that the net will appear. You are willing to do the necessary work required–in actualizing your dreams. My bet is that the slowness, the feminine urge of nothingness, the receptivity, the doing less however…is where your edges and challenges actually *live*. The thought of 'doing less' may bring up the *most* resistance yet…as it goes against everything you *learned* to become. **It's time to remember…it's time to come undone.** *The Art of Receiving is your very nature.* It is an embodiment that allows for an Unfuckwithable life–where everything you want, wants you. The *Art of Receiving* is an unconditional frequency…there are no rules or limitations as to what you can have, or how you can have it. There is no forcing or efforting—there is only pure alignment. ***This alignment isn't only your bold inspired action, but it also includes your innate ability to lean back into pure nothingness and receive.*** The next few chapters will go into the details of my own personal journey from burnt out and doing wayyy too much, into luxury receptivity and doing less. Within these chapters I trust and know that your own journey will begin to resonate, and you too will begin to heal your internalized productivity wounds and old programs of misaligned hustle. These next few paragraphs will shine light on your unique path as a high achieving individual and shine light on where you may be depriving yourself, and denying yourself of the rest and regenerative practices that your body so deeply needs and desires. **The *Art of Receiving* really is an art...and there is a fuck tonne of deconditioning and reprogramming that is required in the process.**

On our journey together in this chapter I will guide you into the unlearning and *hold you* through the healing. We will dive deep into rewiring, re-programming and deconditioning the misaligned hustle, internalized trauma, and fear of "not enoughness" with every last word on these pages. We will heal the productivity wound and return to your innate harmony as a divine being. **I will guide you into TRUE Unfuckwithableness—which is the ULTIMATE self love.** This means loving ALL parts of ourselves—even our "lazy", "unproductive", and deemed "un-loveable" parts. You will actually come to find that these "less productive" parts of you are actually the missing ingredients, and the nourishment that your energetic frequency and material capacity *requires* to get you to your next level. **We will begin to understand the true power in our sacred rest...and not just the "rest" that society deems as acceptable.** A new paradigm of rest where your very existence and purpose is being fuelled in an ongoing, revitalizing, and nourishing manner. Not just the "rest" parts of ourselves that meditate, journal, and stretch... not just the productive rest parts that we are consciously attributing to our success (yoga, guided breathwork etc.), but the *rest* parts of ourselves that live in the true *nothingness*. The restful activities that seemingly have nothing to do with any form of self development or spiritual awakening. The restful activities that are deemed "lazy, irresponsible and procrastinatory". *What I have come to discover is that the rich nothingness is actually the most nourishing and productive rest that you can take.*

Our egoic and controlling parts of ourselves love to disguise our true vulnerabilities and old programs. I see this in the high achievers who pretend they're taking 'rest' when they're actually meditating, doing yoga and breathwork to achieve their goals. As if they aren't worthy of just simply resting...resting without a purpose. *There are sneaky layers to this–I know this because I lived this.* I used to only allow myself rest when it was manifestation meditations, a massage for my body optimization or guided breathwork to release something in me so I could create space for more. Rest was a means to an end... a means to achieve more–always seeking–even in the "rest". This was so extractive in nature...disguised as self loving. The truth is–all of these incredible life-giving activities (yoga, meditation, breathwork etc.) are fucking fabulous–but they are not rest. They are not forms of clean–pure–rest. There's nothing wrong with these activities. They were absolutely forms of bettering myself (and to this day I live for these practices all day long). What I know now however, is that these practices aren't *true rest*...they are activities, and they are *work.*

My conscious meditation, yoga classes, breathwork practices etc etc...all of these modalities that I was doing regularly, I was considering my *rest.* I tricked my internal *high achieving productivity whore* that I was 'resting'...when really I was just infusing my productivity and obsession with self development into my rest. I wondered why I was fatigued, burnt out and experiencing the energetic and physiological symptoms of low grade stress when my days were seemingly restful and broken up with these nourishing activities. These activities were wonderful for me, and they still are. **The problem was, I was only allowing myself the 'rest' that I considered to be *productive*.** In that reality...I was not fully receiving. In that reality I was still being controlled by the illusion of separation. In that reality I was attempting to control outcomes. In that reality I was denying the part of myself…who just wanted to rest to rest. The part of me who needed to know she was loved, supported and worthy for simply– existing. I would only rest as a means of spiritual or self development. That rest isn't rest– that rest is not pure, clean uninterrupted nothingness. **That rest was still a means to an end and therefore extractive in nature.** It is what I call, the *"nothingness rest"* that actually serves your feminine nature. *It is the nothingness rest that actually opens you up to receiving.* You are worthy of rest because you are worthy–period. You are as they say "a human being…not a human doing". **The fact is that when you truly honor this nothingness you WILL naturalize more material results in your reality because you have created the space for it–*you are truly open.*** The paradox now is that I don't want you to do it (nothingness rest) because it is productive and will lead to more results, I want you to do it because *your body wants it.*

Nothingness rest in actuality is the MOST
productive thing you can do…
AND I hope you just do it for the fuck of it.

No agenda, no controlling outcomes, no "if I do this, I get that"...
No more fucking control, and contortion of self, and call it "rest".
Rest is rest.
Yoga is yoga.
Meditation is meditation.
Breath work is breathWORK.
And Rest is REST.

Nothingness IS the catalyst of creativity and the incubator of divine intervention. The nothingness is the space where the magic can actually land without control or interference. "Nothingness Rest" is: staring blankly into space, naps, falling into bliss as you watch the stars, cuddling and kissing slowly with no sense of urgency, one too many episodes of your favorite show, accidentally falling asleep at the beach, or losing track of time watching the waves crash in. These acts of nothingness are so fucking rich in our experience of life on Earth...our existence as BEINGS. Our reality as souls having a human experience depends on our BEINGNESS. **Rest because it feels fucking good, not because it will get you somewhere.** Do it with no other agenda than for the fuck of it. That my love is living in alignment with the *Art of Receiving...and* THAT my love is BEING Unfuckwithable. Your ultimate self love, receptivity, and Unfuckwithable-ness is you LOVING yourself wholly and completely. Loving the cookie and chip eating version of you as much as the pilates going green juice sipping version of you. Loving the napping and Netflix watching part of you that just wants to BE. Unbothered, alone, and at rest. **These parts of you are *as* instrumental in your success as the meditating, aligned action taking, and outwardly expressing parts of yourself– trust that, know that...let that land.** *Breathe in. Breathe out.* You are worthy. *Breathe in. Breathe out.* You are loved and supported. *Breathe in. Breathe out.* It is ALL adding up–always. I invite you through this chapter and beyond to continue the practice of loving *all of you*–whole, fully, and completely. *Practice unraveling into nothingness and opening up to the divine receptivity that is your nature.*

Why do I feel the need to include the definitions of "clean rest" / "nothingness rest, and spend all this time and energy on reprogramming the conditioned, extractive, and capitalistic ideologies that are stripping you from your very nature? **Well babe, many of us are still straddling the paradigms of *alignment and conditioning.*** The straddle between what is actually *life giving* for us versus what is extractive / what has been conditioned into us. I am *finally* fully feeling the actualization of my individual new paradigm in terms of rest, leaning back, and doing less. I've been working on this reprogramming for a long fucking time, and I too still straddle. I spent YEARS in what I call "misaligned hustle"–-and don't get me wrong, I created some incredible results from that. **Then, there came a time where my body whispered...*and then she screamed*.** The extractive ways stopped working for me. I couldn't sustainably create impact, serve, lead, and receive in the ways that were aligned with my infinite potential. *Something had to change.* I have now created a reality where my success is based on my purest alignment, and that alignment is a deep and true honoring of my physical and energetic system. There is no forcing or "efforting". **The reason I can teach so potently on the *Art of Receiving,* is because I have been entrenched in the *contrast* of it for many years.** I experienced burnout so detrimental I lost my menstrual cycle for almost an entire year, had countless injuries, adrenal fatigue,...you name it–my body was begging me to slow down. **Begging me to step into my *true essence* as a divine feminine, receptive, naturally open and surrendered being.**

It took time. **It takes time.** I still catch myself deviating from my alignment. I, myself, have spent the last few years working on undoing, unlearning, and HEALING the productivity wound that has been a very real challenge in my life. I have spent years through highschool, college, university, and my working years being CELEBRATED for my accomplishments, for my achievements...for "doing". All the while behind that external validation, conventional success, and seemingly happy life...my body was BEGGING for TRUE clean rest. Again, I am fucking proud of who I was and what I created through efforting. I bask in the acknowledgment and celebration of my hard work and success–I really do. Truthfully, a big part of my story is being empowered as an Unfuckiwthable woman who takes action and creates with ease. A woman who gives, serves, and produces like a fucking machine. I am a high level woman and action has never been a challenge for me. **But what is truly Unfuckwihtable for me now...is knowing that I am whole, complete, worthy, and MAGNETIC just because I exist.** My beingness, my rest...me doing less is more magnetic than my forcefulness ever was. **My Unfuckwithableness now is knowing that there is more power in the flick of my aligned finger...than any amount of misaligned hustle would ever yield.** Hours producing, forcefulness, trying hard (when it really isn't required) is a paradigm I left behind, and continue to leave behind. **My power lives in my ability to *allow and surrender* to the flow**. My ability to trust in something higher, bigger, and more powerful is what guides me. I am Unfuckwithable because I know how supported I am, and that I don't have to do it all alone. **The reclamation of my innate divine feminine nature as a RECEIVER in this life…is my greatest realization and my biggest upgrade thus far on my journey.**

For many years I had a REALLY hard time resting for long periods of time (and even short periods at that). As I have stated…I could rest if my mind perceived it as "productive". I could attend a retreat, ceremony or yoga class…knowing that it would serve my manifestations. There were always reasons…It was never just resting for the fuck of it. **There had to be conditions for my rest…**If I do XYZ, then I can rest. If I rest then I will have more energy for XYZ. If I meditate I will be 'higher vibe' to actualize XYZ. **I had a really hard time resting for the fuck of it.** Being okay with being unproductive and "lazy" was simply not in my wheelhouse for many years. I actually had a tonne of judgment toward the word lazy and anyone who embodied it…again–the wound and illusion of separation. I built a tonne of success on the concepts and foundations of taking action, motivation, inspiration, and forward movement. I absolutely still stand by these concepts to this day, I am absolutely still a forward moving, action taking boss bitch…but now I know and embody the nuance. The nuance that clean uninterrupted rest with no productive agenda is the most success catalyzing rest you can take…AND, it is to be experienced from a place of desire…not a place of manipulation. Read that again. **The nuance being that the forward movement is so much more effortless and efficient when you do it from a place of alignment.** There is a time for action and there is a time for nothingness. You don;t have to "earn" rest. You don't have to do XYZ to be deserving of regenerative, healing and nourishing rest. You are worthy–period.

Again… *"Efforting doesn't yield results, alignment does".*

What I REALLY want to bring into your consciousness now is the medicine in *doing less.* Slowing down and enjoying the journey. **Practicing stillness and being content with your unique, unrushed process.** Being so proud of yourself for a day of napping and reading. Finding success in an afternoon of nothingness. Being so whole and complete with or without the list of accomplished "to do tasks". Loved whole and completely by you, for you…for just BEING you. *I've been working on this, and I continue working on this.* I'm complex and multidimensional–we all are. I have waves of massive production and energy. I also have waves of stillness, nothingness, and slowness. I love my high energy. I love progress and success. I love my innate ability to thrive, to GIVE, to share, to inspire, and to connect outwardly. But there is SO much medicine in the nothingness. For me specifically, as a 6/2 self projected projector in my human design, and a Taurus sun in my astrology, there is a TONNE of medicine for me in the *delicious hermitting alone time.* (If you don't know anything about astrology or human design–no worries babe. We are all designed uniquely and my specific design is even more attuned to rest than most–I need it more than say a 5/1 generator)--go ahead and google these words and phrases if you feel called to, and discover your own human design and astrological chart) I am so grateful for my innate BEINGNESS that wakes up grateful, happy, excited, and joyful for the day ahead. I love the fact that I crave movement and that it's easy for me to get to yoga or to the gym daily. It's easy for me to make people happy. It's easy for me to be the one everyone counts on and it's easy for me to count on myself. I SO effortlessly love these parts of me. I am, also, learning to love sleepy Haley, lazy Haley, unproductive Haley... I am learning to love Me for all of me. **And babe…I invite you to learn to love ALL of you.**

True unconditional self love is an ever evolving journey of inward discovery–you are fluid–always changing. You will come to discover new parts of yourself. Parts that are easy to love, and parts that take a little more work. I am continuously learning to love the ever evolving "unproductive" parts of me, and the bad ass, boss bitch parts of me. I am loving the me that just *is*–the me that just exists. I am loving the Me that isn't high vibe, happy, succeeding, accomplishing, and uplifting all the time. There is so much medicine in the nothingness and when I decided that 'nothingness' was safe and nourishing for me (and of course for my future), that alignment yielded more and more alignment. **When I made the decision to devote myself to my personal alignment–I was committing to being supported, to leaning back, to doing less, and to knowing that it was safe to surrender.** I also decided that the sides of me that I hadn't yet celebrated as 'valuable' on my path…deserved to be celebrated. **When it comes to encoding the *Art of Receiving,* we are mastering and integrating the embodiment of "unconditional worth"--you are worthy no matter what.** When you can master the ease of alignment and the richness of doing less–magic happens. You begin to operate in regenerative and life giving ways. The extractive conditioned tendencies fall away and you commit to only your personal alignment. The stillness and slowness of our bodies is nothing to rush through, or attempt to change. The lower energy days and seasons aren't a phase to hurry through–but rather a natural part of our flow, and optimal for our holistic wellbeing and success. *Our nothingness requires no urgency…It is all happening in divine order.*

When we can surrender into the slowness and the "art of doing less", we then master the *Art of Receiving.* On the other side of this slowness, is momentum cashing in. **I can promise you that by doing less you will receive more.** Being Unfuckwithable is an unconditional phenomenon where you are actualizing desires, healing, and living your best life *no matter how much you "do" or don't do.* You are worthy–period. I have discovered on my own journey (and I hope you begin to recognize it too) that we are unconditionally worthy of love, wealth, happiness, and wellbeing. We are worthy because we exist–period. This is not dependent upon how much you produce or not. You get to have what you want–because you do. In reality, you will produce *more* from a place of alignment that *actually* yields the results you desire when you do less! **All parts of you deserve equal love.** All parts of you play a role in your healing, wellbeing, and success. **To fully and completely love yourself, you must LOVE (not just accept, not just allow or tolerate) but LOVE all parts of you.** The parts of you that you haven't been conditioned to celebrate…they deserve LOVE. Your sleepy parts, unproductive parts, lazy parts, uncertain parts, scared parts, angry parts–ALL OF YOU IS WORTHY. You in your fullest Unfuckwithable essence is a reclamation of these parts– an allowing of the natural ebbs and flows of your energy in this life. You get to decide that there are no limits to your receiving…there is no separation. You get to receive, because you are worthy just as you are. You get to create, because you have gifts to share. You get to surrender, because it is safe to trust that it is all already divinely orchestrated (because it is). You get to have it all NOW. *Your "efforting" was never required, and your receptivity exists in your ability to release conditions.*

I made a radical decision to not just be of high service in this world, but to also RECEIVE in the highest, most luxurious ways. This is a high level reciprocity that I experience in my life by design, and that experience is available to you now. All the pleasure, wealth, and happiness from a foundation of reciprocal indulgence and service. *Because I want to…because I can.* Because I want to experience the desires of my heart, soul and body. Because there are material things I adore and want more of. Because I want to, because I can. I decided that my service is so high in this world, and I want to receive on the same level. There are experiences I want to experience for the first time, my receiving will allow that. I choose to live a life of ongoing evolution and expansion of my energetic and material standards, so I decided a high level of reciprocity was required. **I decided, and so can you.** I am the queen of service and the queen of receptivity. I serve with devotion and receive with ease. I focus on *rich self care* and rich service of others. I focus on unwinding, nourishing myself and nourishing those in my world. I have mastered the *Art of Receiving* and you will too. This is a new paradigm of devotional giving, rich self care and high level reciprocity. Infinite gifting and infinite opening. Leaning back and receiving, while devotionally serving and giving.

> *When you perceive yourself as valuable…*
> *Luxury becomes a very natural standard.*

Luxury becomes a very natural standard, when you actually value yourself and prioritize feeling good. Luxury is your standard, when you prioritize rest and receiving as a critical part of your success journey. You are in the energy and flow of luxury, **when you focus on your well-being, self care, mindset, wellness, holistic success, pleasure and JOY–*results naturally flow.*** When you perceive yourself as valuable, luxury becomes a very natural standard. Wealth will become natural. Wellness will become natural. Abundance in ALL areas (friendships, money, experiences, love, intimacy, recognition etc etc) becomes NATURAL. Let's really encode this now..lock this in. Lock in and understand your high value in the world. I want you now to SEE yourself as a valuable individual, with valuable: energy, gifts, insight, wisdom, skills– SEE yourself in the fullness of you. Celebrate you. When you value yourself in this way, babe…you naturalize MORE. Affirm: I have an Unfuckwithable embodied confidence, self love, and a KNOWING of who I am AND what I deserve. I have a KNOWING of my unique power, my skills. and gifts. I have a knowing that no matter what, I am of great value to the world and I am ALWAYS available to receive. *Breathe in. Breathe out.* **You are valuable, babe!** Affirm that. Believe that. Know that. Let that encode into every cell in your body. I see YOU only in your highest timeline, now you get to fully see yourself there. The highest timeline of your expression, well being, pleasure, success, wealth, embodied happiness is what we are here for– an orgasmic life. I see you there. I hold you there. I will continue to lead you there as you also hold yourself in this alignment. You are of great value to this world. Your very existence is VALUABLE. And when you perceive yourself as valuable...luxury becomes a natural standard. **Your material world wants to show up for you...But you have to show up for you, first.**

It's the tender care of the body and energetic system that creates results in the material world.

Let's talk about self care. It's not a buzz word or idea...it is necessary when living in alignment as a high level individual. **It's the tender care of the body and energetic system that creates results in the material world.** As an ambitious, high achieving, and driven individual your energy IS your currency—your energetic alignment IS your missing ingredient—the edge that takes you into next levels of success. Clean rest and proper self care is REQUIRED at this level of drive and ambition. There is a HIGH standard of self-care in my world, my client's worlds, and now...in your world. The self-care I'm talking about is deep body self-care, deep emotional self-care and deep spiritual self-care. Self or professionally guided facilitation of clean rest/nothingness, breath work, body work, and energy work is needed, to ENSURE top tier results and top tier wellbeing. **Rich self-care creates top tier energetics, top tier physical beingness, therefore, creating top tier results.** The Unfuckwithable archetype is an archetype of harmonization of the divine femme and the divine masc. This combination of a deep tender honoring of *"Her"* (this is what I call your pleasure body) and high level BOLD MOVES aligned action steps (that "He" / your divine masculine takes,) is what yields aligned beingness and aligned results. This harmony is you co-creating, by harmonizing the energetics of divine feminine and divine masculine—the energetics of duality that exist within you. **When we harmonize the two, we alchemize all that is.** This harmonization could look like this: Your inner divine masc notices the divine feminine's desire for a sexy night in, a night for one...You, your vibrator and the bathtub...your divine masculine creates a spacious evening schedule to ensure your inner divine feminine is taken care of. "He" gets the vibrator charging asap, he fills up the bathtub, and lights the candles…he has created the environment for "her" to rest and receive all night long. *This harmony and role play with your inner masc and inner femme is what creates a life of aligned action and open receptivity* (more on this later this chapter).

Your body was designed for pleasure.

Now, let's dive into pleasure and its role in the *"Art of Receiving"*…**Pleasure is our greatest portal to receiving and luxury receptivity is an awareness of our own innate divine feminine and her natural desires for MORE.** Her desires for beauty, fragrances, luxury, sensuality, textures, wealth…The actualization of these erotic, pleasure filled, and easeful states are **facilitated** by your healthy, aligned, divine masculine within. Pleasure…climax and receptivity go hand in hand. When we open ourselves up to the pleasure portals within our body– we elevate our electromagnetic field for receiving MORE. **The *Art of Receiving* really is an art.** It's a way of being…in flow. Being in flow with the universe, with lovers, with opportunities, with money and success. Being in flow is opening up to receive…in quantum levels, that is. We are talking about receiving that is faster and bigger than your logical mind can comprehend –It takes integration, embodiment, and ongoing upgrading. We have talked about safety in surrender and safety in the unknown. **There is also a layer of safety in receiving that *all* humans on some level must either heal, reprogram or uplevel in order to have the desires of their heart.** Trust that it is SAFE to receive. Trust that you are SAFE to lean back. Trust that you're WORTHY of having it all. This takes work and the work goes deep. But ohhhh baby, the work is soooo worth it. Luckily for you… I have made the work within this chapter (the work to master *The Art of Receiving*) pleasure packed, indulgent, restorative, and expansive. This work is life giving. This work nourishes you. *This work just makes sense to your body and your soul.* This work and the results of this work just feels natural. Together we are diving into all the codes of receiving wealth, love, and aligned opportunities. Receiving it all with ease, with a profound sense of self love, worthiness, and power. **You deserve to unwind and lean back. You deserve to receive.** You *really* deserve it.

Your body tingles from head to toe

You've lost your breath

… yet you've never felt so much sensation

e u p h o r i a

You're at peace (ahhhh…exhale)

Completely surrendered

Yet more ALIVE than ever.

p l e a s u r e

It's the state the soul chose Earth for…

The state your SOUL chose your BODY for

It's the state that generates - creates - attracts and receives MIRACLES

p l e a s u r e

Your body was *designed* for pleasure. **It's pleasure that pulled you from the bliss that your soul knew so well.** Pleasure pulled you to THIS realm. The experience to be FELT fully in your *unrepeatable* precious body. Pleasure is a sensational experience. The human body opens to the sensations of touch, taste, smell, feel, sound…pleasure creates a luxury experience. Pleasure is a part of what I call "luxury receptivity". Sensation is a natural part of your human experience. Your soul chose Earth for this experience, the material world is the land of sensation–the land of pleasure. Pleasure is experiential, and is reserved for the awakened human to experience. The human who is not rushing through the bounty that this life has to offer. More on pleasure and its connection to our unrepeatable precious bodies. Pleasure is the state that creates miracles. Pleasure amplifies innate abundance and unlocks wealth codes deep within you. Pleasure opens you up to MORE. Your body is wealth…you were made for r e a l l y nice things–*designed for pleasure.* Designed by the architect of life, *every inch of you is on purpose.* Pleasure is a cathartic experience. **Pleasure is one of the most spiritually liberating experiences you can have within the container of your human body.** Pleasure is an act of reclamation. Pleasure opens the portals to *all that is.* Pleasure is a catalyst for manifestation. Pleasure is a celebration of self. When you experience pleasure…life celebrates with you! When you experience pleasure, *the creator revels in their success.* It is a life-giving act of sensual empowerment to claim your pleasure and choose experiences that honor your pleasure body.

> **Let's take a rest now and practice opening up**
> **to our desires through our pleasure body…**
> Take a moment to feel yourself. Feel your body.
> Drop in. Now connect to your desires.
> Abundance, connection, opportunity, love, wealth,
> impact…whatever you desire more of…
> *Breathe in. Breathe out.* Can you allow
> pleasure to enter your body?
> *Better yet, can you allow yourself to **notice the***
> ***pleasure that already exists within you?***
> *Breathe in, breathe out…get 5% more*
> *receptive…open up…let it in.*

You are meant to have the best of the best. You were designed perfectly. You hold high standards for yourself, and you get to continue to elevate those standards moment to moment. You are worthy. You are divine. *You are a manifestation of God.* You are open and ready…*ready to receive.* Ready to surrender, *ready to lean the fuck back.* You are ready to HAVE the experiences, opportunities, love and money your soul truly desires. *You are ready to have it–here in the material world.* **When you honor your pleasure, you honor your desires, and you claim your dreams as *yours.*** Pleasure is an honoring of your humanness…your desire to feel, experience, and enjoy life's bounty. Pleasure honors your desire and longing for *actualized physical manifestations.* Pleasure is a healing state–pleasure can only be experienced to its peak from a space of foundation of homeostasis and regulation. *So, if you are intentionally experiencing pleasure– you are opening up to healing states of consciousness and physiology.* When you honor your desires in the material world– you not only liberate your spirit–you heal your body. When you consciously create spaces, environments and experiences that honor your pleasure body you are communicating to your body that you are safe and worthy of experiencing rich self care, pleasure and positive sensation–and this is an act of great self love. This intentional self love is an act of great healing. **And, when you heal yourself–you heal the world.**

My life changed DRASTICALLY when I learned how to receive. Specifically for me, when I learned that the *Art of Receiving was not* something I had to "turn on" –but rather a natural state for me. A state to attune to, *a way of living that I could always meet within myself.* It changed as I I remembered my innate attraction points and my innate receptivity. Innate meaning–it was nothing I had to learn, it was already inside of me…*something to be remembered.* As I learned that pleasure is my birth right and pleasure catalyzes results in my material world faster than any conscious thought or planned intention could ever catalyze. When I learned to receive and remembered the opening that pleasure allowed in my body and therefore my material world, **I instantly stopped the uphill climb.** I stopped swimming upstream and I started to embody fluidity. As I say often–"*Fluidity is an embodied state, flow is something we respond to*". The *Art of Receiving* allowed me to be *"in the flow"*. Moreso, the *Art of Receiving* allowed me to attune to the flow that already exists. *Consciously allowing, and surrendering to the flow of giving and receiving.* Recognizing the naturalness of it–*remembering it and getting out of the way.* Many high level, driven, and ambitious individuals aren't existing in the flow. Many of them are swimming upstream–efforting their way to results. Heavily in their misaligned or 'toxic' masculinity and "forcing" energy. The *Art of Receiving* codes (once integrated) allows one to flow with the nature of life and receive both energetically AND physically the bountiful abundance of the Universe. This bounty comes in the form of friendships, love, money, material wealth, joy, happiness, pleasure, opportunity etc. etc. *You name it–the bounty exists for us and it is always flowing our way.*

When we experience pleasure, we are communicating with our nervous system, our soul, spirit, and *"all that is"* that we are ready and available for *more.* The intentional pleasure communicates safety and openness within our system–we are ready to receive. We place our order with the Universe through bodily sensation. Our bodily sensations are connected to *all that is* (more on this in the Dimension of Openness chapter). Our bodily sensation–or as I like to call it "the pulse of life" communicates with other *life giving energies* that we are alive, connected and open…ready to receive. *The Art of Receiving* really is an art, there is nuance to it. There is undoing, reprogramming and self correcting involved when you fall into old extractive patterning. Conceptually it is quite simple to understand, and experienced and encoded it becomes natural. So let's encode you. *Breathe in. Breathe out.* I know we've covered a lot… and *Oh My God* am I so glad you're here with me! I know we've been taking our time with this chapter. **Art is not something to be rushed…*and neither is pleasure.*** I want to take this work slow with you, and I want you to really immerse yourself in the teachings and integrations of this chapter because the rewards on the other side of these codes are brilliant!

As I've stated…This work has changed my life. AND I am still on the journey alongside you, of upleveling and upgrading my standards and therefore opening up to new integrations to encode as I rise–this is ongoing evolution afterall. The *Art of Receiving* has allowed me to grow in love, service, and impact– beyond my wildest dreams, it keeps getting better and I feel like I'm just getting started! (eek!) **The *Art of Receiving* is the space where desires actually land.** For me this was monumental and IS monumental, because I was caught in the 'seeking energy' for so long that when I discovered the naturalness of the 'allowing' and 'letting desires actually land in my reality energy'–shit got GOOD! The soft landing strip where you are open and in true allowing is the space where the manifestation can properly "complete itself". *It really is the most important part of the process when it comes to actually HAVING what you want.* The *Art of Receiving* changed it all for me. Once encoded...I began earning more money doing what I LOVE–every day. Transforming lives effortlessly through my gifts as a psychic channel and energy medicine practitioner (in a way of such ease and effortlessness). Podcasting, writing, speaking, sharing...all effortlessly and the ease and receptivity expanded my wealth, network, community, and client base. Opportunities just came effortlessly, I was receiving the divine invitations daily and it all felt flowy and natural. My relationship to my own body became so much more tender and communicative. My body was healing and optimizing more and more, I was glowing, radiant and I felt such deep innate respect and safety within myself. My intimate relationship with my Man became deeper, sexier, more honest, more open...more reciprocal. My friendships, family life, and all forms of relating became more reciprocal because I learned how to receive. My experience of food, wine, coffee, sunshine, sex...all of it–became so much more intentional, sensual, and rewarding. **The *Art of Receiving* was not separate from any area of my life.** It continues to deeply guide how I move through each moment, day to day–I am so grateful.

I began living in true harmony. *Inhale I receive...Exhale I give–* was the vibe. My services became higher level. My devotion to give, lead, hold and facilitate became top tier. The *Art of Receiving* allowed me to deeper *devote* because I trusted in the nature of reciprocity. **I was no longer "protecting my energy", but rather entrusting in the natural flow of life.** I KNEW that my devotional service would naturalize high level reciprocity, I knew that my service was life giving because it was always coming from a place of overflow. None of it felt hard. I wasn't "efforting". I wasn't over giving or over sharing. I freely gave, and I freely received. I wasn't contorting myself to ensure everyone else was getting the most out of what I was giving. I just naturally *gave.* The quality of my work, the value, and the worth upgraded massively. **I was living in my deepest devotion to service AND making the decision that I am open and available to receive in infinite ways as well.** I intentionally decided that with this level of service, I must also learn to lean back and receive. **Resting and indulging with *PURE EMBODIED TRUST* that I was supported was *critical* in receiving.** I had to trust that it was safe to lean back, to do less…rest was essential in my embodiment of this harmonized system. These codes unlocked the remembering within myself that reciprocity is NATURAL and this is the way that all life on earth harmoniously exists. The work encoded–it's all easy and natural now. I take good care of myself and my loved ones with OVERFLOW energy. I deeply serve my clients, my community…the WORLD from a place of overflow. I serve in an energy that is truly LIFE GIVING–no extraction. This babe, is the vibe. This was the encoded *Art of Receiving* that changed it all for me. From this point forward, I just kept upgrading my levels of receiving. *I continued to naturalize higher levels of reciprocity, I naturalized exchange of energy and I naturalized fulfillment.*

The *Art of Receiving* is not just a "way of being" –it's also a belief system. The *Art of Receiving* is both a mindset embodied AND an upgraded internalized KNOWING that you are supported. ***Your entire existence becomes about doing only what feels good.*** The *Art of Receiving* allows you to trust that your beingness is enough, and you start to better understand when it's time for you to lean back. *You deepen your trust in the divine unfolding of your life.* You will begin to trust that your experience of wellbeing is of high value and that your self care is of high value– and you begin receiving in alignment with that. The *Art of Receiving* for me was both a devotion to my wellbeing AND a devotion to the actualization of my desires. **I decided that everything I wanted wants me, and that I would not sacrifice any of my wellbeing to have it.** I was making decisions based on pleasure and intuition. I was deepening into the sensations of every experience in my body, my thoughts and my physical reality. Taste, touch, smell…it all became so important. I was regularly having manifesting orgasms where I could see my vision and *feel* its actualization (yes I'm talkin' me, my vibrator, and my desires envisioned). I could see and feel the next level I was bursting into! **It was so *"felt"*.** I saw my desires, dreams and visions and I FELT them land in my body, with the widest opening and allowing. **I surrendered to the pleasure of it all manifesting.** I surrendered to the divine…surrendered to a higher plan. **I surrendered to what was truly meant for me.** No control–pure trust, THIS *is the Art of Receiving.*

When you can be devoted to actualizing your desires and simultaneously surrender to the divine unfolding of those desires…you enter magic land. A level of deep surrender and trust in YOUR personal power AND the power of a *'Higher Love'* encodes within you. **You actually trust…and then your life elevates.** Every inch of you was DESIGNED for pleasure. Pleasure in the material world, pleasure in your thoughts, pleasure in feeling into your desires and pleasure in actually experiencing them in your physical realm. **Your experience and embodiment of pleasure is the most empowering and cathartic thing you can 'do'.** Your experience of pleasure empowers you, and simultaneously empowers the world by raising the collective vibration. **Pleasure is the state that the soul came to Earth for.** Let that land, let all the bullshit and dramas of the world quiet now, and actually SEE the truth–the truth that your SOUL CHOSE EARTH TO EXPERIENCE PLEASURE. Not to rush through life with urgency–but to slow down and actually BE. Breathe into that truth–release the borrowed traumas of this hustling and bustling world and step into your true nature–*choose your New Earth, New Paradigm…CHOOSE your New World.* **Affirm this with me:**

When I take care of Me, I take care of the world. Breathe that in. When you take care of you...you serve life, and as we know already...*Life serves life all day long.* **Let your pleasure be a contribution to the world– and of life giving generosity to self.** This life giving generosity to self NATURALLY serves the collective. We are all in union, there is no separation. **Your wellbeing is collective wellbeing.** This is the *Dimension of Openness,* and nothing is separate (more on this in the next chapter). This is a oneness consciousness that creates powerful portals of collective ascension–**and it starts with you.**

The collective ascension starts with You...
Your wellbeing. Your self care. Your pleasure.
Your receptivity. Your service. Your generosity.
ALL from a grounded and high level foundation of ***overflow.***

When you're overflowing with goodness, you can't help but to spread it everywhere. *"Taken care of, and always taking care"* –is the vibe. **You are supported–infinitely.** Let that truth land– and if that doesn't feel true for you yet– then the missing ingredient is your awareness of the infinite support that is always surrounding you and within you. Your breath, your heart beat, your entire organ system is working FOR you. The sun, the air, the Earth is SERVING you now, and always. God, consciousness, spirit, the Universe is one intentional breath away–your awareness of the support is the key that unlocks the results of that support to land. You *ALLOWING* that support in, is the missing ingredient. The support is here for you now. **The *Art of Receiving* beyond the embodiment of it, is also a high vibrational and highly life-giving belief system that you get to decide to program now.** This life of high level reciprocity. A life of *aligned giving and aligned receiving*...a life of overflow. This life is of HIGH service. This life is available now–it starts with you. This life is bountiful, nourishing, healing and rewarding as fuck. I know this, I TRUST this, and I *GET* to live it. This belief system/way of life is life-giving and regenerative to all. I benefit from the rewards of this belief system, *and you get to live this way too.* By this point in the chapter, my intention for you is that you are already opening wider. Feeling into 10% more openness in your physical body, and therefore expanding your energetic capacity. *You are dialing up the overflow.* My intention for you, is that you are now leaning into surrender and the frequency of "allowing". Opening up and softening the landing strip. **The soft landing strip is where your desires softly and easefully land into your reality.**

An unobstructed and unblocked system
is an open and receptive system.

It is important to always acknowledge and empower ourselves as co creators. *We aren't doing it all alone,* we are infinitely supported AND we are responsible for being the leaders of our lives. **There is action required, and it is the aligned action that precedes the receiving.** There is a divine masculine container that *sets* the environment for receiving. There is work in the undoing and rewiring of the old "try hard" and "efforting" ways of extraction. This work requires a held intentional space set by your inner divine masc for the inner divine femme to heal and open. The soft landing strip exists once obstructions have been cleared. **There is necessary action that you must take to create an unobstructed, open and therefore receptive system.** Your job is to clear the obstructions, melt into the softness within your body. Open up your energetic capacity, widen the landing strip through deep conscious breath and allow your system to receive with ease. **The soft landing strip is a conscious alignment of both action and nothingness.** A flow between movement and lean back that opens up a clear portal of receiving. Your body AND energetic system are now stationed in the "allowing" frequency. **You have cleared obstructions, and created space for your desires to land.** There is a nuanced harmony between taking aligned action and knowing when enough is enough. The harmony of your inner divine fem and masc allow for effortless co creation.

The flow between "doing your part", and knowing when it's time to lean back. *This formula of 'flow' is unique to each of us, and we must practice BEING with ourselves to understand our individual peak alignment.*

I want you to receive. I want you to feel the rich luxury of a regulated system...of true homeostasis in the body. You deserve this opening. You are strong enough to take the necessary action, and it is safe to trust and lean back. **You are worthy of receiving the desires of your heart and basking in unrushed pleasure.** The entire world benefits from your experience of rich self care, love and pleasure. Individual, collective, and ancestral healing occurs in the embodiment and unapologetic experience of PLEASURE. Because of the dimension of openness, when we heal...we heal all life on Earth. Not only are you healing yourself, you are healing timelines of humans who went before you. Not only are you empowering yourself, you are writing new stories and changing cycles for those who will come after. You are basking in pleasure now, and you are simultaneously harmonizing yourself with the nature of the planet. You are syncing back up to the natural rhythms of Mother Earth. The *Art of Receiving* was already encoded in our DNA as earthlings and in our frequency as energetic beings. **It is our responsibility to reclaim it.** When we embody pleasure...and encode the *Art of Receiving* we are elevating the collective consciousness, and therefore the lived realities of our fellow brothers and sisters. We support all life here on Earth, and we empower the generations to come. ***This was always your nature.*** It is your turn and time now to claim it. This entire chapter is a great remembering, *simply the key to unlocking portals of receiving that are already innate within you.* The undoing, rewiring, reprogramming, and the actual work is YOU claiming your right to pleasure and abundance. The work is you deciding that ease is your nature, and that the extractive ways of existing are no longer your truth. You choose reciprocity, you choose high service, and, you CHOOSE to receive. **Taking care of YOU is of high service to the world.**

Breathe in. Breathe out…And let this land.

You receiving a lot of money is of high service to the world.
You having more orgasms is of high service to the world.
You experiencing unrushed and uninterrupted
rest is of high service to the world.
You having a big impact, and being SEEN in your
power is of high service to the world.
You overflowing in JOY & PLEASURE is of high
service to the world.

It's time to CLAIM it and it's time to LIVE it.

Let's dive into the importance of what I call "The Body portal". **We manifest through the body portal.** As spiritual beings having a human experience, we can sometimes forget the naturalization process of primal indulgences. **Sometimes we forget that our body is the portal to our greatest ascension.** When you have had your "spiritual awakening" and you are very aware of your spiritual beingness—it becomes tempting at times to "forget the body" and exist primarily in the "unseen realms". This quantum/energy field experience is fabulous and if you haven't existed there yet I highly encourage you to spend some time in the energetics of that. However…there is SO MUCH POWER in the human body. **There is an incredible opportunity for actualization, spiritual ascension, and alchemy to occur within the container of the human body.** This ascension requires your deep honoring and understanding of the body *as* spiritual. *The realm of infinite possibility is not separate from your humanness.* You get to experience the infinite realms within the body. **The *Art of Receiving* and pretty well all of my work is designed and devoted to spiritual liberation *through* the body portal.** Your SOUL CHOSE EARTH. Your soul CHOSE your BODY. And your body is the PORTAL to your ascended reality. It can be tempting to deny the body and exist only within the energetic realms when you first discover the vastness of your infinite soul. I get that…but the space I find to be the most grounded, rewarding, spiritually liberated, result yielding and fucking euphoric...is the space where my body and spirit become one. I see so many humans identifying as spiritual beings, falling into the escape of their bodies. They have an exquisite meditation practice...but they deny the body and breath work that is so nourishing to their temple and therefore their soul/spirit. They can visualize and dream with ease...but are missing the actualization piece of *actually having those desires manifest* in this precious lifetime. **Your soul CHOSE this body for this unrepeatable period of time on earth.** Why escape that? Why not integrate *all of it* within the dimension of openness? **This work is about integrating BODY and ENERGY work–they exist in UNION.** There is no separation. *Your body is the most spiritual thing about you...if you let it be.* This is the dimension of openness, babe (more on this in the next chapter).

Don't forget about your body on your Ascension Journey.

The body is the portal to your greatest receiving. There is nothing more cathartic, empowering, and PLEASURE FILLED than *having and holding* your desires. Manifesting (making real) the desires of your soul–is literally the reason why your soul chose Earth. **Your soul signed up for the physical experience.** As a NEW paradigm thought leader, psychic channel, spiritual teacher, and facilitator, it is extremely obvious to me just how spiritual the material realm really is. There is no separation, and your relationship to *all that exists* (tangible or not) IS part of your spirituality in practice. Therefore, it has become part of my life's purpose and life's work to empower spiritual beings in their experience of the material world–to be one of abundance, and integral wealth. My work brings your awareness to the "SPIRITUALNESS" of your body, the "SPIRITUALNESS" of money, and the "SPIRITUALNESS" of the tangible material world. **There is NO separation.** If it exists for you to experience (and it actually fulfills you and is instrumental in you living your highest timeline) it is GOOD FOR YOU– and therefore good for the collective. Again, spiritually placing oneself on a hierarchy of "better than" for not *desiring the material experience* is frankly an illusion of separation and an egoic distortion in itself. So Babe..simply own what you want. Claim it and get ready to receive it. You're not 'less spiritual' for wanting more money, driving a luxury car, and buying a Chanel bag. Your desires were God given–divinely placed within you, so claim them. Your desires of the physical realm may also be more experiential and sensual in nature. These more physical desires (cuddles, sex, physical intimacy, sensual pleasure etc.) are profound spiritual experiences to engage in within the containment of the human body. Your material desires may be more rustic in nature, or "more simple", like having land and wanting your own chickens. These material desires are also spiritual in nature, and still OF THE EARTH. You may desire and naturalize all of the above if you're anything like me. **The important note is that ALL desires of the material world (if they are TRUE for you) are spiritual in nature.** Your spirit is fulfilled by the achievement of your physical desires manifesting–there is no separation. *Stay in your lane and trust the desires of your heart.*

Part of the illusion of separation that many spiritual people fall into, is this escapism into 'higher realms' or 'lighter densities'. The physical realm often gets labeled as dense and painful by spiritual teachers–and it is…it can be. But when you blindly cling to the *stories of density* you miss out on the *reality of the lightness* that is here. I want to awaken you to the magic that exists in the Earth realm, so you can begin to experience the *"spirit liberation through the body portal"* that I speak of. **Some of the countless miracles of the Earth:** The soft fur of a precious new puppy, a newborn baby squeezing your finger, the effervescence of champagne on your tongue, the warmth of hot coffee on your lips, the inner tingles of sensation building up to your climax. The containment of a big and firm hug, the depth of massage, the warmth of the sun on your back, the feeling of success in your BODY as you drive your brand new car, the warm summer rain on your face, the butterflies in your belly when something magical is about to happen…you get the point…there is MAGIC and LIGHTNESS available on Earth, and we get to exist within multiple realms all at once. The most sensual, healing and activating experience for your inner divine feminine however, is to actually **have and hold her desires.** To actually experience it in the physical material world. *We are of the earth and anything that can be experienced here is a manifestation of God.* **Your job is to discern what material desires are true for you in this lifetime.** What material desires actually fulfill you? What physical experiences actually nourish you? The architect of life created you and created everything that exists within nature–there is no separation. You can trust your desires, they are true for you. **They are natural for you, and it actually takes more resistance and work to deny yourself of them than it does to just surrender to their divine place in your life.** If you want it you get to have it. Let love be your discernment as you decide what your TRUE desires are. *Remember…we manifest what is actually true for us.* It is written in our soul contract…written in the stars. We can't fuck it up…we can only slow it down. So…Babe–get the fuck out of the way, decide what you want and allow it in. *No matter how "spiritual" or "3D" it may seem–if it's true for you–it's meant for you. We will be going into understanding if a desire is "true for you" in the coming paragraphs.* Breathe into the harmony of where you are now, and where you are headed. Grateful, present, yet always moving forward.

Pleasure is the portal to your greatest receiving.

When we open ourselves up to the pleasure portals within our body–we elevate our electromagnetic field for receiving MORE. We are communicating with our nervous system, our soul, spirit and ALL that *is*. Important note: I have an honors clinical degree in Kinesiology and 6 years of post secondary studies under my belt in anatomy, physiology. I have studied the nervous system, organ systems, and the entire human body in DEPTH and DETAIL. Our pleasure experience is closely connected to the nervous system. Our experience of pleasure is determined by sensation that is coordinated between our sensory receptors and our nervous system in communication. Much like receiving money, gifts, love etc... pleasure is a state that requires opening and therefore a healthy parasympathetic nervous system. Pleasure is an experience that facilitates *opening*. In contrast–a constricted body is not open to receive. Our sensory organs and our sex organs receive parasympathetic innervation that creates dilation therefore increasing blood flow to the surfaces of our pleasure centers. This parasympathetic response is only available to an open and receptive system. An open receptive system is a system that is experiencing parasympathetic responses through perceived homeostasis. This homeostasis is our energy of rest, leaning back and surrendering. *Are you starting to understand now how it is all connected?* Pleasure is our greatest portal to receiving. Luxury receptivity is an awareness of our own innate divine feminine and her natural desires for beauty, luxury, and all in all...more. The feminine is always yearning for more. Our level of openness and homeostasis play a massive role in our ability to receive. Pleasure, climax, and receptivity go hand in hand.

Up until this point I have been speaking about feminine energetics, not specifically about female bodies. Whether you are anatomically male or female or somewhere along the spectrum– you have an inner divine feminine and an inner divine masculine energetic component within yourself. Now I want to talk about the unique role that pleasure plays and the respective nuances and challenges of it for women. Pleasure, climax and orgasm (specifically in female bodies) is much more nuanced and complex anatomically. Receptivity which we know to be directly linked to our physiological state and energetic capacity is also a more nuanced conversation for women. Opening up, surrendering and RECEIVING anything is a multifactorial conversation–based on various vectors of oppression that many women have experienced. For many generations there has been a cultural imbalance in women's empowerment and experience of personal power. Empowerment as we know, is directly linked to pleasure, the *Art of Receiving* and financial power dynamics at large.

Because of this, there is reprogramming and evolution required individually and collectively. There is healing required on various levels. It is nuanced to be a woman effortlessly receiving money...it is nuanced to be a woman effortlessly experiencing orgasm. There are historical, societal and physiological nuances at play. There are connections between pleasure, money and power...Feel me? **This is a high level and high quality conversation to be having, and there is A LOT to acknowledge.** I will not be able to touch it all within the confines of these pages–but please begin to recognize the individual nuances and multifactorial nature of this conversation. Begin to insert your own past, present, ancestral and societal experience, meaning and reality into this conversation to better understand where your own healing and work lies. Begin to recognize where your empowerment exists and where you can support the collective rise in TRUE coherence and unity.

I am personally very well positioned to bring the topic of receiving pleasure and receiving money (insert whatever tangible desire you have) to the forefront. I took 4 years of back to back schooling of social justice courses, women's studies and deeply studied social determinants of health–*informing me in depth of the nuances of individual lived realities with money, support and ultimately one's ability to trust.* I have a clinical degree in Kinesiology where I understood human anatomy, biomechanics, physiology and function like the back of my hand. My experience studying the human body in post secondary, clinical placements, university, college and in understanding the nervous system, sensory organ systems and my studies and unique understanding of the psyche with the nature of my life's work, client base, and education. I work predominantly with high achieving women who are operated in a top tier of financial success, impact and life's purpose. I have also spent years working with a client base who were in the depths and magic of experiencing motherhood, the intricacies, challenges and beauty of it was my work to facilitate. I worked in pre and post natal fitness and pelvic floor physiotherapy where I began to understand natural cycles, physiology, and the biomechanics of the female sex organs. I also quickly understood the impact psychology, emotion, perceived safety, and pleasure plays in the biomechanics and physiology of a woman's body.

My intricate lived experience as a wealthy woman who has done her fair share of deconditioning and reprogramming places me *here* with empowerment. I live in a healthy, optimized and thriving body that allows me to regulate. I have been well positioned in life with an incredible family system, parenting, mentors and friendships. I have been so empowered and privileged and I have also experienced the overwhelm of losing trust, living in scarcity, having the rug ripped out from underneath me completely shattering my understanding and safety. I experienced what is known as *'sexual dysfunction'*, I had such intense ongoing co-contraction in my pelvic floor I couldn't even insert a tampon, let alone be intimate. My body closed up–I experienced the physiological and psychological trauma of feeling like you cannot trust anyone, let life itself. I immersed myself into healing, spiritual, emotional, physical support to reclaim my pleasure, my power, my right to holistic wealth. **I have done the deep work, and I have re-learned to trust.** Now, I live a life of wealth, flow, alignment, life-giving intimacy, deep love, stunning relationships, thriving wellbeing and I have an Unfuckwithable trust in the knowing that I am INFINITELY supported by *all that is*. I have more orgasms than I can count on a monthly basis. I have lived and studied the connection between the physical body, emotional and energetic state and one's ability to RECEIVE. *I have experienced co-contraction within my finances and within my physical body.* I have seen first hand how *constriction energy* differs from *allowing energy* in terms of both orgasm and receiving more money. I am super fucking passionate about the interconnectedness of pleasure and wealth, AND, I am insanely passionate about empowering women around the topic of pleasure and trust!

I always knew I would be a best selling author, well known, and well regarded for my insights. Since I can remember, I planned on writing a book and I thought my first book was going to be called

"The Coregasm" ...Titled after my first accidental orgasm–yes accidental. Now, I have experienced and continue to experience over 5 *different types* (yes there are different types) of orgasm...on purpose (wink wink) and regularly. Talk about *"Thank You More Please"* vibes. At the time of my first and accidental orgasm...I was doing lower abdominal exercises (leg lifts to be exact) and with one too many repetitions *(or just the right amount rather)* I experienced my first *"blended exercise induced orgasm"*. I was just a young high schooler. I serendipitously and honestly accidentally had my first orgasm, while doing a lower ab exercise. God bless lower leg lifts. *So, unlike most high school girls who unfortunately spend a lot of time engaging in performative pleasure, I was blessed with an accidental orgasm early on which set my standards HIGH for what I, and my beautiful vulva, was/were available for.* As I'm sure you can imagine, I spent a lot of time on my yoga mat attempting to recreate the experience many times over. Now it's automatic, on demand, and something I can achieve within 30 seconds of doing that specific exercise. I have the coregasm mastered–which is why I was inspired to write a book on it. So, it's only fair that I include a small portion of the pleasure chapter to what I call–*"the coregasm"*. Now, I have countless types of orgasms through self pleasure, time with my partner, time with my vibrator, time on the yoga mat and time with just my breathwork. I have mastered pleasure and it is a self mastery that continues to evolve. **The interconnectedness between personal pleasure and wealth energetics and actualization is so closely interconnected that it blows my mind.** The biggest relationship, I would say, is based on the nervous system. *When your body feels safe, it opens and when it opens you can effortlessly receive–more.* More pleasure, more opportunity, more money etc etc. This is a very good time to start communicating safety *to and with* yourself through your body and energy system. Start self pleasuring even in simple ways like running your hands across your collarbone, or tugging your own hair. **I encourage you to land in the playground that is your body and begin to infuse your desires into the experience.**

Breathe in. Breathe out. This gets to be easy.
Place your order with the universe, open up, receive…
and say "Thank You More Please" as it drops in.

You heard me mention "manifesting orgasms" earlier and I bet you couldn't wait to dive deeper into that. So, here we go…manifesting orgasms are a common practice that I include in my weekly self care. Whether I'm receiving from my partner or having a solo date with my vibrator, I consciously tune in to pleasure, desire, and receiving. I tune into the sensuality of the physical pleasure I am experiencing. I am tuning into the desires of my heart and soul. I tune into the frequency of receiving–*I associate this with receiving penetration, climax or pleasure in general.* **I begin to create nuanced circuitry between my brain body connected and the pleasure I receive being connected to receiving my desires.** This circuitry again–is nuanced, complex, and individual based on who is experiencing it. When I am experiencing pleasure…be it sexual, sensual or experiential. I am consciously linking the experience to desires manifesting. **I am consciously programming my mind-body connection to associate pleasure with receiving. I am wiring my brain to feel safety in the opening, safety in the space between pleasure, and climax and safety in the experience of having and holding** *more.* This is why *intentional pleasure work* is SO healing and SO cathartic. **Pleasure work is reclamation work–it is deeply empowering.** I have been leading a women's retreat called, *"The Art of Receiving"* for years that is all about the healing and catharsis in pleasure. The work I do within that retreat has inspired this chapter. *Pleasure is a nuanced topic and experience–it can be complicated based on individuals' pasts, histories, and traumas.* Whether you have experienced sexual trauma or money trauma–*your body has kept score, and has likely closed off for safety.* This makes sense–this is actually a safety response. **The reclamation work here is around creating safety in the opening, safety in pleasure and therefore safety in receiving.**

You are worthy and deserving of healing–worthy
and deserving of empowering yourself.
No matter what happened to you–you are safe now,
and you can reclaim your pleasure.
You can now reclaim your experience of receiving through this
work.

Let's dive into *creation portals* and how they relate to pleasure and the *Art of Receiving*. The lower energy centers in our bodies are the centers tied closely to our physical experience of pleasure. Interestingly enough, they are also closely tied to our ability to generate and receive financial wealth, our experience of safety and our reality of stability. Our lower centers are the Sacral Chakra (our pleasure and creativity chakra) and our Root chakra (our safety and reproductive chakra). The sacral chakra can be connected to, with a gentle yet firm touch to the lower belly and womb space. This chakra can be balanced, unlocked, and optimized through pleasure practices. Self pleasure opens creativity portals within this chakra that can be generative and regenerative in our wealth production and our experience of freedom, joy, and fun in this lifetime. Our root chakra can be connected to, with a gentle yet firm touch to the base of our spine and/or the vulva, or groin region. This chakra can be balanced, unlocked, and optimized through pleasure practices. **Conscious self pleasure creates safety, regulation, and the experience of trust and surrender within the body.** When the body feels safe to experience pleasure, the body opens up, and is better optimized to receive material wealth. We can balance the sacral and root chakra through not only pleasure, but also other nervous system regulating practices that we will go into in the coming paragraphs.

Self pleasuring is an experience that can be as *sexual* or as *asexual* as you desire. Self pleasuring can literally be you sitting on the grass, in the sun, slowly eating a juicy peach and letting the fresh air kiss your cheeks. **Self pleasuring can be felt in any conscious creation of an environment that nourishes your**

sensual experience–be it touch, taste, smell or sight. I personally am a 6/2 self projected projector and a Taurus sun who has life partnered with a Scorpio, Projector, High End Chef and Artist. *I think you can imagine the importance, and the diversity of pleasure in my life.* But without borrowing any ideologies of what pleasure is based on my experience–start to self inquire and get curious about what pleasure is for you, then start self-pleasuring– often. **There is nothing more Unfuckwithable as mastering pleasure–on your own terms.** The physical vessel, that is your stunning body, is capable of pleasure that will blow your mind. *Pleasure that will ignite fires within you to create, to express, to feel, to awaken, and to LIVE so very fully.* Pleasure is foundational in living in *lust* with life. Pleasure is a portal that opens you up to massive receiving. Safety in receiving more and fulfillment in receiving what is actually true for you. The mind-body connection is so *intricate* and so *experienced* in our self pleasure journey–*get curious.* The psyche, emotional, and energetic connections to the sensual and sexual body are extremely interconnected–*get playful.* And, the material world is so deeply connected to the nervous systems perception of safety and therefore openness to more–*get more surrendered.* **Pleasure is what amplifies the experience of ALIVENESS–and we are HERE to fully live my love.**

So, back to not forgetting about our body on our ascension journeys…*let's talk about the actual body portal and the role that wellness plays in the Art of Receiving.* Nervous System (NS) regulation is necessary–as you call in, experience and embody new levels of your highest self (be it with career, wealth, relationships or health) you will come to realize that your body really does call the shots and determine your level of evolution. *Nervous system regulation isn't just a bonus–it is required.* Our 'human' will sacrifice desired realities for comfort every single time. If the nervous system does not feel held, safe, and nourished…the nervous system will act up, dysregulate and force you into safety (which is also the experience of comfort to the NS). **The practice of regulating your nervous system is** foundational when calling in new levels of alignment, success and expansion. *When you regulate your NS you communicate safety to your body...the 'new' or 'unchartered territories' of evolution begin to feel comfortable and safe–this allows us to grow exponentially AND sustainably.* Knowing that your body will always choose comfort–consciously creating comfort and safety in the new and expansive realities will allow your body to grow with you. *You can thrive together: highest self, soul/spirit and physical body in union.*

In the next few paragraphs we will explore how the nervous system works, how you can regulate it and co create with it. We will uncover how you can honor your body and its needs as you live an unconventional and Unfuckwithable life. *We will dive into the juice of how you can have everything you fucking want from a place of grounded regulation (woooowee!) As we covered in chapter 4...societal programming has perpetuated the ideology that living an unconventional life is dangerous.* This work is about allowing you to KNOW you are safe AND know that you can live a life GUSHING in love,, you can be TRULY free and you can walk your TRUEST path courageously. It can be risky, scary and unsettling OR it can be wildly successful, stable, and safe to live an unconventional life. **You get to choose.** I want to kick off by saying that even after encoding the *Art of Receiving*, doing years of self care, self development, high level spiritual practices, and being pretty top fucking tier when it comes to embodiment and observation of myself...I still have to continuously come back to regulating myself and creating safety in *"the now"*. **It is an ongoing, ever evolving journey of meeting myself where I'm at, creating regulation, ensuring my mind, body and spirit are in coherence, and then expanding into what's next for me.** Loving awareness in each moment, is the quickest way to neutralizing emotions/regulating and therefore experiencing your desired reality.

The *Art of Receiving* requires a high level, and all encompassing conversation of the role that *safety* plays in receiving. The actual function and physiology of what is happening within the nervous system is what either supports or inhibits our ability to receive. **The optimization, homeostasis, and wellbeing of our energetic and physical systems is a major key in opening up to *more*.** The *Art of Receiving* really is an art...a way of being–being in flow with the universe, lovers, opportunities, money, and success. Opening up to receive (love, pleasure, money, opportunity etc etc) in what we like to call "quantum" levels (aka way bigger, better and faster than your conscious mind can comprehend) takes nervous system optimization. It takes integration, embodiment, and upgrading. **Your body must be in a state of wellbeing, homeostasis, and nervous system regulation to experience *opening*.** So that you can trust that you are safe to *lean back* and trust that it's *safe to receive*. **So you can trust that you are worthy of having it.** This takes work, the work goes deep...and the work is soooo worth it. **Your wellness (or lack thereof) is an indicator of your ability to receive more.** When it comes to having *more* in alignment– your wellbeing IS the foundation. *An open, receptive and harmonized system is a system that feels safe, stable, and well.* **This level of well being is not just foundational...it is necessary in the NEW paradigm of receiving.** Remember back to the chapter on the NEW paradigm of wealth and how it was REGENERATIVE, not extractive? Ah-ha...back to that. **Your level of receiving is based on your level of openness and your level of openness is based on your level of safety.** Your level of safety is based on: your perceived stability, groundedness, and your perceived ability to trust. **Your level of safety is determined by your nervous system.** EVERYONE'S nervous system is unique. This is why some people feel safe skydiving and others don't. Some people feel safe being an entrepreneur and existing in the "riskier" realms of financial stability–others don't. Some people wear their heart on their sleeves–others don't. **If you know you desire a certain life, lifestyle, experience or material thing–in order to have it...you must feel SAFE having it.**

How we ARE is based on our nervous system's association with *fear or safety*. What we HAVE is based on our bodies perceived safety of having it. **It is already clear to me, that if you are reading this book–you're a badass.** You are someone who is here to squeeze ALL the yummy juices out of this life. I KNOW that your level of perceived safety is on a much more rebellious, bad ass, revolutionary, more brave, and courageous level than the average person. You are unconventional and your fear response likely looks different than the girl who is scared to speak up, works a 'safe' yet unfulfilling job with a guaranteed paycheck, and has to run all her decisions by her husband. **You aren't living in an old fear paradigm like most.** You are likely more bold in your action, than a boring life of mundane societally conditioned behaviors that will label you, *a good girl with a good job.* This being said…you likely have a higher capacity within your nervous system. **You likely can create more safety in an unconventional lifestyle and begin to naturalize it as stable**. However–there is still a tonne of safety work required, because with bigger visions come greater levels of expansion. Great expansion requires greater regulation. **You are still a human babe, and your body needs to be in optimized coherence with your big beautiful souls desires.**

For me, when I graduated University and dove right into entrepreneurship, I didn't feel a tonne of fear around the "risk" or the "instability" of not having a guaranteed salary or paycheck. I instead, clung to the belief that I would make fuck tonnes of money in unconventional ways and out earn anyone who would take a salaried position my age out of Uni (and of course I did). I CHOSE to create safety in an experience that an old paradigm would label as "risky". I saw my Mom do it as an entrepreneur. I put myself in rooms with successful entrepreneurs, I received mentorship from multi-millionaire entrepreneurs. I began to create an entire community and network with successful, high earning, extremely stable, and safe entrepreneurs. *I was regulating my nervous system without even knowing it.* I was proving to my subconscious mind that it was safe, healthy, successful, and GOOD to exist in this type of lifestyle to reap the rewards and live my purpose…there was no fear. Because this felt safe for me, it was.

My nervous system didn't freak out, it felt comfortable and frankly normal to live an unconventional life. I founded a tech startup, I was working as a personal trainer and beginning to uncover my gifts as a psychic channel and energy medicine practitioner. This was all normal (lol). I didn't even think I was being bold or brave–it was just a standard. Again, I was well positioned with parents who empowered me that I could be,do and have anything I set my mind and heart on. I witnessed my family succeed as entrepreneurs, and I began to naturally create friendships of like minded individuals–and we thrived.

I ended up closing my tech company–it was no longer aligned. Again, this wasn't scary. I didn't have fear around the: time, love, money and energy I had invested into it. I didn't see any of it as a "waste", li simply trusted that that journey had ended. Around this time I also released all of my steady income through personal training clients (this was one of my businesses before going all in on what I do now). I was making great money fresh out of Uni and had incredible clients, and it was all guaranteed–safe and regulated for me. Yet, I knew it was time for more expanded alignment. I gave up my career as a personal trainer and jumped into new territory…I went ALL IN on my work as a psychic channel, thought leader and energy worker. Naturally–I thrived. My body was not registering any of these "leaps of faith" as scary–I had perceived all of it as very natural and progressive. It just felt right. I trusted, and I moved. Fast forward, months after becoming self employed, incorporating my company, being in the top 1% of people my age, living a truly free and joyful life, and working in ways that supported my body, alignment and being successful as fuck doing it…*I did started to feel the fear.* My nervous system started to cap out. The unknown started to feel scary. It no longer felt safe. Not knowing what my next month's income would be was no longer exciting and expansive–it was constricting and scary. By this point on my journey I was a homeowner, I had payments for my luxury car, I had investments and I was fully in the identity of a high level wealthy and successful woman doing what I loved. **I got myself there–I was living it, and NOW it felt scary for my nervous system.**

Now I have "big girl" expenses. I had future paced and casted energetic projections for the lifestyle that I knew was meant for me, and I started living it. *This is a boujee lifestyle let me tell you. I had created an abundant life for myself that needed to be maintained...and in my reality–it needs to constantly upgrade (Hi, ever yearning divine feminine within me).* Despite earning really good money, something switched in me. Maybe an illusion of scarcity or a perceived deficiency? Maybe a very real fear that it would all run out? Nonetheless, my nervous system began to experience instability and dysregulation. **Again–the body portal is the portal in which we manifest through.** My body portal was in dysregulation. It is important to note that the nervous system legit runs the show physiologically, biomechanically, anatomically, and systematically. I started to feel the sympathetic (fight, flight, freeze and fawn) response more often in my body. I started to doubt myself. I started to constrict...both energetically and physically. I started to stress–my body did not feel safe. I started to fear (and fear is the root of all illness). I was not experiencing homeostasis as my baseline frequency anymore, I was experiencing low grade stress. I knew this experience because I had experienced low grade stress, control, and dysregulation energetically and physically in the past. This time around was different–it was mostly connected to money. I was not embodied in the *Art of Receiving*. Rather, I was experiencing dysregulation, feast and famine, and lots of distortion in my experience of my abundance. **I was scared of the life that I had created.** Some people are scared shitless that they never make the move–that wasn't my journey. I courageously made the moves no problem– my dysregulation and fear only set in when I HAD it. **Here is where observation and embodiment comes in.**

Thankfully, I had integrated the codes of the *Art of Receiving* by this point on my journey. I understood exactly what was going on. **I knew that it was within my power to regulate my nervous system.** It was important to release the obstructions, calm down my nervous system, create safety within the present moment, and upgrade my physiology and energetics to a state of surrender. *When we do the work–we understand surrender is the only option.*

With every new level of my growth as a thought leader, healer and high level individual living this life by design...I drop into the work. I still experience moments of dysregulation. I consciously bring my nervous system to a state of regulation and homeostasis, every step of the way. I consciously process the emotions that are present for me. I consciously create homeostasis within myself, and tap into my internal and inherent safety. I consciously optimize my physical vessel...my temple through self care, yoga, breathe work, and energy work. I consciously program my mind to SEE the safety in the unknown. **I consciously program my mind to know that I am supported and there is a divine plan unfolding. A divine plan that is much more abundant and successful than I could have ever 'efforted' into creation.** I consciously place myself in environments that positively represent the lifestyle I desire as: *safe, stable, and healthy.* I consciously do the work of hypnosis, internal rewiring, and subconscious reprogramming to release old patterning. I remove illusions of fear and distortion. **I am always in ongoing communication with my body–*I am safe.*** I am constantly communicating with my physical body that we are healthy, vital, thriving and always optimizing. **I am consciously and constantly programming my physical body for wellbeing.** I take the aligned action to keep my body in an optimized state of homeostasis through the ways I move, eat, and rest. I prioritize sleep. I surround myself with positive energy and I know that the world is always responding to my frequency–*so I optimize it.* **I have a conscious practice of coming back to my center and elevating my vibration.**

The nervous system runs the show. The nervous system is *optimized* when there is a high level of mind, body, and spirit coherence. When you are empowered with the knowledge that the NS is so powerful–we can consciously regulate and optimize it. *We cannot forget about our body on our ascension journeys my love.* **The body will literally shut down when it does not feel safe.** Our body must constantly be supported, held, and regulated to properly relieve stress. Your body must have the time and space to rest, recharge, and regenerate. Your body needs spaciousness (what I call strategic spaciousness) to recalibrate to its higher frequency. Your body needs spaciousness to receive. The nervous system is ideally in a parasympathetic state 99% of the time. Ideally, we are resting and digesting. **Ideally, our body is in its *thrival* majority of the time.** When the nervous system is regulated and we are experiencing homeostasis, we rise faster and more powerfully than the average human. *What is someone's ceiling becomes our floor.* **We have SO MUCH MORE CAPACITY.** More SPACE to earn, receive, attract, do, create, and build because we are operating on a higher coherence and from a grounded homeostatic environment.

Don't rush back into the doing...
let your body rest, and be at ease, in homeostasis,
before bursting back into expansion.

When our nervous system is supported, we have more capacity. This larger capacity is monumental in having a soft open and receptive landing strip. **When we are well, healthy, and vital, we have the spaciousness to accept and receive *more*.** My go to nervous system regulation practices are: breath work (calming myself with intentional breaths), affirmations (programming thoughts and beliefs that I am safe, it is safe to rest, safe to have more, safe to uplevel) and emotional processing (actually letting my body speak, expressing the emotions, letting my emotions be heard, allowing myself to fully feel the fear response that is present instead of shutting it down and bypassing my bodies very real needs). In order to properly optimize, to heal and to rise we CANNOT bypass what our body is communicating to us. *Personally for me, when I experience nervous system dysregulation–the answer almost ALWAYS is to rest.* God bless my Man for always checking in on me–telling me to rest, encouraging me to do less and to take breaks. *As a high achiever with SO MUCH CREATIVITY to give to the world–I can get a little wrapped up in the "doing" energy.* **See what is true for you now babe**...is REST the answer for your regulation? Or is your answer to move? Check in with yourself–come home to yourself, and regulate. Often, when we are experiencing fight or flight however–

the body has difficulty resting. This is where my practices of yoga, breath work and movement really come in, and once you're back to regulation… rest. Chill, lounge, do fucking nothing–*and let your body naturally recalibrate to its higher frequency.* **Rest is MEDICINE, and it heals the nervous system every single time.**

Now, let us dive into my absolute favorite topic, *which is the topic of desire.* First off–nothing is off the table. Everything is accessible to you. *Now… Let's go deep.* When we talk about desire in this book–we are talking about SOUL desire. **We're talking purpose, path, material desires that are effortless and NATURAL for you in this incarnation.** Experiences that your soul CRAVED when it chose Earth. The desires that are INEVITABLE for you– because they are TRUE for you. We're talking about the love of your life and the spirit liberating sexiness you craved when your soul chose this body. We're talking about the rich, sensual lived reality of wealth and abundance that is so so so MEANT for you. The SOUL desire space is a paradigm your conscious mind can't "think up" this realm is by no means logical. This realm is the realm of knowing. The realm of certainty–a certainty that cannot be backed by logic only backed by an innate knowing. This realm is vast, expansive, and is unlimited. *This realm is the natural journey, the path of least resistance, your soul path that is within the hands of the divine and your very alignment.* Your desires are no coincidence. Your desires are uniquely yours.Your desires are both the roadmap and the destination to your soul's purpose. The journey gets to be as abundant, expansive, and luxurious as the destination. **You are aware that the desires of your heart are natural for you, to be expected, and very much here or on their way.** *Breathe that in…your desires are NATURAL for you.*

*The world would be a very different place if
more people trusted their desires.*

*Honored the pulls within, and allowed
their intuition to guide them.*

*Start listening to your inner knowingness
and watch your world transform.*

Our body and energy system will tell us if our desires are *true* for us. The way we begin to understand our soul desires is by working within our body portal. We tap into our soul desires and understand them by uncovering our subconscious mind. *Breathe in. Breathe out.* Drop consciously into your subconscious mind, drop into your subtle body. Consciously slow your heart rate down. Begin to tap into the divinity within you. *Attune* to the spaces within your heart, mind, and body that you don't always notice. *Breathe in. Breathe out.* Tap into your truest desires. Our subconscious mind houses the information about our desires. It houses our capabilities of actualizing those desires, and it houses the programs that may be blocking those desires. So let's dive into some ways we can begin to communicate with our subconscious mind. *Let's discover what we truly want, and let's discover what needs to be reprogrammed and rewired to actualize those desires with ease.*

My favorite practice to tap into the unknown realms of our desires is: *manifesting orgasms.* Where we see what we didn't even know we wanted, and we see beyond what our conscious mind knows to be possible. **Manifesting orgasms will show us the desires we didn't even know we wanted.** *When our body is open, expanded and vibrating in a higher coherence we are in unity with our mind, body and spirit–we see the unseen.* Meditation and visualization practices will also show us desires we didn't even know we wanted. Our chakra system is open and optimized– connecting to our greater purpose. Our greater purpose directs our desires as they are deeply interconnected. Journaling practices will also open our eyes up to desires that were encoded in our very genetic sequencing that we didn't even know we desired. Any energy work, body work or breath work (if properly facilitated) will open you up to a plethora of desires that are TRUE and meant for you. *This congruence of mind, body, spirit connection shows you what your conscious mind could not articulate.* Your subconscious mind shows a wider capacity of possibilities within varying realms. **The visions you are shown in this congruent state are *true* for you.** As opposed to what your limited and conscious mind could *think up* based on its conditioning and learned possibilities.

These interconnected states within the subconscious mind are showing you the infinite realms. You are shown what is natural and meant for you. You are shown what to be expected in your future, in these highly connected states. When we open ourselves up to the subconscious mind not only are we seeing what desires are there and meant for us, we also can see where we may be subconsciously blocking ourselves from having the desires of our heart. The subconscious mind also shows us the limitation, the old patterning and outdated programming that our conscious mind has bypassed. We see where we need to refine, heal and upgrade. My favorite way to reprogram my subconscious mind is through ongoing observation and correction of old thoughts and beliefs. I also receive hypnosis and provide my clients with energetic upgrades and subconscious reprogramming through various modalities. *Our subconscious mind is best accessed in theta and trance-like states, where we are more open and receptive to healing and positive suggestions.* **Our subconscious mind holds answers, we can heal and alchemize when we become familiar with the more subtle codes and energies within our system.**

When you play in the realm of conscious desire…
You are always limited.

God has a bigger and better plan, babe. *When you play in the subconscious mind and within more 'subtle energy' you see with new eyes–you see the divine orchestration of it all.* When you play in the subconscious mind with your desires (and yes it's as fun, quantum and limitless as it sounds) then you understand how *true* they are for you. You then get the affirmation, the validation, the answer from your highest self. You get the clear knowing that these desires are CERTAIN for you–that these desires are MEANT for you. From this place, they become inevitable. The desires that are actually designed and meant for you, are not the desires that your conscious mind can think up–they're even bigger than that. Conscious desire is limited...by logic and conditioning. *Often conscious desires are borrowed from society, borrowed ideas of what we think we should want.* Or from limited conditioning that says "this is all you CAN have" or "this is all that's possible". **You don't feel as though these borrowed desires are inevitable for you, because they're not actually yours.** Borrowed desires are not encoded...they're not *soul given.* Conditioned desires are limited, they are based on conscious processing of what is realistic and logical–not based on the infinite potential that *is* your truth.

Your Soul desires however, ARE uniquely yours. Your Soul desires are inevitable. Your soul desires are not fleeting. Your SOUL, GOD GIVEN DESIRES are the ones that you just KNOW are meant for you. Even if it makes no sense...you know they are yours. *They feel so true for you...because they are.* We're talking infinite realms here. **This is why surrender is such a key piece of the *Art of Receiving*, because in order to receive what the universe has in store for you–you must get out of the way.** Your conscious and conditioned mind could never think up the "how" of these desires..because the conscious mind isn't designed to. Soul given desires are limitless, infinite AND inevitable. We're talking paradigms your conscious mind can't think up. *This realm is divine–this realm is expansive–this realm is CERTAIN...and THIS realm is the realm we play in.* The work within this chapter (and this book for that matter) is concerned with you receiving ALL forms of desires that are meant for you. The desires that you think up in fleeting ways, the desires that you consciously want and the desires that are so much bigger and better than what your gorgeous brain could ever even imagine. This work is holding you in the quantum as well as grounding you in the material realm. The work ensures that you are attuned to your desires, embodied to the frequency and regulated to have and hold them in the material world. You GET to have fleeting material desires. You get to have deep purpose driven desires. There is no hierarchy. There is no separation. You get to have everything you've ever wanted. You get to consciously co-create AND you get to lean the fuck back and surrender to what God has in store for you.

Infinite Wealth
Limitless Love
Expansive Freedom
Soul Aligned Purpose

Now, let's talk about fleeting desires or what some may call "untrue desires". This is again—a nuanced topic. I am a stand for having our fleeting desires, I know there is room and space for them on our journey of true fulfillment AND I also see them as distractive (DISTRACTIVE - not destructive). I see distractive (yes I made this word up—get used to it) desires come up, and take up precious space in my clients' lives all the time. These are the desires that aren't actually true for you…but your ego fixates on them. In truth, your ego fixates on them not because you actually want them…but rather as a sneaky subconscious misalignment and block. *Your ego fixates on untrue desires as a means of procrastination and deviation from your path.* Remember—you manifest what is TRUE for you. You GET what you want. **Your ego, however, loves to attach itself to these untrue desires as a means of staying in the wanting versus actually living in the having.** Your TRUE soul desires are actually circulating in your vortex…much closer…ready to drop in. So let this land for a moment…***If you really wanted it. You would have it.***

If you want to know what is true for you, and you want to know what you actually want…look at your life. **What you have is a direct reflection of what you are available for.** What your standards are, what is presently TRUE for you. *Take a little survey—what do you love? What needs to be released? What needs to be upgraded?* **If you have things or experiences you know for certain that you DON'T want…you need to look at the subconscious desire that is keeping them in your reality.** The subconscious desire to stay small, stagnant or comfortable (I warned you this was a nuanced high level conversation). **We actually HAVE what we want.** What we have in our reality is what we want *either consciously or unconsciously. So, if you* don't have what you *"want"* it's because you either don't actually want it (it is not TRUE for you) OR it just hasn't manifested YET. If you are manifesting something you *think* you want... and you're fed up because you don't have it *yet,* you are likely manifesting something that is not true for you. The ego likes to keep us here– because it is perceived as *"safer"* than the potential identity upgrade of BEING the Unfuckwithbale human who actually HAS their soul desires and LIVES there dream life. In many ways it's more comfortable, and safe to just have "pipe dreams" that you never actually experience...Feel me?

This energy of "not having" is a frequency of lack...a frequency of not enoughness..a frequency of scarcity or stagnancy in a void. When your ego lures you into a frequency of "not having" you miss out on what is actually TRUE for you. *If you are wasting your time focusing on a desire that you don't actually want–you're distracting yourself from the present moment.* You're distracting yourself from your TRUTH..from your SOUL desires. There is a BIG difference when it comes to not having our SOULS desires *YET*. If it just hasn't manifested *yet*–you will KNOW in your bones that it's happening. You will NOT get wrapped up in scarcity or fear because you are LIVING in your alignment and you KNOW that it's all adding up. You know that you are ALIVE in the great unfolding of the manifestation(s). You KNOW that you are ALIVE in the dream. *You know it's all unfolding perfectly, and you can carry on your merry way. Again–your SOUL desires are uniquely yours–they are guaranteed and they are inevitable.*

So let's refine the meaning of *TRUE* desire...If it WAS soul given you would: A) Have it already or be experiencing it already OR B) You wouldn't be worried about having it, because you'd KNOW it's on its way. You KNOW it's meant for you and you KNOW it's inevitable. *Therefore, you have surrendered to divine timing.* **Therefore, you are ACTUALLY embodied and in flow with the *Art of Receiving.*** You know it's inevitable–Period. *From that place of knowing and within the dimension of openness (more on this in the next chapter), you KNOW that there is an alternate reality, paradigm or realm available in which you have it.* **You are not stuck in the illusion of separation because you know that your future self exists with you currently and that your future self WILL have it.** This is a state that is only available to experience when you are co-creating desires that are actually TRUE for you...SOUL given...GOD given desires. PSA: Again, I want to be clear–you CAN manifest untrue or fleeting desires...people do it all the time, I do it all the time...The difference is, they often take more efforting, struggle, hustle, and work to manifest AND they don't feel as rewarding when they actualize. **So... you can spend your life chasing OR you can lean into surrender and effortlessly create and magnetize your desires.**

Once we open up to the quantum field, to our soul space, to the dimension of openness...we can effortlessly communicate with our higher self/source consciousness. We understand our TRUE desires. When we communicate within these higher realms, we begin to understand what we *really* want. We see with new eyes...what are the truest desires of our heart. We lock in on the big questions like–Why did our soul choose Earth? We get the answers. Often, the soul desires are much more textured, sensual, descriptive, and experiential than, *"I want ten thousand dollars overnight"*. Staying in the example of financial desires..the soul financial desires are more like, "I want to live a life where I am infinitely supported by money, where everything I desire to do I do with ease because money just shows up for me". Get it? **So, tap in now...*what are your true soul desires?*** When we actually get clear on the feelings of our desires and the experience of them–we can refine. We can refine our lifestyles to attune to the wealth, opportunity, and love that you desire. The experiential, taste, touch, sensual realities of our desires begin to be experienced in our environments. You can then effortlessly embody the frequency match for that in which you desire. **From this aligned frequency–you start to experience the desires as**

real, natural and *to be expected* in your lived reality. When you are in a more connected, mindful, open, and receptive space...the desires of your soul communicate clearly *to and with you.* You start to notice that on some level...you are already experiencing *"like frequencies".* Those *like frequencies* are meant to be further indulged in...with more gratitude and more presence. You will also begin to see what is NOT of the like frequency. What experiences and energies don't match the vibe. You are then encouraged to release those *ways of being* and manage the role you play in these interactions and experiences. **Ensure you are vibrating at the aligned frequency–ensure you are doing your part as the co creator.** From this energy of presence, high level awareness, and embodied openness...*you are existing as your highest self.*

From there you know...

A. Your desires have been SOUL given.
B. You know they're on their way.
C. Your only job is to stay in alignment with them.
D. They can collapse into your material reality at any moment (yay!)

You're ready now. You're now aligned. The rest is up to divine timing. **That divine timeline gets accelerated through conscious decision.** Deciding powerfully that you are ready, devoted, and that you trust in the unfolding. Making a choice, declaring your readiness and openness are the actions you must take. **When these actions are done in alignment–they accelerate the process of receiving.** BECAUSE you know that you are Unfuckwithable–you know you are whole and complete no matter what...*so there's no rush.* **You are unrushed, present and focused on living life–doing you and doing it well.** When we talk about *soul desires*, there is a knowing that the desires are highly integral. Humans are innately good. Humans come into the earth from the stars as little angelic beings ready and excited for the life that lies ahead. Our soul desires are programmed into us within our very DNA. Within our soul bodies, energy bodies. and physical bodies. Our soul desires are highly integral. They are created by divine, source consciousness. The desires of your soul are created from love. Love yields love. Love yields abundance. Love yields healing. This is why no matter how "superficial" or "material" or seemingly selfish your desires may be…when they come from the soul space you can trust them as true and integral.

When you KNOW yourself–everything is easy. You trust yourself, you trust your desires, you trust your impulses..you trust your *knowings*. When you let LOVE be your discernment, you can understand where your desire is coming from. **If that desire is indeed a soul and heartfelt desire–imprinted within you, then you know the desire is of high integrity. It is good for you, good for the collective, and good for the world.** As you walk toward your desires on your aligned path…you WILL be shown the way. You WILLl be rewarded when you walk with alignment. In contrast–you will likely be deviated from the path when you move with extractive, misaligned intentions or actions. *There is this phenomenon called "Universal Protection" –often we are redirected, stopped or realigned when we try to walk the wrong path–so stay intentional, and stay aware babe.* The vibe here as always is–lead yourself and allow yourself to be led. It is essential to lead with desire, and pay attention to the impulses, intuitive nudges and information along your path. Always connect back to your "why" to your mission, your purpose and your reasoning for wanting what you want. Living an aligned life, and living your purpose WILL be a life of integrity–guaranteed. Integrity looks different for everyone–however my simple definition of being integral is this: living in a way that is aligned with your TRUTH, your purest, most grounded, centered truth… of WHO you are and HOW you want to live. Trust yourself. Trust Your Desires. Allow Yourself to want it. Take the aligned and inspired action where needed. Declare that it's yours. Navigate the highs and the lows. Surrender to the path. Trust the unfolding…and receive. **You get to have what you want AND wholeheartedly KNOW that there is a divine plan orchestrating the unfolding of it all.**

Life is WAY too good... to not get the absolute most out of it.
So claim those desires powerfully, do your part and
leave the rest up to the divine.

When you live as an integral human being you are living with a higher consciousness. You are living with an understanding of the interconnectedness of all life. You are living with an understanding that there is no separation–knowing we are all connected in oneness and that we are brilliant, individual, and unique simultaneously. **When you live with integrity and you consciously exist within the dimension of openness. When you exist in the *Dimension of Openness,* you can confidently know that your desires are meant for you, and leading you to the next natural evolution of your *life by design* and your purpose.** Important note: when I talk about Integrity–this is NOT a borrowed identity or fear based programming about what being a "good human" means. Again, this is about living in alignment with YOUR truth. *This alignment with your truth requires ongoing introspection, intentional living, and conscious attunement to your higher self.* This life comes down to intentional thoughts, beliefs, and actions. This life comes down to actual embodiment as the HIGH level individual who leads themself, trusts themself, moves with life, and knows that they are supported. From this conscious understanding of what desires are TRUE for us and of the highest good for collective ascension–we can dive into the juicy topic of divine feminine energy and the never ending yearning for MORE.

It's time to dive into the divine feminine yearning within each of us. This divine feminine yearning is our desire for more. *When we are the conscious embodiment of our divine feminine, we can trust these desires and move toward them powerfully.* We have made it to the last topic of this *Art of Receiving* chapter– I introduce to you the topic of "polarity". **Polarity–the phenomenon of Feminine and masculine energetics and embodiments.** Sacred polarity is the understanding of ourselves as both divine feminine and divine masculine beings. Polarity is the knowing that we get to ***self fulfill*** our masculine and feminine needs and desires. The deepest and most high level form of unity within self through our innate polarities. The power in holding the duality of vulnerability and power—creative freedom and successful execution. **This is polarity.** The high level individual holds the space for their inner divine masculine and divine feminine to work in harmony…to own the innate magnetism and power of each version and parts of themself. **Creating unity within ourselves allows us to have the richest experience on Earth and in our bodies—*all the while actualizing our souls desires.***

A little look inside my harmonization and the reason I am successful, immensely supportive as a facilitator, powerful as a leader, AND effortlessly able to receive in abundant aligned ways. **I have done the work to consciously harmonize my divine feminine and masculine energies.** It is my very harmonization that allowed me to channel this entire book, write it, edit it, successfully execute each process, and birth it into the world for you to read it now. I have an incredible balance between my energies. I have a stunning balance between wanting and doing—AND leaning back. **This balance for me has manifested due to my ever evolving desire for more.** This *desire for more* is my inner feminine. The desire to just exist and have it all be enough is my inner masculine. *My feminine wants more and my masculine wants to experience that more.* The masculine wants the exhale. The satisfaction and success knowing enough has been done and now is time to rest. The feminine keeps wanting, yearning, creating, desiring, existing in the *neverending liberation of the infinite.* **The masculine wants the results of these manifestations, the masculine will do the work…but the masculine needs the rest.** The feminine wants and wants, AND she also needs to lean back. She also desires nothingness. I have learned to optimize my system by co creating with both my inner masc, and my inner fem. It has taken time and devotion to build and regulate this balance. In essence, I'm not afraid to want what I want unapologetically, and I'm not afraid to do the work to devotionally make it happen. I am comfortable doing my part, and also knowing when enough is enough. **I know when it's my turn to make the moves, and I know when its time for me to chill the fuck out.** I'm willing to want something so bad that I walk toward it powerfully in aligned action each day… AND (again honouring that divine feminine within) leaning the fuck back and surrendering to the divine timing of it all. ***Nonetheless, I am unapologetic in my yearning for more.***

"My desires are like water to Me… I need them."

When your dreams are so big, SO important, and you are SO devoted to actualizing them, it feels like a hunger that can't be FULLY satiated until you are actually LIVING this dream as your reality. **The paradox is–once you are actually living your dream–your next dream will present itself.** I personally spend a lot of my life *in the wanting, in the desire, and in the drive* because I have MASSIVE dreams for myself and for this world. I want to create a massive impact, I want my work to be FELT and integrated across the entire Globe. I also want to experience rich self care, rest and solitude. I want to BASK in ALL the success that I have created, and I want to achieve the very achievable MORE that I desire and that I deserve. These polarities require harmony and congruence between my fem and masc within. **This life requires my devotional and dominant action AND my submissive lean back.** I will always want more, I will always SEE and KNOW the *more* that is SO available to me. **I will always dream bigger than the average human–and so will you.** I often remind myself and my clients that just because we may be living YOUR dream life … doesn't mean we're living our dream life–yet. *Because it KEEPS GETTING BETTER.* The better it gets the better it gets. **This ongoing yearning for more is the combination between a healthy feminine and an unsatisfied masculine.** Ultimately, to achieve this harmony–a healthy conversation between both parts of your inner being is required…

So! Let's role play here.

Inner Femme – "I just want moreeeeee, I know there's more, I can see it, taste it and FEEL it."

Inner Masc – "I know babe, I see it and feel it too. It's beautiful that you want so much more...you want it because it's meant for you...we're gonna have it together."

Inner Femme – "Okay so let's make it happen, let's do it now...let's go."

Inner Masc – " I know you're excited babe, I love that about you. But let's also bask in what is here now...the success here now. While we're doing that, let's let the universe do its part."

Inner Femme – "Oh, okay, I'm down for a bath."

Inner Masc – "Same, lets rest and receive."

This roleplay is an example of how to harmonize the yearning for more with the success and presence that is already here. The harmony of loving where you are in the moment, and knowing there is more out there in the future. *This role play also supports a very excited inner feminine into knowing that even without creating and wanting there is still momentum building and movement happening within the divine intervention from source.* The *Art of Receiving* **is not just all about leaning back to receive, it is also about understanding when it is aligned to make moves and take action.** The divine masculine has a natural desire to take action that is aligned with the mission. The divine feminine feels the inspired action through her creativity, flow, and freedom. *Together this union creates the perfect harmony for action and receiving.* **The feminine and masculine share the ideal for success, satisfaction, pleasure, and joy.** They want to feel as though they are basking in the fruits of their labor. They both have a desire for a life well lived, and together can co-create that with the universe and *all that is* in a regenerative way. Being in a flow of gratitude AND wanting more is a magical place to be. Being so grateful and present where you are...while simultaneously courageously walking toward more.

As high level ambitious individuals there will always be a yearning for more–this is not something to dim within yourself–but rather something to understand and optimize. The work often in this case is to create safety and pleasure in where you are now. The regulation of this harmony is key. Regulating one's system to a healthy balance of action taking and resting/receiving. **The healthy balance that allows one to trust and surrender to the divine path.** This harmony is an ongoing evolution–a living, breathing, transforming phenomenon. It is our conscious awareness (that is the divine masculine within) that is always noticing when more consciousness and intention must be infused. The divine feminine is always feeling into situations, what feels good, nourishing, and *right* in her being. Taking note, and allowing that feeling to lead the way.

Some examples of our Inner divine masculine and inner divine feminine...
So you can begin to understand the flow,
harmony, and relationship between these
two sides of your inner being.

1.Your divine masculine loves to nurture your divine feminine from a state of overflow. Your divine feminine loves to be nurtured. When you nurture your divine feminine, your divine masculine is energized to give more, and your divine feminine is open to receive more–Overflow vibes.

2.Your divine femme loves to feel free, to play, to dance, and to know she's taken care of. Your divine masculine loves to create a safe space for her to fully explore and experience all the textures of life.

Your divine masculine creates safe containers for your divine feminine to explore within. There is high level reciprocity occurring in this dynamic. Mutually beneficial exchanges of energy.

3.When your divine masculine takes care of your divine feminine– you develop self trust. *You trust that you've got you.* When your inner masc supports your inner femme you experience the most deep sense of trust within yourself. This self trust creates an ability to surrender to the divine unfolding of your life.

This is fully embodied self leadership and luxury receptivity.

Now, back to that hunger…I want to make it clear that the *hunger for more* is a healthy thing. **It is healthy to strive for more.** Where it becomes unbalanced is when we fall into the illusion of scarcity or lack. The imbalance happens in the illusion of separation. When we think we are not enough until we have the *"more"*. The Universe communicates in frequency. If the frequency of the desire for *more* is a frequency of lack…you will stay in the lack frequency. If the frequency of the desire for *more* is the frequency of excitement in receiving…you will find yourself in the frequency of *having and receiving*. Personally, my dreams, my path…the life I am HERE on Earth feels necessary to me–the desires are beyond want–they are just MEANT for me. *My desire is like fucking water to me– I need it.* That is my shameless truth. I want what I want. I let myself want it. *I allow my inner feminine that yearns, to fully yearn.* There is no distortion in my desired frequency. There is no pretending I don't want what I want. My desires are shameless, and the journey there is shameless. When the desires drop in (as they do) the celebration is shameless. There is no distorted pretending that I don't want what I want. **I am clear to my divine feminine, to my masculine, to the Universe, to God, to source and anyone who will listen– that I WANT WHAT I WANT.** I make that clear, all the livelong day. The nuance here though…is that I have trained my higher self and my divine feminine to *create groundedness in my wanting*. The *wanting* doesn't come across as "not enoughness". The wanting doesn't change frequency to lack. **The wanting stays clear and clean as *excited anticipation.*** The wanting doesn't become a frequency of scarcity. **Being Unfuckwithable means knowing you can have everything you desire AND that you are whole and complete with or without it.**

Be hungry... But don't stay hungry.

I have had many visions of myself as a HUNGRY lioness... I find it nourishing to see myself as a woman who wants more and knows that she gets to have it. There is medicine in the *wanting.* There is activation and aliveness *in the hunger.* **It only becomes extractive, no longer life-giving and scarce when you** *stay hungry. Feel me?* **Be hungry...but don't stay hungry.** There is a natural gestation period for all desires to birth into the world. A natural unfolding and series of events....A natural bridge of incidence. It is not natural or healthy to say in a frequency of wanting–your homeostasis is you HAVING. So fully drop in to what is true and alive in your reality–now. **When you experience the hunger for more...you activate the desire.** If you create a frequency of, "where is it?", "I need it now.", "why isn't it here yet?", "I'm not full without it." etc etc.Then you perpetuate the *hunger* and you stay in a frequency of lack. **As we know in this world of energetics–when we are IN a frequency we naturally continue to match that frequency.** So lack frequencies equate to more lack, *and that's not the vibe.* **You didn't make it to chapter 9 almost to chapter 10 to be in** *lack frequencies.* You came here, and you made it this far to experience abundance frequencies. You came here to elevate to a higher standard and baseline frequency of MORE–always dropping in.

Passion is the precursor to pleasure.

Now, let's dive into passion and pleasure in relation to the divine masculine and feminine within us. Passion is the energy and experience that we all crave. Our divine feminine wants the passion leading up to the pleasure, and our divine masculine wants the pleasure and satisfaction of the actual experience. *The divine masculine wants the feeling of being satiated. The divine feminine wants the lust for more.* Think about sexual tension–we've all experienced it...this feeling of *wanting* is actually a divine feminine experience. It is a desire for more and there is pleasure in the desire for more. There is also pleasure in the actual *experience of more.* **Just like sexual tension, pleasure can be experienced in our journey to having the physical manifestation of desires.** Again, I call this the "clim(b)ax" for a reason. We get to experience pleasure on the journey–this is where we guide our inner masculine into enjoying this *in between state.* The divine feminine gets to be led into enjoying the actualization of the desire. **Together they create a team of always creating and experiencing more.** Passion is why we're here. Just like pleasure, every cell in our body is wired for pleasure, and naturally your brain is wired to desire passion. **Passion is the precursor to pleasure.** Every inch of you was made for pleasure. The embodiment of both passion moving toward our desire, and the pleasure in the actual experience of having it– is what we came here for. Pleasure without the lead up, isn't as satisfying. **We are here for unrushed passion and unrushed pleasure.** This sacred *unrushing* (also another made up word by me) requires high level communication and teamwork between the inner divine femme and the inner divine masc.

This harmony creates a life well lived.
It really feels like the natural flow of "inhale
I receive…exhale I give".
Breathe that in…big inhale…receive for 3,2,1
now let it go…big exhale…exhale give.
Inhale, I receive. Exhale, I give.

Pause and repeat this for a few moments
now before moving on.
You deserve this breath break. You deserve to
harmonize your system.

Before we dive into the homework, I want to talk about the importance of divine feminine empowerment, reclamation, and a coming home of our nature as divine feminine beings. **Again, no matter who you are, what your sexed organs were when you** arrived on Earth, and no matter how you identify now–you have an inner divine feminine within you. This is the part of you who is capable of SO MUCH creation, liberation, and MAGIC. This feminine energy within, is also a part of you who has been: hushed, harmed, and contorted either in this lifetime or lifetimes before. *The Art of Receiving is about divine feminine RECLAMATION and EMPOWERMENT.* We have had lifetimes of pain, trauma, and heartbreak. The divine feminine carries new life–the divine feminine births new creativity, ideologies, and paths into existence. *The divine feminine within IS the visionary.* She builds new realities by standing in her truth. The divine feminine leads the New Earth, and the divine masculine supports the building of this reality. **But it is the divine feminine who envisions this harmonious, regenerative, and bountiful reality for all.** We can create new pathways, realities, and paradigms through divine feminine leadership. When we are clearly envisioning forward, and being supported by our inner divine masculine–we can build what we came here to build. **We can be the purest magnet to our desires when we OWN our inner vulnerability AND lead with our personal power.**

Our sensuality, our goddess codes, our ability to attract and receive: wealth, love, pleasure, and opportunity through these unlocked codes is a reclamation of our truth as divine feminine beings. We are infinitely creative. We are infinitely wild and free. We are here to pave new paths through our innate brilliance and embodiment as *harmonized souls.* The polarity harmonization and its role within the *Art of Receiving* is complex, nuanced and it's unique. The polarity harmonization is sexy and powerful. It's dominant and it's submissive. This polarity work honors ALL of your edges and all your gorgeous details. **Every inch of you is explored and celebrated.** These codes allow you to heal, awaken, and thrive. As a spiritual person experiencing life in human form. As someone who desires more abundance, pleasure, love, and a life they are TRULY obsessed with–you are someone who is harmonized. **You are balanced and ready to dance with desire and walk with gratitude.** You get to be all of you. You get to have it all now, while you navigate the furthest corners of yourself. Your divine femme and divine masc work together to provide your infinite soul with the most fulfilling life in the material world. Trust the pulls, trust the desires and listen to the whispers of your body–the whispers of infinite wisdom. *Let your feminine envision, let your masculine hold you, and let your highest self lead.*

This is the *Art of Receiving*, and you have mastered it.

Now let us dive deep into the homework. We will work with some high level (yet super fun) polarity concepts. Polarity work within our own system (our own internal yin and yang) when embodied and experienced creates MASSIVE shifts in alignment. You take more action, you rest more, you give more, you receive more, and your life EXPANDS. Tasks that you've been meaning to get done, that you've been putting off or avoiding, GET DONE. Your creativity is flowing. Opportunities arise. Harmony and balance is achieved as a new baseline internal state. Success elevates. Wealth elevates. Love elevates. You have a newfound certainty in the unfolding. An inner sense of safety, stability, and security unfolds.

You gain deeper levels of self trust. You know you are taken care of. You know your desires are natural, and to be expected. Dive into these examples, then begin to create your own.

High Level polarity concepts: Begin to play with these in your day to day realities

It's time to role play with yourself...

Scenario 1: Your inner fem is exhausted and wants to sleep in later than is aligned for you... your inner divine masc says let's get up Babe, let's have an amazing day, I'm going to make you coffee and a nourishing breakfast. Instantly– your internal energy shifts. You're up. You're thriving. Your divine masc led your divine femme. Good aligned choices were made. Everyone was taken care of.

Scenario 2: Your inner fem wants to take the day to get creative work done, wants to journal, meditate, walk, and rest. Your inner divine masculine creates a container of safety for this to play out–sets up the space, clears the schedule, lights the candles, creates a soft, and mailable schedule for the day. This schedule includes all the juicy fun events as well as some essentials like any to do's that need to be done). Your divine femme gets to play, rest, and create in freedom your divine masc created as the container and environment for that to easily occur.

Scenario 3: Your inner divine femme see's herself enjoying a restorative night in. She is having snacks, wine, and watching her fav show. Your inner divine masc creates the ambience, prepares the snacks, sets up the blankets, and picks up the wine. Your divine femme then leans back and enjoys a night in–as desired.

*In all 3 scenarios, (please add and start to embody and experience your own) it is YOU AND YOU BABE. Your inner masc leads your inner femme. It's like this highest self management system where your human is always supported and your soul and spirit are too. EVERYONE wins. High level polarity work, embodied, and integrated like this creates the most successful foundations for thrival. It is YOU and YOU. Time to practice this fun and insanely rewarding role play.

When we are in flow–we are always playing in this balance.
The vibe becomes, "What does my divine feminine need from me today?"
"What does my divine masculine need from me today?"
"How can I support this part of me to feel fulfilled and satisfied?"

This flow is a successful dynamic in which you're flowing between desire, aligned action, success, and satisfaction.
Take a few moments to drop into your breath.
Take out your journal, land in the "now moment".

Breathe in. Breathe out. Be here now.

1. Bring awareness to how you're moving through life–are you embodying the *Art of Receiving?*
2. Do you feel successful?
3. If you do feel successful…Is it sustainable?
4. If you feel far from successful…are you truly living life by your own design? Are you truly living in alignment? Are you doing your part? Are you doing too much?
5. What would exponential evolution look like for you?
6.Do you feel that your evolution has a growth potential? Is it sustainable? Can it evolve?
7.Do you feel as though you can continue to evolve exponentially without overdoing it, burning out or harming your body?
8.Is there a way that you could surrender deeper to a *divine plan*?
9.Is there a way you could create more intentional containment, healthy environments and containers in your life for your divine feminine to create, play, and receive?
10.Could you create more containers for your divine masculine to rest, recharge, and bask in the satisfaction of what is here now?

You have done your part, now it's time to REAP your rewards.
It's time to BASK in the joy of what you have created–My god have you EARNED it!

I celebrate you Babe for making it this far.
I celebrate you for being so present with
this juicy and extended chapter.
You have encoded the *"Art of Receiving"*…
Now it is time to live it.

It is time to lean back and surrender to the *divine plan*.
To truly embody the harmony of giving and receiving.
You're beyond worthy of a life you're obsessed with.
A life that nourishes you–one where you feel so good,
AND you have everything you want.

You deserve a life where you feel regulated
and clear where you are,
AND you know that *more* is always on the way.

You deserve to receive.

CHAPTER 10

THE DIMENSION OF OPENNESS

Life is so beautiful–it will break your heart
Open, unraveled and alive.
Grounded in the knowing that you are everything,
and everything is you.
360 degree awareness…(and beyond) of the
interconnectedness of all that is.
Every thought, feeling, experience and image surrounding you–
pulses to the same rhythm.
There is no separation–It's all connected…
This is the Dimension of Openness.

My entire reality upgraded immensely when I understood (and then actually saw) ongoing evidence of the interconnectedness of all that is. The power of my thought, speech, vitality and intentions could change life across the world. Nothing was the same, everything was different, when I actually began to embody the consciousness of *union with all that is.* When I understood the *Dimension of Openness* as this time-space-reality, that is not separate from any paradigm, realm, or consciousness–*it is all coexisting all the time.* When I studied quantum physics, I understood energy and began to choose the timelines I wanted to exist within my awakened mind. But that wasn't even it–there was more. It wasn't until recently, when I understood the deeper layers–the phenomenon of the *Dimension of Openness.* I actually knew in my bones that there is NO separation. There is no hierarchy. There is no pedestal of realms. There is no 3D, 5D, or beyond–there just *is* the *Dimension of Openness.* There just *is* an ongoing time-space-reality with no separation.

There just *is* an infinite intercommunication between the past, present and future. There just *is* a choice in every single moment to shift. There is no separation–but rather an infinite opening, and shared space for *all that is.* **An expansive capacity for LIFE to hold all of us, in all our paradigms, all at once.** There is no separation between us and those who have gone before. There is no separation between humanity and plantlife. There is no separation between planet Earth and Mars. There is no separation between intergalactic beings, and the most grounded Earthlings. *There is no separation between who you are now, and who you desire to be.* There is no separation–there is simply openness. Openness to the infinite paradigms and realms that are always coexisting. There *are* higher frequencies and dimensions yes…But they coexist, unbothered and unattached to the lower ones. There is no escaping. There is only an opening. *Opening up to the infinite realm of all that is–the infinite realm that is the Dimension of Openness.*

The amount of freedom that I experience in my day to day KNOWING wholeheartedly that I can shift dimensions at any moment *is unparalleled.* The freedom in knowing for certain, that I can shift into new paradigms at any moment throughout the day. The freedom in knowing that I have the power to change the channel. The freedom in knowing that I am actually truly FREE, and that my physical material reality can shift and upgrade at any moment when I exist in the dimension of openness. **The freedom and ALIVENESS in knowing that I am alive in the unfolding of my dream life–it's all happening now.** I experience infinite freedom knowing that there is always a better feeling realm available…Within this exact moment, here and now. There is no separation. There is no space between. There is simply interconnectedness. I feel free and grounded knowing that I can turn on my owl head, I can spin my consciousness around into 360 degree awareness, and actually SEE with my third eye, *all of the ways in which I am supported.*

With the infinite awareness of the *Dimension of Openness,* I can effortlessly see, and feel the support that is here and now, for me to receive. The resources, opportunities, experiences and people that are here and now, ready to support me. **The groundedness and safety in knowing that I am supported above and supported below.** I can open to the realms that I know to be here connected to me, and bask in the bounty that is infinitely available. *The Dimension of Openness has an infinite capacity.* There is no start and no end. The *Dimension of Openness* proves to me that if I can think of it, feel into it, or even imagine it as possible– that I CAN have, and hold it. The *Dimension of Openness* does not require anything to change–*other than our very perspective.* **Our very awareness is what shifts our frequency, and catalyzes the results.** A simple yet profound knowing that *all that is,* interconnects and communicates within various realms to support our manifestation(s). What we want and what life wants for us–actualizes with a collective consciousness that transcends far beyond Earth. Our perspective and energetic capacity when attuned to the infinite realms of *"all that is,"* becomes magnetic to actualized material results.

Bigger Vision.
Bigger Alignment.
Bigger Surrender.

Frankly–any illusion of: us vs them, or this realm vs that realm, or hierarchies of spirituality, self development or religion...Are simply illusions of separation. Illusions rooted in fear. Illusions that deny the truth of interconnectedness. *Everything is happening, all together, all at once–no separation.* Our very existence is realized on the fundamental TRUTH, that we are all connected. Explore this with me–and insert your own examples as they arise...Your thoughts change physical matter. An old friend crosses your mind, later that week they send you a message–they were thinking of you too. You close your eyes and communicate with the water–it responds to you. You set a simple intention–your material reality shows up to validate that intention. *Supernatural humans, or as I call them–*

high level individuals, have been communicating with nature for thousands of years. The collective wisdom of First Nations peoples, and their relationship to nature, and their union with *all of existence* to create and serve life–is the wisdom of *The Dimension of Openness.* Our dream state, each night is an example of our consciousness traveling and exploring the vast interconnectedness of *The Dimension of Openness.* The more we tune in, and tap into our very existence (and the creation of our existence) we can quickly recognize the vast union of it all. The vastness–so infinite, quickly becomes oneness. **Our individuation leads to our collective union.** There is no escaping the interconnectedness of it all. As you dive deep in your journey of healing, awakening and in alchemizing this life–you will see and more importantly FEEL ***the truth that it is all happening at once.***

Our ancestors were doing it long before there were words for it. Now, thought leaders are creating new innovations for the future based on *The Dimension of Openness.* We co create and interconnect with all that exists–whether we are conscious of it or not. Every text message you send, or every time you go into your Instagram app…You are connecting within a *Dimension of Openness* (perhaps not consciously all the time)…But you *are* connected). Each time you exchange energy with a food or beverage…With sunlight or water…You are existing within the ever connected *Dimension of Openness. Everything you are ingesting or experiencing is aware of you, and your connection to it.* ***Everything you interact with is interacting with you…You are always giving and receiving.*** Surfers are communicating with their waves–co creating the experience. Gardeners are co creating with nature to regenerate plant life. Farmers co create with the land to create life giving foods. Renewable energy, technology and kinetic energy that serves our life today (and sometimes dis-serves based on the consciousness of those using it) is created based on the foundational principles of the *Dimension of Openness.* Animals across all ecosystems are communicating, and co creating habitats, life, death and rebirth cycles in unison.

We are interconnected whether we are conscious of it or not– in everything we do and everything we BE. Your conscious awareness of it–IS the missing ingredient, this awareness IS what catalyzes faster reactions. Your awareness of this *Dimension of Openness*–is the nutrient that expedites all healing, creation, and regeneration here on Earth, AND in the cosmos. **You will always have free will–to choose which paradigm you exist within.** You can always choose separation, fear and conditional love. But the *Dimension of Openness* is always available to you. **You're already existing in it–but it is your *awareness* of this existence that yields the benefits of it.** Your awareness however, and active participation within this dimension, is the missing piece–to the acceleration of your wildest dreams.

We are always in circular motion, circular movement and circular fluidity within the *Dimension of Openness*. Life on Earth, and life within the energetic realms, exist in circular fluidity– always moving. There are no cells at rest–there is no real energy at rest–it is always evolving, and always moving. **It's all happening now–it's all happening at once.** The *Dimension of Openness* is this ever changing, ever evolving, always shifting, always moving–in flow. The flow always exists–your job is to be fluid. Your job is to respond to the flow, with fluidity. **Your job is to actualize more flow in your life by existing in circular motion.** There is constant manifestation–you are always manifesting. There is constant giving–you are always giving. There is constant receiving–you are always receiving. **You are alive and you cannot turn off that aliveness.** You are powerful, and you cannot truth off that power. It's all happening now. When we are aware of this circular flow–we can immediately lock in the belief system that it's all happening now, and all happening at once, it's all happening for us, and it's all adding up.

There is no separation, and even when it seems like nothing is happening–it's all happening. When you are in a more edgy/challenging season of life, you KNOW for certain that the movement is leading you to your next evolution. When you are in an aligned, abundant, effortlessly flowing season of life where everything is dropping in, and you feel like you're on top of the fucking world…You KNOW that it is always amplifying and evolving–it just gets better. There is ALWAYS cyclical changing occurring within your physical body, your personal energy field, and cyclical changing within the united energy fields surrounding you. **You cannot escape movement and fluidity.** The only way you can block the movement is by denying the true nature, that IS ever-evolving circular flow. When you become aware and attuned to the ever evolving movement, fluidity and interconnectedness of *all that is* –you experience the rich nutrients, and missing ingredients of your manifestation(s). **You wholeheartedly BELIEVE.** *You notice, you see, and you become aware of the ever evolving fluidity of life.*

There are over 4 million bits of information coming into our mind at all times, our nervous system is constantly processing. **We are always connected.** In order to stay well amongst this infinite realm of interconnectedness we must become conscious of it. We must recognize the vastness, and ultimately the oneness of it. We must naturalize and neutralize the ongoing stimuli through mindfulness. **This mindfulness is the awareness that there is no separation–it is all happening now and we may as well fully experience it.** We must *slow down* to receive the benefits of the regenerative *speed up*. We are always connected…There is no escaping. **There is only shifting realities through consciousness and perspective.** Life is happening now–our awareness of the emotions, energies and fleeting feelings that arise are a way of regulating. Not becoming overwhelmed by *all that is*–but by connecting deeper to it. There is no separation, because of the *Dimension of Openness,* and the TRUTH that everything is happening all at once.

There is no stagnancy–only life giving generation. *But you must CHOOSE it.* I have become a master of constantly regenerating my energy…Constantly existing in life giving ways that serve self, which serve life, which serve the collective which serve the planet, which serve the Universe. *I have decided that there is no separation–and I am always in the co creative flow.* Always giving and receiving. Always trusting in the flow. I understand that there is no separation, and therefore there is nothing I have to do in order to heal, or change, or uplevel, or manifest…Other than simply **choose** the perspective that there is a paradigm available now, where all these desired events are happening.

I don't need to escape to a week-long retreat to heal–*unless I want to.* I don't need to journal for months straight on my ideal reality–*unless I want to.* I don't have to do any self development, spiritual practices as a means to an end–*unless I want to.* Within the *Dimension of Openness* there are no rules or conditions that say "if I do _____ then I get _____". **Our dimension and this consciousness has far expanded beyond conditional love.** This is a free, ever evolving energetic and physical reality of openness. No amount of self developing or obedience to your practice will make you worthy–*you already are.* You get to receive because you are worthy–period. Open up my love–it's here, it's now. **You are alive in the unfolding of it.**

> *"What I've come to discover is that doing what I want*
> *is the most abundance yielding thing I can do"*
> *-Haley Bowler-Cooke*

What I've come to discover, integrate and embody is that doing what I WANT is me in my most sustainable alignment. Doing what I want is the most nourishing and productive choice I can ever make. Because I trust myself, I trust the *infinite supportive energy that exists all around and within me,* and I trust the desires of my body…I know that when I listen to my heart's desires–I'm supported and I am led. Because I am devoted to my alignment…doing what I WANT naturally looks like taking really good care of my mind, body and soul. **Without rules or control– I naturally do the things that support me.** Doing what I WANT

---

allows my business to grow in ways I didn't even see coming and expands me into new and higher portals of receiving. Doing what I want allows me to listen to the desires of my body and eat, move and self care in ways that support my healthiest and most alive physical embodiment. Doing what I want allows me to take care of myself fully, so I can show up wholeheartedly and in pure overflow, for those in my life. Doing what I WANT serves me, serves you and it serves the collective.

Take some time here, breathe in...**Do you trust yourself to do what you want?** The vibe here is dropping the rules and letting yourself out of whatever weird controlling cage you put yourself in–*in the name of self development.* **The new vibration is here babes and it is solely led on love.** The *Dimension of Openness* is a dimension in which there is NO SEPARATION. So...Let love be your discernment. *Breathe in...Breathe out.* Are the rigid self-development practices STILL aligned for You? (Again...maybe they are–they once served me, and served me well)...OR are you ready to let your PLEASURE BODY lead you? I promise you she won't do you wrong. *Your willingness to lean into the truth of unity in all that exists, is the answer to your exponential evolution.* There are no more rules, or conditions–*there is simply existing in what is and choosing what feels better.* **There is always a realm available, in any given moment for your desires to become true for you–a lived reality for you.**

When operating in the *Dimension of Openness,* there is no limit to what is available. There are no conditions as to *when or how* you can receive it. **It is ALL happening–now.** This dimension is you in full embodiment and interconnectedness with your truth *as* divinity. This dimension is–*you* embodied in your truth–as a *manifestation of God.* Your connection to source consciousness is direct, readily available and NATURAL. The *Dimension of Openness* is a chosen reality where you know in every cell in your body that you are supported, it is all connected, it is all adding up AND it is happening–now. The *Dimension of Openness* does not fall into the illusion of separation, or the distortion of disunion. **This dimension does not require years of healing, years of self**

development or *any experience at all.* This dimension just asks for your awareness of everything as infinite. Everything as open. Everything as fluid. **This dimension just asks for your wholehearted surrender to the path of alignment.** The path of surrender and the *actual* embodied trust that it is all happening for you–now. The dimension of openness honors all parts of ourselves and all parts of everything. **The *Dimension of Openness* allows us to exist within ANY potential reality, as real and TRUE for us–when we decide.** When we choose to turn on that channel, when we attune to the frequency of fluidity…Of infinite abundance, love and wellbeing…We enter the realm of possibility. When we turn on that channel, we enter the realm of fluidity, and we become consciously ALIVE in this life. This is the DIMENSION OF OPENNESS–where we work in the quantum realm, where time and space don't exist…**We then bring the energetics of *infinity,* INTO the material dimension.** So we can LIVE in this way, a way of infinite capacities. No conditions. No rigidity–pure flow…The way of our highest timeline.

*You're more divine than you know, more powerful
than you think…Now, act accordingly.*

Let's dive deeper into some of the nuances within the *Dimension of Openness.* As you rise, your standards rise. As you choose to exist within higher realms, as you choose to tap into the truth that is the Dimension of Openness, certain frequencies no longer align. Certain energies no longer vibrate on your level. Your frequency has elevated, and there is no longer congruence with certain outdated realms. Certain things upgrade with you, and certain things fall off. As you rise there are new energetic standards as to what comes WITH you. As to what you experience within *your Dimension of Openness.* When I fully integrated into the *Dimension of Openness,* I became allergic to many old paradigms of thinking, believing and behaving. **Time and money scarcity simply did not match the truth of the infinite abundance of *all that is* inside the open and fluid realms.**

There was no congruency between scarcity and the *Dimension of Openness*–it just didn't make sense. I had to powerfully **decide,** to leave behind old conditioned thoughts, and beliefs around what was possible. I had to get clear on what was actually my truth, what was actually available and *real* for me…And step into the infinite realms of surrender powerfully. I had to step into the infinite realms within the *Dimension of Openness,* and say yes to God's plan. Constriction, control, scarcity, lack, seeking and forcing energy no longer made sense within *this* chosen dimension. It no longer felt right, or even possible to feel scarcity…Because I knew in every cell in my body that there is nothing BUT abundance. What was once a possible thought or belief, was being disproved over and over again–by the truth that is *the Dimension of Openness.* Infinite realities, surrender, alignment, possibilities beyond my own imagination or control became the only possible truth.

I started to loosen my reins. I started to feel the benefits of this level of surrender. I started to see the evidence in my material reality. **My standards of living continued to rise and my level of trust and knowing elevated with it.** It simply didn't make sense to fear the unknown anymore. It simply didn't make sense to force or control anymore. *It just encoded within me that it was all adding up perfectly.* There was a much more divine plan unfolding and working out for me. It was my surrender to this divinity that would actualize the reality of my desires–and beyond. Most people spend their entire life resisting this natural flow and unfolding, that they miss out on the desires of their heart, and the desires that LIFE has for them. *They don't get to experience the Universes path of least resistance and overflow of abundance because they spend so much time fighting against it.* Most people never experience God's plan and the infinite bounty of it because they spend so much time in fear of the unknown and resistance to the present moment. When you powerfully choose to surrender and exist within the *Dimension of Openness* you encode the belief system that it is all adding up. You know there is nothing to fear and that everything is happening in divine order. You know that in your action AND in your rest you are co creating. You know that stagnancy is an illusion, and that it is all happening now. **You know that it is all unfolding in divine order, and you stop getting in the way.** You stop allowing external markers to determine your level of belief, and you hold a knowing so powerfully within yourself–*a knowing that is Unfuckwithable.*

PSA
Ducks will never be in a row
Timing will never be perfect
and you waiting for it to be… is the biggest
procrastination in the books.

So long as you attempt to be in control…You're moving slower than God's plan for you. Drop the perfection and make the moves. *The Dimension of Openness gives you a free pass– always.* There are no distorted perceptions of perfection–there is simply an ongoing check in with self *"Is this a YES in my body?"* "Does this align with my highest timeline?" "Is love the leading energy here?" If the answer is yes–move. If you are trying to grip or control–you are subscribing to a much more basic, less abundant and way less aligned path. **The Universe has a much more easeful path of least resistance laid out for you.** This path can only be discovered through TRUE surrender. Decide that the timing is divine, and MOVE with it. **The Universe moves when YOU decide.** FLOW with the desire, and the yearning within you–and TAKE FLIGHT on your dreams. Most people are creating constriction and limitation in all areas of their lives–therefore, blocking and limiting the levels of receiving that are actually so available and so natural for them. They create timelines like this "I will be married with kids by age 30" "I will be a multimillionaire by the end of this year" "I will find my soulmate this month!" etc etc etc…They create rules and timelines around when certain desires will land–*therefore creating unnecessary pressure and resistance.* This level of control is repelling to what is actually natural for you, and already unfolding for you within your unique path. *Your control and forcefulness is not speeding up God's plan–it is slowing it down.* Your forcefulness is not in congruence with the *Dimension of Openness.* Your rules have created limitations. Your confines of *when and how* certain things will align/desires will manifest, is creating blockages and resistance in your NATURAL, already divinely orchestrated path. Your rules about *how and when* xyz will manifest for you is not only creating resistance to the natural unfolding of it all...It is also creating unnecessary pressure. Pressure repels our natural ease, flow and openness. **Pressure is an illusion.** There is no scarcity. Time is NOT running out. Money is NOT running out. Energy is NOT running out. You are infinite, and it is ALL unfolding in perfect order.

You can be a slave to time...or you can be the master of time

The confines of your rules, and the pressure of your timing, IS what is creating resistance in your unfolding. You create an obscure rule about how this month will be the month where you receive your first 5 figures in business, and in doing so, you create a weird amount of pressure around it, and when it looks like it's not happening...You throw in the towel...Give up...Unplug energetically, and physically and completely deviate from the path. You set a controlling goal to measure your level of worthiness and success, and then pull the plug as soon as you think it is not happening for you. **MEANWHILE your highest timeline is always available, the *Dimension of Openness* where it is all adding up (without your control and rules), and God's divine plan for you is unfolding naturally behind the scenes.** *When you create pressure, rules, limitations, conditions, and when you unplug because your plan doesn't go perfectly...You drop the momentum, and lose out on the magic.* It's shocking how many people are throwing in their towel as the end of months and years approach...They figure that if their desire has not yet manifested within the illusion of time, and the confines of the *man-made calendar year*–that it's just not happening for them (eye roll-yawn-lofuckingl). Most people forget their connection to *all that is,* and forget the truth–that is an ongoing aliveness and fluidity with life that is *always unfolding.* Most people fall into the *group think* and collective egoic shadow, of slowing down their momentum (physically and energetically) as their high pressure, delusional timeline approaches. They forget that divine timing is always happening and unfolding FOR them. But YOU are not most people. You are rare, you are brilliant and you are CHOOSING a life by design. You are consciously moving toward life within the *Dimension of Openness* and you are beginning to see all that is as a co creation, ever evolving and always happening for you. **If you really want what you say you want...You will BEND time.** You will exist within the *Dimension of Openness* and KNOW that time is an illusion that speeds up or slows down based on your level of presence with where you are, and your allowing of surrender to *what is.* When you exist with life as fluid, and understand that you are ALIVE and it is all happening now…You will become the master of time. **You will allow time to be neutral to you, so you can go on doing your thing, working your magic and being the powerful, brilliant, stunning individual that you are.**

Now, let's dive into what my personal wellbeing, self care practices, energetic upgrading and holistic existence looks like in the *Dimension of Openness.* When I started my spiritual journey, my business, my service/life's work, my soul path etc....I was TOTALLY the queen of rituals and routines. I was fucking diligent…Don't fuck with my routine…Don't take me away from my morning meditation, or my daily practice…Oh my God, it would have DERAILED me back then. I was rigid as fuck…And that truthfully served me for *that time* on my journey. But now…Within the *Dimension of Openness*…There is no room for control. **Control is an illusion.** The new Earth, this new vibration…For me at least, is way more open and WAY less rigid. There are no rules around my self care and self development practices anymore. *Everything I do is connected to my evolution, my feeling good and the unfolding of my dreams and desires.* My life now, is a hell of a lot more intuitive, flowy, aligned and natural. It's NATURAL to treat myself, and it's NATURAL to take amazing care of my temple…There is no control over how that looks. It's NATURAL to devote hours on end to my service, my work, my business, my creativity, my clients and my channel. It is NATURAL for me to include standardized spiritual and self development rituals into my day. **It's natural for me to do incredible things for my body, mind and spirit–it's just natural.** There is no control. It is natural for me to crave vegetables, high quality protein and take myself to the gym or yoga studio AND it's NATURAL to be a lazy lizard in human form, and take the rest I know I need. I am devoted to honoring the desires of my body–no rules, no cap, no limits. Simply intuitively honoring what my body needs at any point in time. It's NATURAL to allow pleasure, desire, my inner wants and needs to be felt and heard. **I don't have to be sitting on my meditation cushion to hear the desires of my soul–I'm always tuned in.** There's no reason to schedule a journaling session or a breathwork session every day, unless my inner yearning calls for it. *There are no rules here.*

"I don't fuck with schedules and rituals in that way anymore"

-Haley Bowler-Cooke said on a podcast interview in 2021

My LIFE is a self care practice. My life is a ritual. My focus is alignment moment to moment. I'm not carving out an hour a day to be spiritual, to heal or to manifest. **I'm manifesting, healing and being spiritual all day long.** My joy is spiritual. My anger is spiritual. My naps are spiritual. My sex is spiritual. My yoga practice is spiritual. My road rage is spiritual. My coffee ceremonies are spiritual. My one too many glasses of wine is spiritual. My conversations are spiritual. My solitude is spiritual. *It is all part of this life.* There is no separation. My focus is living my truth moment to moment. There is no hierarchy of spirituality. When I'm doing breathwork with my deepest devotion and intention, and when I'm horizontal watching luxury real estate shows and mainlining pringles I AM SPIRITUAL. There is no separation. There is no hierarchy. There are no rules or limits in my world. I let that control go longgggggg ago. I do me, I do pleasure, and I do alignment–period. I work intentionally as fuck on my life, life's work, relationships, wellness, clients ascension, creations, services and my channel. I also enjoy just *simply fucking living.*

Rituals, routines and strict self development schedules may work for you now, at this point on your journey. It is fabulous if you find a routine that is aligned for you, just make sure it is actually *true* for you. But don't think that just because some guru, some coach or some man standing on a box told you that xyz was the answer– that it is now a practice that you must submit to, and be obedient to until the day you die. There is a lot of sneaky scarcity and illusions of separation that creep their way into the spiritual and self development world, and I want you to intentionally practice dropping into your body and your own truth before committing to any regimes. I want you to be completely empowered aka UNFUCKWITHABLE in your own body, being and divinity to know what is actually aligned for you. When I get asked about consistency, or habits, or routines or rituals– I'm always like *"I just do me".* I consistently do what I want. My decision making process is literally an ongoing introspection of "what do I WANT to do today?" "What do I desire?" "How do I desire to feel?" "What do I WANT?" **Because of the *Art of Receiving,* because of remembering who the fuck I am, because of leaning into edges and finding true surrender..because of staying in my own fucking lane...I have a pretty clear understanding of what is actually serving me.** I gave up the cages of fear based routines and rituals long ago. Now, I do tons of ritualistic work–but from a place of–YUM, this would be fun and helpful...Not from a place of–If I don't do this I won't heal, manifest etc etc. *There are NO RULES in the Dimension of Openness...It is ALWAYS adding up.* Let LOVE be your discernment, and make moves based on your actual inner truth (which is love).

Self indulgence is my middle name. *Living life by design–joyful and Unfuckwithable-y (eek) in my own lane is my vibe.* **My energy**

is my currency—period. I do what makes my mind feel good. I do what makes my body good. I do what makes my energy feel good. I do what makes my LIFE feel good. What feels good shifts and rearranges day to day, moment to moment…So strict routines don't really vibe with my ever changing body and emotional system. Again—stay in YOUR own lane, what feels like alignment to YOU is likely wildly different than what feels good for me. It will definitely be different from the "5 steps to a successful life morning routine" process and whatever else you see trending or being preached in the self help industry. If you wanted to live a life riddled with rules and structures that feel like cages…You wouldn't be choosing *The Dimension of Openness,* and you wouldn't be reading this book. You GET to live in alignment with what feels good for YOU.

My job here again…is to simply bring you home to yourself. Breathe in. Breathe out. Start now…Start living in alignment with what actually feels good for you, and watch your success quickly follow. YOU are the source. YOUR energy is your currency. For me this looks like having top tier standards of living. Top tier self care and a FOCUS on my energy as my currency. My life's work is an extension of me. My money is an extension of me. My love is an extension of me. My service is an extension of me. So the focus is always…Me! (big smile) and inevitably, I get to SERVE the world infinitely. I get to be generous with my time, love, money, gifts and energy. I get to help, support, lead and facilitate. I get to give give give give giveeee—because my focus is always, me. Naturally, when we exist in overflow we GIVE MORE. We live in reciprocity and we flow with the exchange of *all that is.* **No attachment or control—just pure overflow.** This *Dimension of Openness* for me in (terms of self care and self development practices) is this: no illusion of structures, systems, rigid outlines and routines that don't serve my personal alignment. I don't submit to rules someone said I should follow, if they don't actually support my individual evolution. **No one knows me better than I know me, and my job—is empowering you to know YOU.** So babe, be very discerning of what self help and self development rituals are designed for you. Be conscious of which ones truly serve YOU, and which ones are just rebranded old paradigms of limitation and rigidity. YOU ARE THE SOURCE. Your wellbeing is number one. Your self awareness yields that wellbeing, and you are of HIGH FUCKING VALUE. So, DO YOU and do it well.

Let's dive into the nuance of self compassion and forgiveness within the *Dimension of Openness.* **Awareness is observation without judgment.** The same way you sometimes need to vent and don't need "fixing" to feel better...In the same way, you can also notice your thoughts without understanding why they are there. You can notice actions. You can feel your emotions. You can become aware of contraction and expansion within your body, without turning it into a full blown investigation. Holding space for someone you love is listening, and validating without feeling the pressure to change things or fix things...The same goes for loving awareness of *self.* **Observe what's coming up, observe your patterns, observe your state...And letting that observation be enough.** This is a practice that is so profoundly healing and alchemizing within this dimension. For example–this practice may look like a moment of intentional body awareness– "Oh I am aware my body is constricting when this thought/encounter arises" or "I'm aware of my sense of bliss and peace when this is happening" or "Oh that was an interesting thought that doesn't feel like my highest self" or "I'm feeling really anxious...I'm just going to observe 'my human' experience this anxiousness for a bit." *This all sounds simple–and it really is.* The hard work however, is the practice of choosing observation when your egoic mind is so conditioned to fix things. These micro shifts of conscious awareness, and these micro shifts within our BEING is what skyrockets our manifestations, healing and personal fulfillment. As always...It's a practice, it takes alignment, and alignment takes time. The key here is LOVING awareness or observation without any judgment, or any need to fix things.

I know that time is an illusion...*AND sometimes...Alignment takes time.* Because of everyone's unique conditioning–simply deciding to leap into a reality of joy, pleasure, ease, alignment, support, wealth and purpose isn't always *easy*. It isn't always instant. Your unique life experiences, traumas, challenges, conditions, programs and cycles actually REQUIRE your attention, your healing, your awareness, your reprogramming and rewiring. The *Dimension of Openness* doesn't care whether you've rewired or healed–it is a dimension that is available to you now. It is a dimension where there are no misaligned frequencies– simply fluidity and loving existence with ALL that is. Because of our pre-programming, however, to naturalize this way of living…To naturalize your desires and truly properly surrender to them…*The inner work is required.* The "work" piece EVENTUALLY leads you to the *Dimension of Openness* where it is EASY…Fucking beautiful and fucking EASY. ***There is no gate keeping at the "doors" of the Dimension of Openness–you are welcome here anytime…AND entering the dimension of openness willingly…Now that often takes integration, alignment and time…YES time.*** To live effortlessly, easefully and successfully ever evolving within the Dimension of Openness–you must practice aligning to the path. PRACTICE, DEVOTION, and CONSISTENCY of and within the work is required for your inner belief to be in congruence with this free flowing dimension. The work being staying in your lane, walking forward powerfully while basking in the richness of the now…The *Dimension of Openness* is a consciousness and way of living that says "It's all here now, it's unfolding now, its happening now…There is no separation…I am the source AND I am supported and connected to *all that is*". The *Dimension of Openness* is YOU already healed, already wealthy, already aligned, already in your purpose, and on your path. There is nothing you have to change–you can hop into this timeline now. This dimension/paradigm/realm/REALITY is available to you– now…AND you must be present to the level of belief and consciousness you are experiencing in the presence of "now". The *Dimension of Openness* is a realm that is so fucking beautiful…A realm that most people feel they can only experience within confines and conditions of containment. Most people feel they need to escape to actualize this reality–on special occasions, through plant medicine, in retreat, in ceremony, or within specific containers. **The truth is however–it's all happening now. This dimension is right here, and ready for you to claim it.**

This new Earth, new vibration…The DIMENSION OF OPENNESS…It's where I live, it's where my clients live, and it's where I encourage you to live. There is a time and a season for diligent, rigid rituals, and there is a time and season for striving and efforting. We are always evolving and upgrading into new realms. I wouldn't be in the *Dimension of Openness,* if I hadn't first experienced my spiritual awakening, and the need for obedience to my rituals. I wouldn't be *here,* if I wasn't first in my season of 'efforting' and diligent practice–I needed those boundaries to stay on my path. But like I said before, there's a season for boundaries but once you evolve into a higher level…All you need is standards babe. **There's a season for discipline, then the season quickly upgrades into intuitive devotion.** Take a breath now, and without rushing ahead, honor what season you're in. *Breathe it in, take your time.* Does that season feel true for you? Does that season feel GOOD for you? Be true and real with yourself…You may require diligence right now…or maybe you're ready for more flow. If you're in the diligent self love, self care, self development practicing season of your journey and it still feels GOOD…EMPOWERING and forward moving for you–Keeeeeep going with it Queen/King…You're meant to be in it. You are BUILDING foundations and that's fucking BEAUTIFUL. But if you're trapping yourself in a cage or limitation with the shiny wrapper of *self help spirituality and wellness practices*…Babe–it is time to let yourself out of jail. Stop treating your body like a slave and start letting your body, your alignment and your intuitive knowing of what's good for you–lead the way.

When operating in a dimension of openness there is no limit to what is available. There are no polarizing, rigid or hard absolutes–There is only fluidity. There are no hierarchies. No dragged out processes–simply a moment to moment choosing that it is all here now. It is all connected now. **It's all happening now.** There is simply a *decision* to exist within the dimension of openness. The POWERFUL decision to choose a dimension where you are supported, where it is all adding up for you. By choosing this dimension, you are choosing to receive the infinite support that is available across ALL realms. You are rapidly graduating through each dimensional reality of ascension and achieving an experience and existence where there is NO separation–no 3D, no 5D…There is simply interconnectedness. **There are no conditions as to when or how you can receive what it is you desire–you simply attune to the dimension of openness.** It appears that everything is happening all at once…*because it is.* This reality is available now–no matter what your story has been up until this point. This dimension of BEING unfuckwithable and living a life of Thank You, More Please. This reality of alignment, infinite love, wealth, wellbeing, walking your path and purpose powerfully–it is a choice here and now. You can choose powerfully now to step into this dimension. There is no gatekeeping–the dimension is here. **Your highest self, your guides, source consciousness WANTS you to step into this frequency now.** It is available now.

The Dimension of Openness is truly the most exciting and esoteric, yet grounded and regulated experience and reality to exist within. This dimension is a nuanced, yet simple reality to exist within–*and it is SO life giving.* It is so simple to choose the *Dimension of Openness,* the dimension of alignment, ease and surrender…This dimension is readily available. This dimension is a choice, belief system, and an ongoing evolving paradigm–circular and *aways* in flow…It's a series of wirings, firings, and programming of your highest good. This dimension is here now–and ready for you to attune to it. Your attuning to this dimension is determined by your level of alignment with it…Determined by your level of belief that this life gets to be easeful, surrendered, beautiful and successful. There are levels to this–there is a nuance, a dance, a multidimensional and multifactorial approach that I like to teach on and explain. I feel the need to explain WHY not everyone is simply existing within this dimension. I like to explain the reasoning of *WHY* everyone can't and won't just decide to live this way. The *Dimension of Openness* IS accessible now…Yes…AND it often requires a conscious alignment practice (be it days, weeks, or years) to start to understand the infinite realities that are available now. It requires alignment AND sometimes that alignment takes time to encode, and to become naturalized in your beautifully unique and intricate human system. As much as this dimension is available now to everyone–it is also a dimension that only few humans will exist within, at this time on Earth. You must actually be in alignment with the power of this dimension–it must actually be TRUE for you in order to receive the benefits of it. Remember–fake trust isn't the vibe here…So, keep going and you will eventually trust. Keep going, and you will eventually surrender. Keep going, and you will eventually be led into the lived reality OF the *Dimension of Openness.* This dimension is here now…Available now, AND you may likely need to take your own path to get to this level of experienced reality. **Stay devoted–it's all adding up.**

Your experience of the Dimension of Openness will depend on your level of coherence with it. Like any manifestation…If you are matching the frequency of it–you will continue to experience it (and beyond). **Your level of coherence with the Dimension of Openness, comes down to your alignment with it.** Your alignment is the tell tale vibration determining if it is TRUE for you. Just like trust is not a tactic…*Alignment isn't either.* You can't just decide to live in the *Dimension of Openness* and instantly see the results of this dimension, if it isn't actually true for you…*Yet.* It must be and FEEL true for you, in order to powerfully DECIDE to live in that reality, and experience the rewards. The decision is available to you now–your experience of the reality of that decision (or not) will tell you your level of alignment. Feel me? As I love to say "DECIDE and the Universe will get you ready". So you can decide now, that the Dimension of Openness sounds like a vibe you're into, and you can continue to decide that you will live with this open fluidity, and eventually as promised…You WILL reap the rewards. You will commit to this path, and realign when needed…Every test, challenge and edge will simply strengthen your alignment to this path–and eventually, you will find yourself walking this path easefully and actually *living* this reality. **No matter who you are and what your journey has been up until this point–you get to decide now.** It's not a matter of time–whether you just started your spiritual consciousness journey or you've been at it for decades…You can decide NOW to choose the *Dimension of Openness.* You can decide to live this way, align to it over and over and reap the rewards along the way. It is available now to you. ***Importantly…I will say it again–it does however require your alignment.*** Your alignment with this level of trust, devotion and surrender. Your coherence with such a nuanced high level realm–takes alignment.

The dimension of openness is infinitely available *now.* **You can simply choose to continue to turn that channel on for the rest of your life.** You can decide now that that is *JUST HOW YOU LIVE.* The catch here IS…it takes TIME, devotion to your own path and often the experience of lots of varying dimensional realities. The varying dimensional realities will eventually lead you to the *Dimension of Openness* (by varying dimensions I mean 3D, 4D, 5D etc.). The varying dimensions get you closer to the CHOSEN reality of the *Dimension of Openness*…AND you can choose and live within the chosen dimension now. **If it is true for you now–claim it.** If you need more time for integration–*take it.* Don't rush your path…If the *Dimension of Openness* feels obscure, far away or not real or true for you *yet*…Keep going. Keep rising into *higher* dimensions, and eventually you will come to the space of surrender. A space where you understand in every cell in your body, in your mind, heart, consciousness…You understand it in your BONES–that the *Dimension of Openness* is here now, and that there is NO separation. You understand that you get to choose it over and over and over again.

The *Dimension of Openness* is the consciousness and paradigm I choose…*It is aligned for me–true for me.* It makes sense to me…it feels natural to me…There are no rules, no limits…everything is infinite. All happening, all the time…all at once–it makes the most sense. This dimension feels natural...It feels right, it feels true. I am not only *connected* to *all that is* when I sit on my meditation cushion. I am not only *connected* to spirit when I channel. I am not only in *devotion* when I pray. I am not only in *union* when I lay out my yoga mat, or when I consciously connect to source...I am ALWAYS connected–I am always aligning. I am always in my *work*. I am always on my path. **I am always existing within the *Dimension of Openness* by simply knowing I exist within it.** I reap the rewards of this flow simply by knowing I am in the flow. I know it is all adding up...it's all happening now. **I am alive in this life. My life is unfolding now, and my desires are dropping in now...*It's all happening now.***

Woooooowwwwweeee my love–we really went deep. **The *Dimension of Openness* is my absolute favorite dimension to channel about, speak on, teach on and exist within.** It really is the purest, truest and most natural way of existing. The embodiment of a soul experiencing life on Earth in a very high level manner. It is nuanced, complex to conceptualize but SO natural, and simple to live...*A true remembering...A true knowing.* **I encourage you to read over this chapter many times until it just locks in and lands.** It takes some time to align properly to this vibration, and my *knowing* is that the more you integrate the channeled wisdom within this chapter, and begin to experience it in your lived reality–the faster you will begin to exist within this dimension, and reap all the gorgeous rewards of it. **It is all happening now.** You are infinitely supported and everything is going according to plan. Take a step back, surrender deeper, and open up to the energy of allowing–*you are interconnected to all of it, and it is unfolding perfectly in divine order.*

Now...For the homework portion of this chapter, I want to keep it potent and simple...I will be giving you ONE task...the task will be to begin affirming to yourself, breathing into the affirmation and beginning to experience the programming of the belief that...

"It is all adding up…It is all happening now…
It's happening all at once…I can't turn it off,
I can't even slow it down…
It's happening for me–NOW…
I am ALIVE in my dream life"
Your desires are happening now.
Your healing is happening now.
It is all happening–now. Affirm this, integrate this. Breathe it in
"It is all adding up…It is all happening now".

Breathe that in, affirm, repeat it and let it encode all day long.

Let the potency, and truth of this lengthy affirmation encode you. Let this affirmation upgrade you, and relieve you of any illusions of pressure or separation. Let this knowing integrate into your system, and allow you to surrender deeper. Let this knowing guide your actions, thoughts and intentions. Let this knowing expand, and open you UP, to more and more *aligned* receiving…More opportunity, more love, more wealth and more wellbeing.

It is all adding up…It is all happening now.

CHAPTER 11

BEING UNFUCKWITHABLE

Your existence is unrepeatable…
And that is something to celebrate.

Every last cell in your body was created with divine intention.
You are truly one of a kind. You ARE unrepeatable. You are
cosmic brilliance. You are radiant. You are of the Earth and of the
stars. You are so uniquely individuated, yet completely
encompassed in the oneness of *all that is.* You are rare, wild and
free. You are loved beyond measure. You are infinitely supported.
You are infinitely powerful and you are HERE ON PURPOSE. **You
are UNFUCKWITHABLE.** The processes of self discovery and
empowerment within this book, has created an undeniably
magnetic embodiment, and wildly profound self concept within
you–*the world sees and feels it too.* You understand yourself as
powerful, rare and unique. You have individuated to such a high
level, that you naturalized yourself into the *Dimension of
Openness.* You have ACHIEVED the alchemy of *individuation*
INTO pure *oneness.* You are living, breathing and stunningly
embodied in the *Dimension of Openness.* You understand
yourself as a never ending INsourced powerful creator, AND you
understand ALL beings to hold the same power in their *own
unique way.* You (unlike most however), have actually tapped into
it. **You've turned on your power and attuned your frequency
to a higher baseline.** *You are empowered in completion
now…*You are intensely aware of your gifts and you WALK with
that certainty. You are more confident than ever, in your own
innate brilliance–and you hold a HIGH standard of living. **You are
fuelled with the overflow of love, supportive energy,**

abundance and high level consciousness. Fully empowered… *You are a walking embodiment of Unfuckwithableness.* This empowerment allows you to naturally support the collective ascension. Your empowerment is an invitation to those around you to see themselves in their own unique power, and to rise to their own highest timeline. **You are Unfuckwithable, and your very existence is a permission slip to the rest of the world to elevate into their own Unfuckwithableness, too.**

When you know who you are… everything is easy

Being unfuckwithable is about observing your life while simultaneously embodying the sensations of it. When you do this…You enter a very high level of existence. You have come to the point in your life where you KNOW that it is all happening *now.* **You know that you are alive in the dream…*ALIVE in your dream life.*** You have your "owl head" turned all the way on, and you can see with new eyes…You see with 360 degree awareness. You see that it has all added up to now, and there is even MORE magic on the way. *You see and feel the never ending, ever evolving, gifts and bounty of this life.* Being Unfuckwithable is you *knowing* that you are powerful–always…Always open to create, always open to receive. You know what success means to you…*And you effortlessly achieve and receive it.* You know what wealth means to you…*And you effortlessly experience it.* **You know that happiness, joy and wellbeing is always available.** You let *fulfillment* be the focus–and you KNOW that abundance naturally follows. You know who you are, and you know your truth. You live life in a grounded yet ever evolving…And *open to miracles* manner. You are in flow. You DON'T need *much* to live a spiritual, successful and fulfilling life…But once you ARE living a spiritual and fulfilling life…It seems counterintuitive, and frankly distorted to deny yourself of the infinite MORE that is so available to you. It seems silly to stay in any illusion of lack and scarcity (disguised as martyr archetypal benevolence), when you understand the infinite abundance, of *all that is.* **BEING Unfuckwithable is about KNOWING that you are SO whole and complete as you are, you don't need anything outside of you to fill your *already full* completeness...AND you KNOW that if you DO hold a desire for *more,* that you are worthy and capable of having it.** You know that anything you desire from a place of truth, certainty and personal power is MEANT for you—and READILY available now. *You ARE Unfuckwithable, and it is all happening FOR you.*

The Universe is working for You – It's all adding up now
You don't have to rush it – You don't have to control it
We've got You.
Place your order with us.
Stay aligned – Intentional and focused – Then let it go
The rest is up to us.

Living life as an UNFUCKWITHABLE being, is really just a coming home to your truth, and to your true nature. Beyond *living* that true nature, you are a walking embodiment of it—you are proudly expressing that truth to the entire world. *Being Unfuckwithable is an act of rebellion, in a world of constriction and distortion.* Being Unfuckwithable is a remembering of your innate divinity, and being a walking embodiment of that level of freedom...*A walking permission slip, to all who will bravely walk forward in their own unique embodiment of freedom.* Being Unfuckwithable requires a high level of discernment...A very intentional level of awareness of your own energy, and of the energies that attempt to interact with you. **Your holistic wellbeing must be top tier.** Your energy must be clean, your mental health must be regulated, your spiritual consciousness must be open, and your physical body must be strong and thriving. **There is a high level of personal power required to live life *Unfuckwithably,* and this level requires you to take good fucking care of your body and energy system.** When you consciously attune your energetic and physical system to optimization, you BECOME Unfuckwithable, and you can BE the steward of your life...You can lead the way while also allowing yourself to be led. You are led by divinity, led by truth, led by a consciousness that is LIFE GIVING (not extractive or distorted), and you can exist in a paradigm that serves you, your life, and your purpose *infinitely*. As I am writing this book...In early 2023, we are in a unique time on Earth...A time where your truest self awareness, sovereignty and consciousness is being put to the test. It is critical for you to stay strengthened, stay in your thrival, stay aware, and stay truly ALIVE.

As we kick off this juicy, and all encompassing chapter let's get you connected to your INsourced aliveness, your highest frequency energy, and your innate personal power.

Here is a list of ways to ensure you are primed for an Unfuckwithable life:

-move your body with love, move your body often
-avoid stagnancy, choose fluidity
-eat intuitively, nourish your body in ways that actually support your unique body
-consciously and regularly cleanse your energy
-get fuck tonnes of sunshine
-stop wasting your time
-stop multitasking, be present
-be focused, dial your energy on what you are present to
-stop fucking around on your phone, use your phone for tasks then get off of it, use your devices—don't let your devices use you
-get out in nature daily
- if you feel stiff—stand up and stretch, don't sit for too long
-drink a tonne of clean/pure/chlorine free water
-be mindful when you eat, be mindful when you drink, show gratitude to what you ingest
-meditate, be centered, focus on grounding yourself
-surround yourself with good people

-clean and purify your environments
-tie up loose ends, brain dump and clear your mind often
-cold plunge, consciously purify your body and energy with water and crystals
-make a conscious practice of decluttering, purging and releasing energy and material 'things'

Focus on your energy as your currency, and take good fucking care of your gorgeous body!

As you walk the walk as an Unfuckwithable human, and exist within an ever evolving new paradigm…It is necessary to let LOVE be your discernment, and let your highest knowing lead your daily actions and intentions. It is more necessary than ever before to diligently notice what is serving you…What is life giving, and what is not. As you rise, and as the collective rises in ascension and awakening, there can also be a rise in polarizing energies. To ensure your energy is pure, your path is true for you, and that you are aligned…Make a conscious practice of checking in with LOVE as your discernment. Check in with the feeling of wellbeing, check in with what is life giving, and what feels nourishing to you. Let love be your discernment when it comes to your beliefs, thoughts, and ways of interacting. *Let love be your discernment when it comes to anything and everything–a constant check in of "does this feel right, good and TRUE for me?"* **You're already doing this, you are already living this…I simply invite you into even more diligent awareness of it.** Doing it bigger now…And more intentionally now. I invite you into a higher level of awareness of the importance of YOUR energy, and the energy you connect with. As you walk courageously forward in your new paradigm, let your connection to what is ACTUALLY REAL, and TRUE for you, be strengthened. **Connect deeper to the real people in your life.** Connect deeper to nature…Actually touch, witness, feel and immerse yourself in nature regularly. Pay attention to vibration…The vibration within AND around you…Pay attention to the vibration coming off other people, environments, and things. Be diligent about the energy you participate in (on your devices/technology/media)...Check in–is the vibration of a certain song, movie, instagram reel, tik tok, conversation etc. of light, life serving and high vibration? Or is it extractive...Is it holding a darkness that does not feel of service to your evolution, and to life on Earth? *If it is not of a high and/or life giving vibration...Why are you interacting with it?*

There is SO much nuance to this conversation around being Unfuckwithable, and existing in a heavily programmed society. So let me clear this up–being Unfuckwithable is NOT about being "high vibe" all the time...It's not about always being in a good or positive mood...***But it is ABSOLUTELY about being REAL.*** We want to ensure that there is rich, raw, realness in ALL that we interact with. Even when we're sad, heart broken, in pain etc. we get to *choose* that there is a healing and shifting frequency here that *moves* us...A frequency of depth, raw truth, and alchemy–a frequency of being ALIVE. Being Unfuckwithable is a constant reactivation, and strengthening, of your own connection to the divinity within you. **You are a manifestation of God–as you already know...You are *not* separate.** You are a soul having a human experience. You are of a high level caliber, a rare individual...AND you also exist within a heavily programmed society. There are countless distractions and distortions surrounding your material environment at any moment in the day...***Being Unfuckwithable is an ongoing CHOOSING of who you want to be, and how you want to live.*** This requires diligent and ongoing intentional activation of your own intuition and internal compass...*An ongoing check in of: "What impulse is there for you?" "What information is arising now?"* Constantly strengthening your intuition, and constantly checking in with: "What is being communicated now?" In this heavily brainwashed, controlled and programmed society you MUST powerfully CHOOSE your own sovereignty, again and again.

Being Unfuckwithable is an unwavering, clear and focussed path...We are powerful and stable in our paradigm...AND there are old, outdated and expired paradigms that *still* exist. The heavily programmed world exists...And even though you are in the *Dimension of Openness,* and riding much higher above those paradigms and illusions...You will STILL come up to them on your path. As you deepen your self actualization, and further awaken into your highest timeline (that is always ever-evolving), you will vibrate at a much more clear frequency, a frequency that does not allow the old, expired systems to penetrate you...*AND they will still be there.* No matter how far along you are on your journey of highest self actualization...You will STILL most likely come up to edges, expired systems and outdated ways of existing...***It is in THESE moments that you realign yourself to YOUR truth, and deepen the strength of YOUR paradigm.*** These illusionary and extractive systems sneak up, not only through people and environments...But also through technology and devices...So—use your devices, *but don't let your devices use you.* Stop outsourcing your intellect...stop googling every last question your mind comes up with...YOU have the answers. Be discerning about what is LIFE GIVING, versus what is extractive, when it comes to what you consume. *Be intentional in your own frequency, check in with yourself often—How are YOU being felt?...When people think of you, or feel into your energy...What do they feel?* Also be intentional about what frequencies surround you...How do you feel around certain people/places/things? **When you can consciously attune yourself to the energies around and within you, you can clearly decide what feels good and what doesn't.** When you powerfully tap into the actual frequency of what is occurring around you, and within you—you can better empower yourself to choose what is meant for you, and what is not. You can actually FREE yourself of the illusions, and you can open yourself up more powerfully to *all that is* within the *Dimension of Openness.*

When you are living life on a high level of constant evolution (as you are by now, if you have been present to these integrations)...***Who you were last week doesn't even match to who you are today.*** Who you were doesn't even come close to who you are now. You are evolving at RAPID speeds...Rapid evolution in both energetics and in your material world. Internal shifts occur, and the results show up externally–fast. This is why the processes within this book have been regulating you, taking you through the necessary safety work, and the energetic and physical regulation that is required to naturalize these rapid levels of evolution. You have been guided to create intuitive rituals of RICH self care, you have been practicing living intentionally and presently, and you have been led to *lead yourself.* You have been guided to observe and embody your beautiful life. *You have truly come SO FAR!*

With this quick evolution–there is rapid transformation, and that transformation appears both internally and externally, within the *Dimension of Openness.* **Your internal world elevates, and your external reality upgrades.** This rapid evolution that you are experiencing, REQUIRES regular "check ins"…It is SO nourishing to slow down and to recognize just how far you've come–*slow down to speed up.* It is so nutrient dense to our healing, and to our desire actualization, to really honor ALL of your evolutions–*to celebrate each milestone, and each season.* **Honor just how far you've come, honor your growth, and honor the journey of *all* the various versions of you…*The versions of you, that led you here.*** Let's do this together now…*Breathe in…Breathe out.* Notice yourself, drop in…Notice where you are now, and notice where you were…Notice the growing pains/the edges between then and now. Notice the growth and evolution…*Notice the lessons, the teachings, and the medicine that exists within each of the versions of you.* Notice the revelations…The "aha" moments in every season. *What was the focus last month, and what is it now?* What was the theme last year…And what is it now? Notice yourself, witness your brilliance and honor your bravery and devotion. ***There are rich nutrients, and healing nervous system regulation, in slowing down, to see all that you are, and all that you have become.*** Now celebrate all that you are…Take a moment here, to be so fucking proud of who you have been, and who you've become. BASK in all your success, growth and evolutions!

Now, let's drop into some more interactive work…
Some ways of being when you exist
AS the Unfuckwithable being.

BEING UNFUCKWITHABLE
vibes / beliefs / levels of reality

"I am so grateful for where I am…AND I know that evolution is natural, and more is always available, and so I say YES to the more that is already here, and yes to the more that is on its way."

"As I live my UNFUCKWITHABLE life, I am constantly disrupting the illusions, with the TRUTH. I am constantly choosing my own innate brilliance, expression and beliefs that are foundational in LOVE, and I am walking with that truth bravely. I am a disruptor of distorted realities of hierarchical power, control and scarcity, and I am the living embodiment of sovereignty and freedom. I disrupt the illusion with the TRUTH, and I walk courageously toward the life that is true for me, and meant for me."

"Most people adapt to the world around them at the price of their own fulfillment…But not me…I am not most people. I create a world that fulfills me. Instead of adapting to expired realities, I create a world that I WANT to exist in. I create a reality that I adore. I create a life that I am proud of. I am not sacrificing, or adapting or trying to fit in…I allow my truth to be free, and I BE fully ME! I choose a life that I am obsessed with. I create a new world, a new paradigm, a new reality, that feels TRUE for me."

"I am available for the blessings that are here now. I am open to the desires that are ready to land now. I am open to deeper levels of enlightenment now. I am open to higher levels of awareness now. I am open to a healthier body now. I am open to healing now. I am open to more joy and euphoria now. I am available to receive what is meant for me now. I open up. I get 1% more receptive, and I receive. Thank You, More Please"

"It is all adding up. It is happening now. I am alive in my dream life, this is my life by design. It's happening now, and so I surrender to it. Everything has added up to this point…It is all landing now. My desires are here now…I feel it, I know it. I am alive in all of it…Seeing it, feeling it, and fully experiencing this unrepeatable moment in time."

"I just know…I have the knowing…It is who I am, it is what I was designed for…If I want it, it is MEANT for me. I trust the timing. I trust God/Universe/Source/Creator…I trust. I just know. I don't have to understand the 'how,' I just KNOW, in every cell in my body, that it is happening for me."

"I just thrive. It is natural for me to thrive. I don't have to make an effort or work hard at it–it is my very nature. I just have to focus on feeling good, and I thrive. I focus on my energetic and physical system…I ask myself–*How can I feel better today?* I naturally do the things that support me–energetically, mentally, emotionally, physically and spiritually. I just thrive. I optimize everything in my life to succeed. I am effortlessly successful, healthy, balanced and happy. I naturally and easily receive. It is simple for me to thrive– and so I will, and so I do, and so it is."

"I am the Main Character and I act like it. Everything I do is meaningful, fulfilling and powerful. I live as though there is a camera crew following me around documenting my extraordinary life by design. My life is a life to be recognized, I am proud of who I am, and devoted to my ever evolving elevation and evolution."

Take a moment, and breathe in all this medicine…Let it all land.

Being Unfuckwithable...
It's an energy thing.
It's a power thing.
It's an ease thing.

Being Unfuckwithable is…
Having what you want.
Magnetizing your desires, love, money and opportunity.
Creating impact, and leaving the world better than you found it.

Being Unfuckwithable is You…
Glowing, radiant and HAPPY
Confident, alluring and CERTAIN
In trust, surrender and OPENNESS

Being Unfuckwithable is a guaranteed life of PURPOSE
You know yourself – you love yourself.
You see YOU, and you see others…For who they truly are.
You are empowered, and you empower those around you.

YOU ARE A BENEVOLENT GENEROUS BEING
You receive in high level ways
You give in high level ways
You experience infinite flow
You experience overflowing abundance

YOU LIVE LIFE WELL
You live life fully
You experience all that your soul came here to experience

Your personal power is Unfuckwithable.
Your alignment is Unfuckwithable.
Your certainty, innate brilliance and essence is Unfuckwithable.

**You being in this state of UNFUCKWITHABLENESS,
is a GIFT to the world.**

BEING Unfuckwithable is the vibe of INsourcing your personal power, in the unique ways that are TRUE for you. Personal power is BEING with uncomfortable emotions, observing them as they arise, and properly processing them. Being Unfuckwithable is an awareness of yourself that goes *beyond* this dimension. Being Unfuckwithable, is integrating the truth that you are not your fleeting emotions, and you are not your shifting energy...Instead you are a powerful consciousness that is aware of yourself...*Aware of ALL OF IT.* **Your Unfuckwithable power is knowing that no matter what kind of mood you're in...No matter how high or low your energy is, and no matter what is happening in your external world...YOU are powerful.** Being Unfuckwithable, is an embodied knowing that YOU are exactly where you need to be, and that everything is unfolding FOR you. You know that you are existing in the *Dimension of Openness,* and that you are INFINITELY supported by *ALL that is...***You wholeheartedly trust that it's all adding up–*and so it is.*** When you are operating in your Unfuckwithableness, you are not waiting for external circumstances to validate what you *already know to be true...*You know it, you move with that knowing, and the universe responds every time–like clockwork. You are Unfuckwithable...**You hold the energy, you stay in devotion, and you are dedicated even when it doesn't look like it's adding up–you stay in it.** You walk with your mission even when it doesn't look like it's making a difference. You walk with your INsourced certainty, and you BE the leading energy that everything around you responds to. You hold the magnet, you hold the energy of elevated knowing, you hold the power, and everything around you rises to meet you there. ***You are the common denominator*–**you know this, and you LIVE this. You release the illusions of timelines, pressure and scarcity. You no longer take score...You don't need to *check* if it's working...You KNOW that it is. You know what you have to do when your action is required, and you do it–powerfully. You know who you want to be, and you be it. You are no longer outsourcing your power for micro hits of dopamine, or external validation. You create your own sense of success, ease and certainty–you create your own insourced joy and fulfillment–you no longer rely on outside sources to make you feel something–*you already ARE it.* **You hold your power, you walk with purpose, and you operate fully as the leading energy of your life.**

Affirm: *"My confidence is something that cannot be shaken. I am unwavering in my power. I am UNFUCKWITHABLE. It's not about circumstances, it's not about what's going well, or what's not…It's the pure essence of the power that I ALWAYS AM, it is that constant access to power that allows me to be unshakeable."* You have access to this level of power now, it's here now–over the many weeks of you integrating the work within this book–you have become it. **By this point on your journey, you are *not only* seeing yourself as Unfuckwithable…But you are actually EMBODYING this way of being–YOU ARE UNFUCKWITHABLE.** By now you are likely already seeing the rewards drop into your material reality. You are truly embodying ALL that you are. Your innate brilliance is in full experience, and full expression…All of you is on display for the world to see. **You are experiencing your power, and you are being recognized for it.** You fully OWN your PUREST power…A power that does not waiver, a power that is not circumstantial–a power that is constant. It's not "when xyz happens, then I am powerful." or "When so and so loves and validates me, then I am powerful." or "When I have x amount of money in my bank account, then I am powerful"…No no no, my love, you are powerful–period. I see you, I actually feel like I know you…The type of person who made it this far, the person who is so focused, driven and dialed into their own self development, yet so open to the divinity of all that is…You are someone who does not go unnoticed. You are rare. You are recognized. You are ambitious, spiritual, individuated AND connected to the oneness within the *Dimension of Openness*. You understand your unique rarity, and you understand the power of interconnectedness. **You really are–one of a kind.** You are someone who is memorable, you are the type of person who cannot be forgotten–you are brilliance embodied, and every last inch of you is gorgeously Unfuckwithable. I effortlessly see you…I see, and FEEL your power. *Now go let it rawr!!*

Your Unfuckwithableness is your ability to hold a grounded certainty, and power through ALL seasons of this precious life. You know there is richness in the full embodiment of the highs AND the lows–you're here for it all. *You know the drill "feel it all to have it all"–plain and simple.* You know that it is in your nature to grow, learn, achieve and move on. **Evolution is NATURAL.** It actually takes more work to slow your evolution down, than it does to speed it up. You know you are always moving and evolving…Always giving, and always receiving–you are highly reciprocal, in your exchange with life, and all the abundance that it has to offer you. You let your desire lead you, and you allow your knowing to pave the way. **You, in your Unfuckwithableness KNOWS that it is safe, and abundance yielding, to lean into new edges and come out on the other side powerfully.** You are willing to experience the temporary discomfort.. For the ever evolving bliss, satisfaction and success. You know that the edges within the growth seasons are beyond worth it. The discomfort is unavoidable–you know this and you hold this (your suffering through the uncomfortableness however, is a choice). Your desire leads you, you hold the certainty, you know you are powerful enough to walk forward with it, you grow, you evolve, and you cash in your rewards along the way–*rinse and repeat.* **Evolution is always occurring.** Growth is your natural state. Evolution is inevitable for you, as are your desires. Evolution is always happening…**We can't turn it off…*We can sure as hell speed it up though.*** Your awareness of your constant evolution is the only missing ingredient to your life by design recipe. Your awareness of the naturalization of your evolution–is the secret sauce. You can always turn on the awareness, you can always attune to the natural flow of life–*and replenish that nutrient.* You are never deficient–*your thrival is just one observation away.* Your awareness, and regulation of your growth, your seasons and the ever evolving movement of this life…ALLOWS you to flow with it (as opposed to working against it). *You in your Unfuckwithableness knows that it is all adding up, knows that it is all happening now.* We are always moving, there is no stagnancy–there is only flow. You in your Unfuckwithableness knows that there is no separation, there is only ever a missing attunement to the naturalization of the growth. You consciously tap in...You consciously attune to the rhythms. **You constantly attune to the ever evolving momentum.** If you ever fall into separation–you bring yourself back to the *Dimension of Openness,* and you remember...You are here, it is happening now...**You are ALIVE in the ongoing evolution, and the ever changing desires, and realities that you consciously exist within.**

A question to ask yourself, as you continue on
your ever evolving evolution over a lifetime...
***What are you still available for that no longer
serves your next level?***
Get real with yourself (if you truly desire the shifts).
Notice what you have been allowing–that
is no longer true for you...
See it, and release it.
*Recognize what you **are truly desiring,** see the new standard,
and become unavailable for anything less.*

The vibe is always–experiencing the fullness of life. Fully immersing yourself in all the joy, euphoria, fun and excitement. Grounding yourself in the neutrality of the seemingly mundane moments in life, and leaning further into surrender in the *nothingness.* There's also no shying away from the shadows, no suppressing the pain, no escaping the uncomfortableness... There's no leaving ANY parts of you behind. ***Being Unfuckwithable, and squeezing the juice out of this life, is about falling in love with ALL of you.*** This energy is about so much more than situational confidence, conditional power or performative happiness. Like I'm confident in certain situations, or I feel powerful, and trustful when all my circumstances are aligned...No babe–we have gone SO much deeper than that. We are operating in the Unfuckwithable, unshakeable and unwavering frequencies of power. **YOU ARE POWERFUL–PERIOD.** Your baseline frequency continues to rise–with every new upgrade. Everything you desire, now desires you. *You are magnetic, effortlessly successful, you ooze POWER and confidence...You are Unfuckwithable.* You trust yourself, you trust your intuitive knowing, you move quickly with the impulses, you take aligned action strategically, and you move with body based intentionality. You know that at every new edge, the new desires are there and ready for you. *You know that what you desire is available for you...It's all so much closer than you think.* You devote to your alignment–your energy is your currency, and you take very fucking good care of yourself. You know that your energetic bandwidth, and your capacity is infinite–there is no cap. **You focus on taking good care of yourself, and serving with purpose, and with deep intention...And you exist in high levels of energetic exchange with the Universe.** High levels of reciprocity is the absolute standard...*Inhale you receive, exhale you give.*

You come to experience your desires as natural, you come to expect them. You have upgraded from the energy of wishing and hoping for it...To knowing its inevitable and excitedly expecting it to manifest...ALL the while, knowing you are whole and complete NO MATTER WHAT. Your success is guaranteed, it's not a fluke– it's certain. *You are Unfuckwithable no matter what, you are good no matter what...But you come to expect it.* **You come to expect that good things will continue to happen for you.** You come to expect that the better it gets, the better it gets. You come to expect that with any door shutting there is a bigger, brighter and better door opening. You live in flow, trust and surrender because you know the Universe has your back, and most importantly, *you know that you've got you.* You have been upgraded to a pure frequency. You have new elevated standards, and you are not energetically available for anything less. **You understand the realm of infinites–and you no longer limit yourself.** You have created spaciousness in your life, to experience inner peace, serenity and ease. You also take powerful action in alignment, when you feel the urge and know it's your time. Your energetic bandwidth is clean and clear–open to receive. You are operating at a high level–therefore you know it's not about boundaries anymore...It's about standards. Your vibration emits an aligned portal to receive on the same, or higher levels of frequency. You have clean, pure and soft landing strips, for all that is aligned to drop in. You embody the energy of BEING Unfuckwithable–and you are devoted fully to the work…You know that it's an inside job, so you go inward. You move, and the universe responds–every time. You put out the signal, and the universe aligns.

On your journey as you continue to evolve over and over again…
You check in with yourself.
*You ask yourself regularly…**What needs cleaned up,***
rearranged, healed or released in my life?

You have become the high level individual, who experiences everything they desire, and everything that life desires for them. **You have been empowered to BE so fully and unapologetically YOU.** You have understood what living your own unique definition of wealth, success, ease, wellness, flow and purpose is for you. **You have opened up to your nature.** You live in thriving aliveness, and you radiate that glow from your inner being. You have defined your desires, you know them to be true for you…You are co creating a life of beauty, wealth, and abundance in your material reality. You experience an inner state of peace and fulfillment. You in your fullness have become so magnetic, so alluring to all that you desire when you own and embody your truest essence. ***You are empowered now, to experience such ease and flow in your manifestation…In your healing, and in your alignment.*** You are now clear, you are focussed, and you have become the master of refinement. You have become the master of your personal standards. You have become empowered to master your own lived reality, and empowered experience of financial abundance (in whatever form feels supportive to you). You have become empowered to be a master manifester of your desires (both tangible and intangible), with A LOT of ease. You understand the huge component that is your ENERGY. Maybe in the past it annoyed you to hear the common phrase *"everything is energy"* –But now, you understand and accept it as true…You accept it as law. You are now educated and empowered by this truth, and allow this truth to lead your beliefs, and perceived reality. You understand it all as deeply connected. *You have learned to be the MASTER of your energy, and therefore the creator of your life.*

You are just living differently now, up and up–you rise. You don't feel the need to explain to those who don't get it…This is just how you live…You own it. You are rare, and you know it. Everyone is beginning to wonder who you are, and how your life is this good?! *Like a magic wand… Abracadabra, you just live this way now–it is natural now…You feel grounded about it all…It's just normal for you.* This rise and elevation is standard, to be expected and completely regulated in your system. You deserve it all…You are worthy–period…You always have been, and you always will be. *You are just more aware of your power now.* You know you have elevated, *and so it is.* You know you are the Main Character, and so you act accordingly. **You have consciously been elevating your frequency this entire journey together.** You have been consciously rising, refining and aligning. You have become more pure, more certain and clear. *You have mastered your OWN energy.* It has become so natural, so effortless, SO embodied. You understand and embody the codes of effortlessly attracting, receiving and creating (not only the frequencies, and feelings within your energy and body that feel sooooo fucking good)…But you know how to create the actual physical material experiences, and tangible results. **You are empowered to actually HAVE the things that you deeply desire.** You love your quantum energetic reality, and you love your physical material world–there is no difference…No separation–and you know this. You feel empowered to be healthy, happy, grounded, and empowered to walk in your purpose powerfully. You also feel empowered to easefully manifest the money in your bank, your dream house, dream car, the relationship of your dreams, your dream interview or show, life changing opportunities, and the infinite resources that are here, in the playground, that *is* planet Earth. You feel confident to manifest any physical, or non-physical thing or experience that you want...You know that your soul given desires are meant for you. You have worked through the process to know what desires are actually TRUE for you, and in that knowledge, you are empowered to manifest them...***You know that it's done...It's yours...It's MEANT FOR YOU.***

You now exist within the energetic reality of oneness...The *Dimension of Openness.* You are living a very elevated experience on Earth–*because you know you are connected to all that is.* You are experiencing the power of divinity, in your every move. You are consciously co creating with source consciousness...You are connected to *all that is.* You actually feel tapped in, and attuned to the infinite realms...You breathe into it, it feels true for you. You are experiencing true co-creation, with life itself. **You are ALIVE.** You exist in flow, and only in ways that are LIFE GIVING. **You are consciously regenerating your energy system and physical body.** You are supported...Held, and connected. Throughout this book, through integrating the work within each chapter, you have UPGRADED your energetic and physical body. You have done the integrations to experience and embody the ultimate BEINGNESS, of your highest self. You have BECOME the match to your desires. You have become the match for what LIFE desires for you. ***You are empowered with the tools, and the identity to actually manifest your desires now...Yes, I mean–now...Not down the road...Not some day...but NOW.*** You know that you manifest what is TRUE for you. You know that you are infinitely supported, and you also know that divine timing is a decision...*The decision that it IS divine timing is now* (you will know when you're ready, or...The Universe will GET you ready). You have integrated the codes of openness...You know you can make the decision to access your desired dimension within the *Dimension of Openness* at any moment in time. You have done the work, and you will continue to do the work. **It's all here now, everything that you desire is real, it exists, and it is available to you.** You have encoded the laws, and the truths of energy. You have upgraded your own frequency with every single reflection, with every single breath in, and breath out. With every intentional awareness, and moment of presence...With every integration of the lessons within each chapter...You have become your highest self. You have come to understand your truest self. You are EMPOWERED. You are ELEVATED. You are READY. **You ARE UNFUCKWITHABLE.**

Being Unfuckwithable means you see your FULL self...Your vulnerabilities, and your power. You see your tender parts, and you see your most strengthened parts. You are willing to fully see, and recognize who you are in the world...As a complete human being, with a past, present and future ahead. You are willing to see yourself as an infinite soul..And you understand that you exist within a much more vast dimension, than the confines of your chronological age, or your physical life on Earth. You hold yourself through the edges, always leaning in further, and coming out powerfully. You are Unfuckwithable, and that means being real, raw and true. You aren't always high vibe and happy–**but no matter what, you're powerful.** You experience the depths of sadness, overwhelm and doubt, but you come back to your center faster and faster every time. **You are a whole fucking human, and you LOVE that about you.** You love your pace, you love your growth, and you love your lessons. You love all the beautiful and joyful events in your life, and you're willing to go to work on the sides of yourself that feel prickly. You unapologetically love the parts of yourself that you find beautiful, and you unconditionally find love for the parts of yourself that aren't as easy to love. **Being Unfuckwithable means unconditional, unlimited–no cap power...You are powerful–period.** Powerful when you're moody and powerful when you're at peace–you're always powerful. Being Unfuckwithable, means that you see yourself as whole, complete, and worthy of love *on* your healing journey (not just at the "end" of it). You know you are worthy of love, and you get to experience that love while you are still healing. You are not something that needs to be fixed...But rather, alive in an ongoing evolution of healing, awakening and thriving...Over and over again. **Being Unfuckwithable also means being so certain that what you're manifesting is on its way, in quantum speeds, *because it is.*** Even if you don't see it yet...Even if it seems like nothing is happening...Even if your physical reality seems to *oppose* the very possibility that it's all adding up...**You KNOW in your bones that it IS happening.** You have an open and receptive energetic and physical system. You choose ease– even in the hard work. You hold on, and lead with a powerful knowing, and a higher perspective, as you navigate the edges. *You trust, you hold on, and you CHOOSE the powerfully enlightened path.* You know you're worth it. You know it's your time. You have fully let go of any struggle, and you welcome in a life of limitless possibility

Being Unfuckwithable...

Is living life in the realm of personal power
No matter what is going on – inside or outside of you... You're at peace
You know it's all unfolding in divine timing
You know it's happening for you
You know that every single synchronicity means that your manifestation is on its way–in quantum speeds
You are also wise enough to know that every single bout of resistance, every block you move through, and every "test" that arises...
Is equally as validating – that your manifestation is on its way.
You're in this *flow* state, where you're good no matter what...
AND you're always available for more
You are Unfuckwithable.

Breathe in...Breathe out.

Connect now to your solar plexus–the space above your belly button–the home of your personal power.
Connect to your core. Connect to your innate knowing.
The part of you that is SOLID.
You know who you are, and you know what you want.
You know what's true for you.

You know how you want to live.

Breathe in...Breathe out...Hold yourself...
Place your hands on your belly...Connect.
Breathe in deeply affirm to yourself
"I am connected to all that is" Breathe that in.
Affirm "I am the source" Breathe that in.
Affirm "I am here on purpose". Breathe it in.
Affirm "Life CHOSE me...The creator CHOSE me...
Now I'm gonna CHOOSE me"

Take a big inhale and hold it for 5,4,3,2,1...
now exhale...let it last for 10,9,8,7,6,5,4,3,2,1.
Breathe in. Breathe out. You are centered. Grounded.
More powerful than ever.

You are UNFUCKWITHABLE

The vibe is ...
No matter what...
My manifestations are on their way.

No matter what...
I am meant to live the life of my dreams.
It's meant for me.
It's safe for me.
It's good for me.

No matter what is going on in my
internal or external world ...
I'm good.
I'm taken care of.
It's all happening for me.

Personal Power is you leading yourself... AND allowing yourself to be led. Holding the vision of your dream reality, your next manifestation, the life you are creating while surrendering to what life has in store for you. Personal power is BEING with uncomfortable emotions... Integrating them, witnessing them and KNOWING that no matter your mood, energy or external circumstances...YOU are powerful and worthy of abundance. You are always exactly where you need to be...Everything is unfolding FOR you. Personal power is this embodied confidence, and strong energy that KNOWS that you are here on purpose, and that everything is aligning FOR you. It's all adding up...Even when your external circumstances aren't ideal... Even when everything feels like it's crumbling around you...Even when you feel SO far from where you want to be...I PROMISE YOU...*It's happening for you.* **Personal power is a DEEP knowing.** The vibe is...No matter what...I know I am _____, I know I am creating _____, and I know that _____ is manifesting for me, in divine timing, and at quantum speeds. Personal power is a CHOICE to return to the vision, to CHOOSE the paradigm in which you want to exist. I CHOOSE the paradigm where I am infinitely free, infinitely wealthy, infinitely happy, and I create infinite impact in this world.

I choose the paradigm where I am a conscious creator, a healer to this Earth realm, and the human beings within it. I choose the paradigm where I am an inspiration, a powerful facilitator, and a high level support system to the collective ascension. *I CHOOSE this reality over and over again.* Even when things on the outside don't seem to add up…Even BEFORE I have the evidence that it's all happening for me…I trust it's happening…I know that I am alive in the journey, and every step counts. *THIS IS PERSONAL POWER.*

You are unshakeable.
You have limitless potential.
You are LIMITLESS!
You know your power, you know who you are.
You KNOW yourself so you exude untouchable confidence.
You feel certain within yourself, and certain about
the life you are creating.

In order to understand BEING Unfuckwithable…You must understand the opposing frequency (the frequency that the wounded ego loves to play in)…This opposing frequency is what we call "Circumstantial Power." *Circumstantial power is when you only feel good when your external circumstances are ideal.* Here is an example of a "good" circumstantial power day: You wake up and feel happy, money is coming in, you're being told how amazing you are, and how beautiful you are, you're having a really good body image day, you got 9-10 hours of sleep, everything is just going your way, you're in the flow–it is amazing. I truly hope that your circumstances are ideal every day–and as you embody this work…The truth is, you WILL experience **so much more** circumstantial power, because you will consciously create successful environments…You're the match for alignment and good things, so you will *naturally* have more of it. Really good days, where everything goes your way will become the baseline standard. Circumstantial power is fucking awesome. Who doesn't love riding that wave when you're in flow. **However, circumstantial power is only one piece of alignment.** The

REAL power, and the real juice, is in your UNCONDITIONAL PERSONAL POWER. This unconditional power is YOU being UNFUCKWITHABLE. If your self perception, your confidence and your perceived worthiness is going to waver on the days that DON'T go as smoothly...You are walking a very fine line babe. You are outsourcing a lot of power to circumstances, which leaves you with a shaky foundation. You are not creating sustainable power and/or results, when you have rules and conditions as to when you are powerful. Personal power on the other hand–is you leading yourself, choosing to be empowered all of the time, and BEING the leading energy of your life. Personal power is BEING the frequency that everything else responds to. **No waiting...** ***You*** ***make the first move.*** You make the choice to be powerful, to decide that things are unfolding for you, and to position yourself in ways that support your alignment and evolution. Personal power and BEING Unfuckwithable, is an ongoing choice to re-calibrate and realign with your power, in the face of both IDEAL and LESS THAN desirable circumstances.

Affirm: *"My emotions are my emotions...They don't waiver nor determine my Personal Power"*

Affirm: *"No matter what is going on outside of me–I know that my internal energy is the leading energy. I know that I am the source, and that everything responds to me. I choose to be powerful–even in difficult scenarios."*

A high level UNFUCKWITHABLE individual, knows that they get to feel and integrate ALL of the emotions that arise on a day to day basis. Even the "low vibe," painful and survival emotions are deserving of love, acceptance and integration. You get curious about your emotions, you observe your emotions, and you process them. You feel your emotions fully...But you don't make the emotions mean anything about you, your power or what you are capable of achieving and experiencing. You are committed and devoted to the work. The "work" is inevitable when you are moving into new realms of possibility. As you constantly evolve, you know that new edges will inevitably arise. The work can be major and/or minor shifts. The work is allowing the emotions that come up, to live, without making them mean anything about who you are, and what you are here to create or experience. You are powerful. It's all inside of you already–claim it. Whether you are in flow, in a sticky spot or navigating the highs and lows...The vibe really is to ENJOY life. Feel the feels–but then fully and efficiently move through them. Feel it all, then move powerfully into the better feeling vibration–you have the power to change your vibration. **You have the power to change your life.** You came here to LIVE, and to bask in the enjoyment of this life–*you didn't come here to suffer.* So–do more of what feels like a *fuck yes* in your body. When you do what you love...You feel more joy. When you feel more joy...You vibrate at a frequency that attracts more joy into your life. When you allow your desires to LEAD you... When you TRULY surrender to what your heart and soul WANT...You quantum leap to your manifestations, while actually LOVING the fuck out of the journey. The vibe becomes *"life is SO good, I don't even need it...But I WANT it, and therefore I get to have it".*

If it's not a fuck yes...It's a no.

Being Unfuckwithable isn't about "protecting" your energy...But rather about regulating and optimizing it. You already know that as you rise...Certain things will fall off...*Certain things don't come with you.* **Additionally, you become much more intentional about where your energy goes.** The Unfuckwithable individual is highly conscious about what they say yes too...They say yes to what is life giving, yes to what is nourishing, and they say yes to what feels like a *fuck yes* in their body. They say yes to the experiences, environments, and the people that align with their highest frequency. They don't do obligatory...They don't do shaming...They don't do fawning...And they certainly don't do people pleasing. **If it's not coming from a place of desire and alignment... It's a dip in standards, and frankly a procrastination to your next evolution.** *You are in the* *fast lane–not everyone drives here.* You are optimizing your energy–always. The average human is living in the simulation of a conditioned limited lifestyle. It takes a rare human to break the simulation, and CHOOSE true freedom…CHOOSE a life gushing in love. It's a radical act of empowerment, devotion, and loving service, to YOU AND the collective, when you choose to do life differently.

I have been called unconventional my whole life. I still have people (as close as can be) who don't understand my life, lifestyle or my work (and I still love the fuck out of them, and they get to love the fuck out of me). I don't need to be validated externally to be loved and supported. **I validate myself**…AND, I am also very intentional about noticing who in my life is on *my team*…Feel me? Optimizing your energy doesn't mean throwing up walls and boundaries…But it *does* mean consciously limiting time with those who don't actually *see* you. Start noticing who DOES elevate and uplift you…And consciously start creating more time with them. Being Unfuckwithable is an ongoing internal conversation, and conscious check in with yourself, about who is supporting your energy, who is life giving, and who is not. As you rise higher and higher, you outgrow certain frequencies, interactions, and ways of being. **Your higher vibe no longer computes with the lower frequencies.** *Optimization means that you are co-creating environments that nourish your vibration.* You will also come to a place of such internal peace, that you CAN still have thriving relationships with people who really don't understand you..But they love you, and want your happiness, and you can ground into the truth that that's all that matters. When you focus on understanding yourself–you don't need those around you to validate you…AND, if you *can* find a squad who see's, validates and understand you…FUCKING RIGHT!! –Cherish them, and hold them close…But always REMEMBER…**You are the source of your own understanding, validation and personal power…** *You are UNFUCKWITHABLE.*

The journey is you living your life.
So truly LIVE it.

Life by design...Living *Unfuckwithably*, and living a life of great achievement and fulfillment...Is not a means to an end. There is no "destination"...*This is evolution over a lifetime.* **There will always be a new ceiling to your floor.** *There will always be a new desire...There will always be a new level.* Get comfortable with ongoing growth. **Life will always show you where you need to heal.** You are in for a beautiful ride my love. Your success, desires and dreams ARE inevitable. It's a matter of... Are you ready and committed NOW? Are you devoted to a constant CHOOSING of the paradigm where your frequency is top tier, where your power is known and felt, and where you experience the infinite realms within the *Dimension of Openness.* **None of this is a means to an end.** This is way deeper than "how to manifest" –I see you as a whole complete soul, having a human experience. **You are so much bigger than the things you will create in this life....YOU are the muse.** You, my love, are the greatest creation. I want to make it clear that you are the gift. You are the unrepeatable miracle...YOU. This work isn't about chasing or seeking...Or even creating things outside of you to feel a type of way. YOU are already whole and complete as you are...This isn't a rate race...But rather a euphoric, nuanced, and embodied, high level experience of life on Earth. **This is a LIFESTYLE.** An ongoing awareness of the infinite realms...The ever evolving form, and the formless. Personal power is you making powerful moves, from desire–not need. **You make moves with certainty– because you just *know.*** There is an infinite intelligence within, and surrounding you...Always communicating your next step to you. **You are infinitely connected.** You regularly check in with the impulses, *and the information is always there.* Personal power is you KNOWING that you are whole and complete as you are, and that everything else is a cherry on top...BUT, we are in the limitless playground of the material world...You are a high level individual, and you are *here* for the cherries (wink wink). ***So...Want it, claim it, and have it babe.***

You decide. You align. You move first.

There is no cap. No limitation.

Nothing is conditional–everything is limitless.

The New Paradigm is a paradigm you get to choose, over and over again.

It is always evolving

Your pace gets faster

You experience more

Living the life of your dreams GETS to be experienced here and now.

The dream will continue to evolve as you do

It's here for you…It's now.

The Unfuckwithable being is NOT obsessing over a past, or a future illusion...*AND they are also not about denying themselves of feeling what they're feeling.* They focus on the present moment…AND they also embody the future pacing excitement (or anxiety) of what's to come…They also honor the nostalgia or the regret of the past. They practice witnessing their wandering minds, and noticing their subtle bodies. They catch themselves if they lose the moment, and they kindly bring themselves back. Most of the time, they land into the fullness of *this* moment…And they allow their soul given desires to lead them. This is you…YOU are Unfuckwithable. **They want what they want, and they know that if they want it, that it's meant for them.** This is you, you GET to have it. You are powerful enough to know that you are ALREADY whole and complete, with or without it…So, you lovingly and joyfully walk the walk on the journey of manifesting it. **You don't seek or chase–instead, you open up wider, and you receive.** Inhale, and get 1% more open…Exhale, and bask in the *knowing* that it's on its way. You get to have it all AND, you *already* have it all (feel me?) You move toward your desires, and want them so badly…While ALSO feeling so whole and complete, just as you are. You move with desire, AND you land in the present moment. You land in the gratitude, and in the wholeness, of right here–right now. You're whole, complete and worthy as you are... *And everything else you desire just gets to AMPLIFY that feeling.*

The Unfuckwithable being is empowered by their circumstances. Regardless of what their life has been thus far, they choose new frequencies that feel better, and more aligned. *They identify the energies, vibes, people and places that FEEL GOOD.* They consciously step into their presence, and into the fast lane of actualization. They actively create an insourced high vibration…AND an external environment of high vibration…from here, they watch themselves constantly moving faster, and closer toward their dream life. **They naturally make more money, have better sex lives, create more impact, feel more joy, have higher depth relationships, and a more fulfilling experience of life on Earth–it is just standard.** They rise up and up…Always expecting better and better experiences. They come to expect good things will happen to them, and they KNOW they are an active co-creator in the actualization process. The UNFUCKWITHABLE being knows that the environments they exist in, will either *support* their desires in manifesting…Or oppose them–*so they choose wisely*…YOU choose wisely. Take a moment now to reflect…***Are your environments nourishing the soil of your intentions?*** Are your environments nurturing your growth? Are your environments aligned, and of a supportive frequency? Take note, meditate, and journal on it…What needs refinement? and/or What can you celebrate and amplify?

You're more divine than you know.

More powerful than you realize.

You're brilliant, stunning and capable.

You're ready.

You're committed.

You have a rare, unique and highly magnetic essence. **The world is ready and awaiting your full reclamation of it.** It is time to unleash allllll that power babe. Your tangible and intangible success IS inevitable. You ARE high level and UNFUCKWITHABLE, both in front of the world…AND behind the scenes. You exist with high integrity for this life, and you walk your purpose. You hold high standards for what you give, and for what you receive. *You are powerful–YOU are Unfuckwithable.* You are alive, always in flow–boundless…Free. You are aware of the infinite and limitless possibilities that exist for you in this life–and you LIVE them. **You know your energy goes well beyond your physical body…Beyond this Earth realm…But you DECIDE to live in SO much pleasure, luxury, impact, abundance and alignment while you're here.** You live a truly beautiful life–you soak up all the abundance, wealth, experience and LOVE that this realm has to offer you. **Day by day, moment to moment, you are more and more empowered.** With every season of growth…You become more and more aligned, more and more successful, more and more evolved and more and more grounded in the now. *You celebrate yourself…You are proud of you…Proud of all that you've been, and all that you've become.*

Your growth and success is both exponential AND sustainable. Your results are expected, your nervous system is regulated, your life is strategically and naturally refined…It is dripping in ease and pleasure. **You take time to reflect, edit and upgrade.** You awaken, heal and rise. You thrive in this life. You just glow, and you effortlessly magnetize everything you want. *Everyone sees you, and wonders HOW you do what you do.* You just do you…At a perfectly aligned, and individualized pace. You have consciously created grounded spaciousness in your life to check in with your OWN internal compass. **You consciously follow your own heart.** You hone in on your craft, you come home to your nature…You amplify, and refine your gifts. *You know that success is an individualized formula…And you know your formula*. You see your momentum stack and cash in…Always. You honor your unique individuality, your unique and varying emotions, your energy body and your own physiology. You recognize your story, conditioning, and your background…But you don't let any of it define you…*You alchemize it.* You have powerfully identified what is actually TRUE for you…*What you actually desire.* You have laid out the soft and clear landing strip for your desires to drop in. **You effortlessly achieve and receive the success that is meant for you.**

PRINCIPLES OF THE UNFUCKWITHABLE BEING

-THEY KNOW that their aligned action is always creating momentum
-THEY TRUST THEMSELVES to rest, to take strategic spaciousness, take a "break" from their work, they have the knowing that they are ALWAYS energetically plugged in
-THEY KNOW they are always alive in their life, and it is all happening now…All adding up…Always cashing in
-THEY HAVE a regulated nervous system that can HOLD duality.
-THEY HOLD the embodied KNOWING that it is SAFE to be uncomfortable
-THE STAY CLEAR in their energetics, they refine, clean up obstructions, heal misalignments, and avoid deviation from the path
-THEY KNOW that their energy IS their currency, and they PRIORITIZE feeling GOOD.
-THEY FOCUS ON top tier baseline frequency –they regulate and optimize how they feel moment to moment
-THEY PRIORITIZE a daily practice of moment to moment honoring, noticing and upgrading of their energy.

BEING UNFUCKWITHABLE is a constant calibration to personal empowerment. **You are worthy of showing up for you.** Forget what happened to you, let go of the victim hood. **Just for this moment…BE the inspiration that YOU need.** Be the source of aliveness FOR you. Inspire and motivate YOURSELF. *Live, breathe and EMBODY the highest level of YOU.* SHOW the world just how powerful you are. There will be time and space on your journey…To feel your pain fully, to hold yourself in the tenderness of it…You need to share it, you need to feel it, you deserve to share your story, and to fully process and honor your pain…But there will ALWAYS come the time, that you remember your power. That you remember who the fuck you ARE! *No matter what happened to you…You are not a victim–you are the HERO of your story.* There comes a time where you rewrite your story, and become the victor of your life, and empowered by your circumstances…*And that time is NOW.* I want to remind you that there is room for ALL parts of you in this work, and on this spiritual/self development journey. **But THIS RIGHT HERE...Is the part where you STAND in your power.** You DECLARE what it is you desire, and you GO THE FUCK AFTER IT!! This tough love is here for you, because I am SO DEEPLY ROOTING FOR YOU. I want to be a constant reminder to you–just how powerful you are–never forget it. **I want the words within these pages to solidify for you, that ANYTHING is possible...And if it is a true desire of your heart...Then it is meant for you, and NATURAL for you to achieve/receive.** Any old outdated beliefs that were forced into your subconscious minds out of fear...*Were never really yours.* You have CLAIMED your truest freedom...Freedom of your body, mind, soul and spirit.

Breathe in, and breathe out babe. You are fucking POWERFUL! Take a massive inhale–feel your entire body electrified and lit up. YOU ARE POWERFUL! One more time–breathe in the biggest breath yet and let out a scream!! Shout out loud to the world!! **"I AM FUCKING POWERFUL!!"** I want to live in a world where we are ALL embodied as our highest selves. A world where we empower, and lift eachother up. I want to live in a world where every child is empowered to BE the true creator of their reality–to know that anything is possible. A world where every single human being knows that they are supported infinitely–that there is always a higher realm, and a new paradigm available for them. **I want to create a world where everyone knows that they have the POWER within themselves to change their own vibration, and to change their own life.**

Nothing is the same, everything is different.

I am proud of you...Proud of the person you've become. The power you've reclaimed and remembered within yourself. I am celebrating your choice to be here, to be embodied in this work...To be ALIVE in this extraordinary life. We are *of* the new Earth, and we are alive in the ever evolving, new paradigm(s). We refuse to settle for the mundane normalcy, or the false sense of security. ***We choose a life by our own design.*** You are reading this because you are RARE. It is safe to know it, it is safe to claim it, and it is safe to TRUST yourself. **Let your life be extraordinary.** Allow the old outdated paradigms of simulations, obligations, and conditioning melt away with each breeze of the new Earth, and each breath in your awakened body. From this point forward, may you lead with LOVE, and do w*hatever the fuck you want,* with your precious life, in your unrepeatable body! *You have been immersed in the work–what a JOURNEY we have had babe.* I see you–I'm amazed by you. It has all added up to now. I know that you are deep in the work, and you are embodied in your UNFUCKWITHABLENESS. Your subtle codes of alignment have been adding up…The work is paying off. It is TIME now, to BASK in the bounty of your hard work. To enjoy the fruits of your labor, and let it all land. *Celebrate you today, celebrate tonight, and celebrate always.* I have successfully LED you…**To LEAD yourself.** You will constantly be evolving, elevating and rising to new heights. I trust that this book will be a guiding compass for you, I trust that over and over again…This book will bring you home to yourself. This book will remind you of your power, and bring you back to your center. **You are so loved.** You are so beautiful, and you are so brilliant, and it has been an HONOR to lead you on this journey of BEING UNFUCKWITHABLE. I would LOVE to hear your review of this book (words of affirmation love language over here–eek!) , make a review online, connect with me, share this book with the ones you love…And of course come back to the work within these chapters, as you need, and as you desire. Dive deeper into my world by finding me on Instagram, by listening to my Podcast…And I invite you to dive even deeper, through my individualized client work within my various containers.

Breathe in…Breathe out…

You have arrived.

Welcome to your New Paradigm.

Nothing will ever be the same...

I love You.

xx Haley

What the gorgeous people are saying…

"Unfuckwithable will have you on top of the world- with laser focused clarity and an induction of potent, high frequency energy, ready to become YOU as your highest, most breathtaking, empowered, unstoppable self. This book is like plugging into the exponential power of the universe,
for a jolt, a remembrance, a reinvigoration, of your purpose here. **Pure, brilliant, alive, this is just what this world was asking for.** Incredible. It's like having the Universe's biggest cheerleader in your back pocket. I'm so grateful for this book. **There is nothing like it.** Captured lightning in a bottle.
This book is POWERFUL. By reading it, you are filled with high frequency, electric, energy."

-Jenna Rose, Artist

"Haley has a way of pulling you into her power, and this book is the embodiment of that.
She draws you into her world, and gives you the pieces you're ready to absorb. Haley's words will help you break free from the limitations that have held you back for far too long and create the life you truly deserve. Unfuckwithable is a divine transmission of energy and a call to action.
Haley's words will ignite your soul, and invite you into your next level.
Unfuckwithable is a loyal companion that you'll return to time and time again."

-Carolyn Chylia, R.Kin, DOMP, FST, clinical hypnotherapist, quantum biofeedback practitioner, CEO + Founder of CareHealthco

"This book is the ultimate journey back to Self. *A turnkey into the realm of the unlimited.* The ultimate permission slip for those ready for truth, power, and reclamation. **To know Haley and to read her words, is to know and witness her Divine ability to call others into their own power, simply by borrowing from her energy field.** This book is now an extension *of* that field; channeled through her at a time when millions of souls are calling in its truth and the freedom that's on the other side. To those ready to do the deep, often uncomfortable work that's required to rise and thrive, **Haley -and this book-is the guide you've been looking for."**

-Lauren Saunders, Artist, Entrepreneur &
Creative Business Mentor

"Unfuckwithable is a highly inspiring book! Just reading the chapters leads to an activation of creativity and connection to one's higher-self. **Haley has dedicated her life to being a new paradigm leader-she is a galactic muse, who can fast-forward us onto our divine path.** While reading **Unfuckwithable**, I was inspired and energized to make internal shifts which have manifested into new adventures in my own Iconic life. Haley's book is insightful and allows for self-reflection thus customizing our high level unique journeys-not just one blueprint for all. **Unfuckwithable, is a path to experiencing self-indulgent love as the energy that makes the world and universe go round."**

-Julie Boyd MSW, RSW
Psychotherapist, Yoga & Meditation Teacher,
Energy Worker, and Author.

"**Unfuckwithable will change the world as we know it.** This book beautifully guides you through a refreshing perspective you didn't know you needed, but can't live without. Haley's words allow you to open your eyes to the infinite possibilities of your life and truly embody your biggest, wildest dreams — one's you didn't even think were possible. **It is enlightening, expansive, and truly ICONIC.** The end of every sentence, every paragraph, and every chapter had me saying *'Thank You, More Please'* to Haley, for blessing us with this divine creation."

-Jenn Baswick, RD, MHSc
The Intuitive Nutritionist, Registered Dietitian,
Certified Intuitive Eating Counselor
Embodiment Coach & Brand Designer

UNFUC
KWITH
ABLE

HALEY BOWLER-COOKE

YOUR AUTHOR...

Hi Gorgeous One, I'm Haley
It's my honor to introduce myself to You, and to lead you
into this deep and expansive journey within Yourself,
as you walk your Highest Timeline...
As you become UNFUCKWITHABLE.

I am a walking embodiment of evolution. Not easily understood or defined. I am truly UNFUCKWITHABLE. I am devoted to service, devoted to ascension, and devoted to living life by my own design. I am devoted to a life that feels and IS successful, pleasure-filled, fulfilling...A life that feels like one big *exhale*. I am a psychic channel, a quantum healer and high level facilitator. I have 6 years of post secondary schooling in the sciences and the human body...The wisdom I teach, facilitate and LIVE however...Comes from a source much more potent, and much more true.

I have a successful career as an energy medicine practitioner, and direct channeler for elite professionals, high earners and entrepreneurs. I run a podcast, I write, I speak, I facilitate and I devote myself, to not only being ALIVE in this work...But to sharing the wisdom and abundance of this work, with the collective. I have dedicated my life to freedom, pleasure and fulfillment–from a space of high level consciousness...And...I am as boujee as they come. I have a KNOWING that my soul chose Earth to not only meditate in lotus, and visualize my desires...But to actually HAVE them.

HALEY BOWLER-COOKE

Psychic Channel, Quantum Healer, Thought Leader
Host of Uplift Lifestyle Podcast
Founder & CEO of Uplift Lifestyle Inc.

As one of my favorite people in the world lovingly put it…"*Understanding Haley is like a constant game of catch up*". I am unapologetically Me, living in a state of lush overflow in self love, confidence, and joy…And I am devoted to evolution over a lifetime. I live a life by my own design. This life is one I have created, co-created, manifested and received. The flow of my life looks like this: intention, drive, alignment and surrender. I live an Iconic life. A life curated by Me, for Me, with the intention, and devotion to collective ascension. I absolutely adore all that I am, and all that I have…AND, I always walk powerfully towards *more. The essence of my life really is…"Thank You…More Please".*

Now, it is my honor to share with You…
All that I know, and all that I am…
For you to remember your own essence
of Unfuckwithableness.

Enjoy Babe.

Photos of Haley shot by: Jenna St.Croix 2022
Cover Designed in collaboration with: Jenna Rose & Haley Bowler-Cooke
Song mentioned at the beginning of the book: Mount Everest - Labrinth

Made in the USA
Monee, IL
17 July 2023

39446294R00193